Critical Leadership

Critical approaches to leadership studies have sought to challenge the normative position of "leadership" as residing solely within the formal leader, and some have gone so far as to undermine the traditionally held assumption of leadership as a "real" phenomenon.

This book offers a critical account of the nature of leadership and management in modern organizations. Specifically, it examines the forces that affect the influence relationships between leaders and followers in a public sector organizational setting, and thus how these relationships inform social influence processes. Although the book focuses on the case of a public sector organization in the UK, the findings are placed in the context of both leadership theory and research across the globe and the dissemination of "New Public Management" world-wide.

By acknowledging the criticisms concerning the weaknesses of conventional or mainstream leadership study, and through the adoption of a critical perspective, *Critical Leadership* provides a deep and rich interpretation of the empirical material on leadership, thus making an outstanding contribution to the current literature.

Paul Evans is Lecturer in Business Analysis at Manchester Business School, UK.

John Hassard is Professor of Organizational Analysis at Manchester Business School, UK, and is a Visiting Fellow in Management Learning at the Judge Business School, Cambridge University, UK. His main research interests lie in the areas of organization theory and change, and he is co-editor of *The Routledge Companion to Organizational Change* (2011).

Paula Hyde is Senior Lecturer in Organization Studies at Manchester Business School, UK, and is co-founder of the cross-faculty Healthcare Workforce Research Network at the Institute of Health Sciences, University of Manchester, UK. Her main research interests lie in the areas of psychodynamic theory and organizational change, and she is co-editor of *Culture and Climate in Health Care Organizations* (2010, Palgrave Macmillan).

Routledge critical studies in public management
Edited by Stephen Osborne

The study and practice of public management has undergone profound changes across the world. Over the last quarter-century, we have seen

- increasing criticism of public administration as the over-arching framework for the provision of public services;
- the rise (and critical appraisal) of the "New Public Management" as an emergent paradigm for the provision of public services;
- the transformation of the "public sector" into the cross-sectoral provision of public services; and
- the growth of the governance of inter-organizational relationships as an essential element in the provision of public services.

In reality these trends have not so much replaced each other as elided or co-existed together – the public policy process has not gone away as a legitimate topic of study, intra-organizational management continues to be essential to the efficient provision of public services, while the governance of inter-organizational and inter-sectoral relationships is now essential to the effective provision of these services.

Further, while the study of public management has been enriched by contribution of a range of insights from the "mainstream" management literature it has also contributed to this literature in such areas as networks and inter-organizational collaboration, innovation and stakeholder theory.

This series is dedicated to presenting and critiquing this important body of theory and empirical study. It will publish books that both explore and evaluate the emergent and developing nature of public administration, management and governance (in theory and practice) and examine the relationship with and contribution to the over-arching disciplines of management and organizational sociology.

Books in the series will be of interest to academics and researchers in this field, students undertaking advanced studies of it as part of their undergraduate or postgraduate degree and reflective policy-makers and practitioners.

13 Critical Leadership
Leader–follower dynamics in a public organization
Paul Evans, John Hassard and Paula Hyde

Critical Leadership

Leader–follower dynamics in a public organization

Paul Evans, John Hassard and Paula Hyde

Routledge
Taylor & Francis Group

LONDON AND NEW YORK

First published 2013
by Routledge
2 Park Square, Milton Park, Abingdon, Oxon OX14 4RN

Simultaneously published in the USA and Canada
by Routledge
711 Third Avenue, New York, NY 10017

Routledge is an imprint of the Taylor and Francis Group, an informa business

© 2013 Paul Evans, John Hassard and Paula Hyde

British Library Cataloguing in Publication Data
A catalogue record for this book is available from the British Library

Library of Congress Cataloging in Publication Data
Evans, Paul, 1943–
Critical leadership : leader-follower dynamics in a public organization /
Paul Evans, John Hassard and Paula Hyde.
    pages cm. – (Routledge critical studies in public management)
    Includes bibliographical references and index.
    1. Public administration. 2. Leadership. I. Hassard, John, 1953–
    II. Hyde, Paula. III. Title.
    JF1351.E92 2013
    352.23'6–dc23   2012049333

ISBN: 978-0-415-53965-4 (hbk)
ISBN: 978-0-203-10800-0 (ebk)

Typeset in Times New Roman
by Wearset Ltd, Boldon, Tyne and Wear

MIX
Paper from
responsible sources
FSC® C013056
www.fsc.org

Printed and bound in Great Britain by
TJ International Ltd, Padstow, Cornwall

A little rebellion now and then is a good thing.

Thomas Jefferson

Contents

PART III
Discussion and conclusions 159

Figures

Abbreviations

ABC	A Big Council: the name used for the organization that was studied in this project, a large unitary authority in the north of England.
ADS	Architect and Design Service: the name used in this book for an internal business unit that was commissioned to undertake ABC's capital works.
CA	Corporate Assessment: an external assessment of the corporate effectiveness of an authority, conducted by members of the government Audit Commission.
CLT	Corporate leadership team: the principal executive committee of the ABC authority.
CPA	Comprehensive Performance Assessment: an external assessment by government auditors on the effectiveness of overall council service provision.
FRLT	Full Range Leadership Theory: a model of leadership (see Figure 2.1).
HRC	Human Resource Consultancy: the name used in this book for the national consulting company employed by ABC to consult on accountability and responsibility among ABC's chief officers.
ICC	International Consulting Company: the name used in this book for the company employed by ABC to implement its model for leadership, cultural and performance development.
JAR	Joint Area Review: an external assessment by OFSTED of ABC's Children's Services function.
LCP1, LCP2	Leadership in the City Programmes 1 and 2: leadership development programmes that were implemented by ABC in the years before this study.
OFSTED	Office for Standards in Education, Children's Services and Skills: a UK government body that regulates and inspects services related to the care of children and young people, education and skills.
NPM	New Public Management (see Chapter 3).
PFI	Private Finance Initiative: Government strategy of utilizing private sector money to finance public sector capital works.

PPPU   Public Private Partnership Unit. A department established within the Chief Executive's Unit of ABC, designed to capture funds available through the PFI scheme.

PSE   Public sector ethos (see Chapter 3).

RACI   Responsibility, Accountability, Communication and Information: a matrix devised by the HRC to assist in consultancy work.

1 Introduction

The problem under investigation

During the last quarter of the twentieth century the interest in leadership gained fresh currency (Kellerman, 2008). There can be little doubt concerning the general view that leadership is an essential commodity contributing to organizational performance. The Business Source Premier online database lists 22,814 separate references for leadership between 1970 and 2000. In the first nine years of this millennium, the same database lists 46,065 references. It is estimated that industry spends an average of $50 billion annually on leadership development (Raelin, 2003). While the resulting contributions have produced insights concerning leadership, there still exist many questions that are yet to be satisfactorily answered (House and Aditya, 1997; Parry and Bryman, 2006; Yukl, 2002).

As part of the reform of public services in the UK, there have been increased calls for the implementation of more effective leadership within the public sector. The complexity of service provision can be appreciated as a series of difficult or intractable problems, and it has been posited that leadership may be the answer in helping to resolve these "wicked problems" (Grint, 2005a). The organization under study in this book, known here as ABC (A Big Council – a large unitary authority in the north of England), formally stated its leadership challenge under an initiative called "From Good to Great" (ABC, 2008 p. 11).

A critical lens is used to examine the dynamics of the relationship between leaders and followers in their normal work context, and the impacts of these dynamics. Critical Theory approaches to social research generally advocate the emancipation of groups marginalized within society (Thomas, 1993). Critical management research aims to follow the spirit of Critical Theory research but focuses on management phenomena (Alvesson and Deetz, 2006a). The leadership literature has been dominated by a functionalist research paradigm (Collinson, 2006) and has thus been based on a limiting set of assumptions representing Western industrial culture, specifically American in character (House and Aditya, 1997). This view of leadership suggests that followers within the relationship are primarily subject to the influence of the leader and that effective leadership is concerned with the mobilization of followers to obtain a specified goal or goals (Bass, 1998; Burns, 1978).

While the value of following is generally underplayed, some studies have acknowledged its importance (Chaleff, 2003; Collinson, 2006; Kellerman, 2008; Kelley, 1992 and 2004; Lundin and Lancaster, 1990; Potter, Rosenbach, and Pittman, 2001; Raelin, 2004; Rosenau, 2004; Seteroff, 2003). Nevertheless, the dynamic influence processes through which the leader elicits and maintains follower support, particularly within a challenging bureaucratic organizational environment, are little understood or commented upon (Avolio *et al.*, 2004; Parry, 1998).

This study examined the dynamics of the leader–follower relationship by exploring the activities of leaders and followers in different work situations. Leaders in this study are considered to be those individuals that are responsible for supervising others in the provision of a service, or part of a service. Followers are considered to be those that are supervised by leaders. Dynamics are taken to be those forces that are active in any direction whose sum reinforces or negates one or more of the forces (Reeves, 1970).

The contexts in which the relationships were played out were chosen because of the leadership potential in each scenario, in combination with the ease of access to each scenario. The leadership potential of scenarios was filtered by the likely occurrence of (a) demonstrating leadership, or (b) involving leadership. Observation of a particular scenario informed the choice of which scenario to observe next, through a desire to follow up, question and interpret the leadership story as it unfolded.

This study presents interpretations of observations, interviews and documentation collected during a 16-month period of fieldwork within one of the UK's largest unitary authorities. Analysis of the evidence collected during the fieldwork is used to illuminate the leader–follower relationship. This study is concerned therefore with the dynamics of the leader–follower relationship and how these dynamics inform social influence processes referred to as leadership in practice.

Aims and objectives of the research

The research aims are briefly outlined here, accompanied by a short statement of how they were achieved.

- To explore the day-to-day work experiences of leaders and followers. The researchers made observations of leaders and followers in pursuit of their normal work routines.
- To identify and explore the main dynamics that comprise and affect the relationship between leaders and followers. The researchers conducted interviews with the principal actors observed, in order to explore their work experiences in depth and to gain understanding of the factors that shaped the practice of work and the relationships between leaders and followers.
- To interpret concepts and conversations concerning the leader–follower relationship. Follow-up interviews were set up to challenge "playfully"

some of the observations and detail of the interviews. A deeper exploration of themes provided the jumping-off point for further questioning and consolidation of understanding. The main themes were applied to work practice, and the relationships between leaders and followers were explored.

- To utilize the interpretations to suggest a framework of the dynamics of the leader–follower relationship from a critical perspective. The researchers discussed and refined theoretical concepts with leaders and followers in order to produce the findings of this study.

The significance of the research

Despite the popularity and availability of leadership-related material, there remains a significant shortfall in knowledge about the concept of leadership (House and Aditya, 1997; Parry and Bryman, 2006; Yukl, 2002). Grint (2005b) states the view that it is not possible to be a leader and a reader and points towards a disparity in understanding and practice, between academics and the field of leadership studies on the one hand and leadership practitioners and organizational development managers on the other. This however does not appear to have diminished the currency of leadership in terms of its perceived value for organizational performance. This view is reinforced by populist management textbooks and hagiographic biographies of "celebrity" business leaders (Calás and Smircich, 1991), and has paved the way toward the dominant position maintained by heroic neo-charismatic leaders (Beyer, 1999). This school of leadership theorizing, referred to as a "messianic discourse", has come to represent the normative position of leadership study (Western, 2008). Driven by the impact of New Public Management (Rhodes, 1991), leadership models have been derived and implemented within various public sector contexts (Alimo-Metcalfe and Alban-Metcalfe, 2004). The successes of such initiatives have been varied (Blackler, 2006).

The results of the study by Blackler resonate with the opinions of many of the key contributors concerning the state of leadership research and the extent to which knowledge has been gained. Much of the concern relates to two distinct issues.

The first is the issue of definition: could it be possible that, as a consequence of widespread variation of definition, leadership scholars are not studying leadership but some other related phenomenon (Rost, 1993)? In reviewing definitions of leadership found in the literature, Yukl (2002) concludes that most leadership scholars would agree that leadership comprises an influence relationship between leaders and followers. In contrast to the mainstream focus on the behaviour, traits and competencies of leaders as individuals, Critical Theory interpretations of leadership focus on exploring the relations between leaders and followers and appreciate leadership to be a socially constructed influence process (Collinson, 2006; Grint, 2005a; Parry, 1998).

Second, it has been suggested that lack of progress may be related to the research design that has traditionally dominated leadership studies.

It may even be suggested that the answer, after considering the enormous resources in terms of money, time, energy and talent spent on (neo-) positivist leadership research as a gigantic experiment testing whether (neo-) positivist methodology works or not, should be no.

(Alvesson, 1996 p. 457)

Conventional approaches are generally taken from the fields of social psychology and management studies and tend therefore to favour positivistic, hypothesis-testing methods (Rost, 1993). It is claimed that there has been a subtle re-writing of existing theory to incorporate new nuances and different terminology, but that these approaches remain inherently contained in the previous literature (Western, 2008). The effectiveness of such methods has been questioned, and researchers are increasingly calling for the application of alternative qualitative methods (Alvesson, 1996; Bryman, 1996; Calás and Smircich, 1991).

Where conducted, critical approaches to leadership studies have sought to challenge the normative position of leadership as residing solely within the formal leader (Collinson, 2006; Grint, 2005b; Western, 2008), and have gone as far as to undermine the traditionally held assumption of leadership as a "real" phenomenon (Alvesson, 1996, 2001; Alvesson and Sveningsson, 2003a, 2003b; Calás and Smircich, 1991; Gemmill and Oakley, 1992). This study acknowledges the criticisms concerning the weaknesses of leadership study, and through the adoption of a critical perspective contributes to the literature in a number of ways.

- By standing outside of the normative functional leadership conceptualizations, the study provides a richer and deeper interpretation of the empirical material.
- Responding to calls for the use of alternate research methodologies, this study adopts a qualitative methodological position (Alvesson, 1996; Bryman, 1996).
- The study seeks to illuminate the dynamics of the relationship between leaders and followers,
- Making interpretations from a Critical Theory standpoint relating to the illustrations given, the study provides conclusions concerning the complexity of leadership practice in an organizational context.

Organization of the book

The book is in three parts. Part I covers the literature and context relevant to the study, and outlines the methodology and design of the research. Part II presents the research data and the authors' interpretations of it. Part III comprises discussion and conclusions.

In Part I, Chapter 2 outlines the literature on leadership studies, beginning with the literature from the school of New Leadership. Following this is a critique of the literature from an historical and methodological perspective. The chapter goes on to examine the literature that takes followers as its primary object of study; the literature that supports a critical perspective of leadership; and finally, studies of leadership conducted from a Critical Theory platform. Chapter 3 establishes the context within which the leader–follower relationship is conducted. It tracks the history of reform and the prevailing currents of research. Chapter 4 deals with methodological considerations, outlining the Critical Theory perspective and the research design.

In Part II, Chapter 5 begins by outlining the presentation and interpretation of the empirical material before setting out the first illustration. This illustration deals with a leadership development seminar held at A Big Council (ABC), the large unitary authority under study. The seminar was referred to internally as "From Good to Great", and its subject matter was directly relevant to this study. The chapter presents an interpretation of the illustration and concludes that ambiguity is a dynamic of the leader–follower relationship. The next illustration, in Chapter 6, deals with a meeting to establish assessments of the authority's Corporate and Children's Services. This illustration was chosen because it illustrates the context within which leader–follower relations are conducted. The chapter makes interpretations related to context and concludes that the environment is a dynamic of the leader–follower relationship.

Chapter 7 concerns a management team meeting chaired by the chief executive. The corporate leadership team is the most senior officer committee in the organization. The meeting illustrates the interplay between leaders and followers; analysis of the meeting demonstrates that the process of acquisition, allocation and utilization of resources is a dynamic of the leader–follower relationship. Chapter 8 focuses on an initiative led by Human Resources concerning a management accountability matrix. This is not an illustration as such but is a composite of a number of observations. It has been presented in this way so as to illustrate the actions of leader and followers. The interpretations made conclude that leaders and followers are engaged in a symbiotic relationship and which comprises an important dynamic between the two.

In Chapter 9, a directors' management team meeting again illustrates the interplay between leaders and followers, and highlights politics as an important dynamic of the leader–follower relationship. Chapter 10 presents meetings between elected politicians and senior managers of the ABC. The interpretations made demonstrate that both leaders and followers are engaged in what is referred to as a game. Playing the game therefore comprises the dynamic in this instance.

Part III brings together the identified dynamics from the previous six chapters to demonstrate how they impact upon and influence each other. The importance of the interplay of the factors of power or control and politics leads to the conclusion that political behaviour and activity correspond with leadership as an observable phenomenon.

Part I

Literature, context, methodology and design

2 Leadership studies

Overview

This chapter is concerned with the literature that relates to leaders, followers and the dynamics of the influence relationship that, in theory, exist between the two. The general or mainstream literature on leadership studies will not be covered here, as space does not permit and because it has been well covered in other sources (e.g. Bryman, 1996; House and Aditya, 1997; Parry and Bryman, 2006; Rickards and Clark, 2006; Yukl, 2002). Instead, the chapter is devoted primarily to the potential for a *critical* approach to leadership theory.

The chapter begins by introducing the leadership literature and elaborates on the potential contribution a Critical Theory view of leadership may bring to what appears to be an already congested subject. The foundations of the Critical Theory perspective and its approach to management studies are outlined. The next section reviews the literature of the New Leadership school and covers the principal theories and theoretical developments. The analysis asserts that the neo-charismatic theories developed and supported by the school have come to represent a normative understanding of leadership theory and practice. This section demonstrates how a normative appreciation of leadership may be applied to the UK public sector.

There follows a critique of the literature. Based upon the contribution of Rost (1993), we make three broad criticisms of the literature, asserting that these shortfalls have compounded the lack of progress concerning leadership understanding: first, that an historical account of leadership studies gives an illusion of progress; second, that confusion concerning definition has retarded understanding and progress; and third, that adoption of functionalist methodologies has effectively reduced understanding of the complexity of the phenomenon, to the detriment of progress.

The conclusions to this section outline the possibility of alternative perspectives of leadership by introducing approaches that can be differentiated from the New Leadership school. These theories, however, remain rooted in the functionalist paradigm and are essentially leader-centric in their construction. While critical of the models of leadership outlined in prior sections, they share epistemological and methodological antecedents with the theories they criticize.

From a Critical Theory perspective, these post-charismatic theories continue to privilege the position of leader over the follower, maintaining the traditional dominance of leaders and their leadership.

The next part of the chapter focuses on the role of the follower in the leader–follower relationship. An increased interest in follower-centric models of leadership has raised the currency of followers in leadership studies. The following three sections therefore contain a review of leadership theories from the perspective of followers. In follower-centric theories, followers are seen as moderators of leaderships. This view of leadership accords a primarily passive role to followers as the recipients of leadership influence. Followers may also be seen as substitutes for leadership. This perspective can be appreciated as an extreme version of followers as moderators of leadership, as it introduces increased independence on the part of followers. The most radical of the three follower perspectives of leadership show how followers construct or represent leaders. The section outlines the literature related to the romance of, and the construction of, identity in leadership processes. This approach has gained most interest from Critical Theory scholars.

We next review the literature of Critical Theory leadership studies, introducing issues of power and politics to the leadership context. The final section draws the literature together in order to draw conclusions about the dynamics of the relationship between leaders and followers as asserted in the extant literature. This part concludes by outlining the literature's significance for the aims and objectives of the research study.

Introduction – why critical leadership research?

Alvesson and Willmott (2001) maintain that management is often treated as a neutral activity due to the mistaken assumption that management is holistic in its effects and works to the benefit of all in the organization. The classic manager, therefore, is an essential component of the rational system as an administrator of efficiency. The leadership literature has followed this tradition and is therefore informed by a techno-rationalist and positivist agenda to favour a dominant management perspective. It is difficult therefore to differentiate between the "efficient manager" and "effective leader" (Alvesson and Willmott, 2001). The objective here is to reinstate the political and social into management theory, challenging the technocratic and functional dominance that undermines the emancipatory potential within the workplace.

Like many areas of management studies, research on leadership has been dominated by neo-positivist and normative assumptions, together with a reliance on rules and procedures for developing objective results and practice (Alvesson and Deetz, 2006a). As demonstrated below, the results of many thousands of leadership studies have proved disappointing. It has been asserted that much of the leadership literature represents an "insider view" (Alvesson and Deetz, 2006a; Western, 2008), in which increased variation and confusion have been received with general disdain, ensuring that the findings do not receive the attention needed in order to develop a more complex and richer understanding of leadership (Alvesson, 1996).

The application of a Critical Theory approach to leadership demands that attention is given to identifying some of the undercurrents, subtleties, and historical and social trends in which leaders operate (Western, 2008). Included within this approach are the different voices that share different perspectives of the phenomenon. In this way the "frozen reality" that may be thought to comprise leadership can be defrosted, allowing established norms to be challenged and greater understanding to be achieved (Alvesson, 1996).

Critical perspectives challenge the traditional orthodoxies of leadership studies by questioning the dominant view that leaders are those in charge and followers are those influenced by leaders (Jackson and Parry, 2008). Such approaches illustrate how underlying assumptions and structural features influence organizational life and how leadership plays its part in this scenario (Western, 2008).

Organizations have become a revered feature of social life, superseding as they have the political and social institutions that were hitherto fundamental in the vital socializing process required by society. Morgan (1997) maintains that organizations have a strong tendency toward domination, leading to the view that organizations comprise one of modernity's most powerful tools of social coercion and dominance of society. This does not mean, however, that the dynamics of power and influences inherent within organizations need always be a negative. Critical Theory perspectives on the dynamics of social relations can help to promote social cohesion through the illumination of potentially harmful socializing processes (Western, 2008).

A Critical Theory approach has no monopoly on truth, but it may provide a valuable resource for stimulating and influencing the development of debate, research, and the practice of leadership in organizations (Alvesson and Willmott, 2001). This perspective has been generally neglected within leadership studies and could be utilized to develop a more holistic appreciation of leadership processes.

A principal objective of Critical Theory studies is to challenge deeply held convictions within society because such convictions stand in the way of allowing a more emancipated society. It will therefore be useful here to look at the development of Critical Theory and the emancipatory goals of the approach.

Development of Critical Theory and central themes

With reference to Alvesson and Willmott (2001), this section will provide an overview of the main themes of Critical Theory.

The term "Critical Theory", as used in this study, refers to the influences and works of the Frankfurt School, which had its origins in the first decades of the twentieth century. At the core of the school's thought is a concern to develop a more rational, enlightened society through a process of critical reflection upon the organization and efficacy of existing institutions and ideologies. While the school demonstrates considerable diversity, there is a common desire to mobilize critical reasoning in order to transform oppressive features of the modern world though non-authoritarian and non-bureaucratic politics. The Frankfurt School introduced the possibility of subjecting established dogmas to critical scrutiny, paving the way for emancipatory change.

Critical Theory has its roots in the Enlightenment, when knowledge based upon empirical observation began to challenge established dogmas that had been protected by tradition and religion. The scholars of the Enlightenment sought to establish knowledge concerning the natural world on a rational, scientific basis. The understanding of scientific knowledge and "rationality" advanced by these thinkers was positivistic or *non-dialectical* (Alvesson and Willmott, 2001 p. 73) That is to say that reality was conceptualized as an ahistorical object world, that exists externally to, and independently of, the scientists' methods of representing this reality. Later the Young Hegelians – notably Marx and Feurbach – challenged the concept of dualism with the historically grounded conception of *dialectical* production or reproduction of social reality, in which subjects and objects are intertwined and mutually constitutive of each other.

The Frankfurt School

Felix Weil established the Frankfurt School in the 1920s and, after a relatively inauspicious start, the school came to prominence under the guidance of Max Horkenheimer in the 1930s. The school aimed to combine social science and philosophy into a politically and practically committed social philosophy. This mission involved a fundamental questioning of the claim that social science can produce objective, value-free knowledge about social reality. Instead of being obliged to discover universal, law-like patterns of social behaviour, members of the school sought to show how patterns of activity (e.g. consumerism, authoritarianism) are constructed within specific historical and societal contexts, and that the methods of representing these patterns are themselves inextricably linked within these contexts. These patterns and methods should be perceived as an historical movement and not a final form of society or science. Underpinning this was a dialectically inspired concern to engender reflection upon, and emancipation from, the contradictions and restrictions inherent in capitalist societies. This should not be read to say that members of the school had overt leftist political views affiliated to the left-Hegelians and Marx. The school declined to align themselves with the interests of orthodox Marxism but did identify with the critical emancipatory intent of the Marxist tradition.

The rise of Fascism in Nazi Germany of the 1930s and 1940s provided many examples of institutions and ideologies that suppressed and impeded an emancipated citizenship. However, as the grip of Nazi Germany tightened over the intelligentsia of the country, many of the members of the school went into exile in the USA. Here they were exposed to, and impressed by, if not also traumatized by, the hyper-materialistic culture of the most advanced capitalist democracy. This experience provoked fresh processes of critical reflection upon the seductive powers of consumerism. Members of the school took particular interest in the effects of mass culture, especially the production and distribution of news and entertainment, which is seen to exert a numbing and homogenizing effect upon the consciousness of the population, inhibiting reflection and normalizing conformity. That is not to say that the media are inherently pacifying or evil. Clearly, they possess the potential to be positive, through education for example. However, their emancipatory capacities appeared to have been subsumed by the commercial and ideological priorities of consumer capitalism.

Later theorists of the Critical Theory tradition have taken seriously the view that the work of earlier critical theorists lacked any rational basis for their views and thus could be said to be little more than a pretentious moralizing by privileged intellectuals. Some contributors in particular have embarked upon a programme intended to establish the rational foundations of Critical Theory. Most radical of these contributions is the conjecture that the structure of human communication at once anticipates and provokes an emancipatory impulse toward the development of a more rational society, in which communication is no longer distorted by the influences of power and domination.

It is worth noting that many traditions of social analysis are highly resistant, if not antagonistic, toward any form of criticism (Alvesson and Willmott, 2001 p. 88). The difficulties in making sense of the development of welfare capitalism and the expansion of consumerism paved the way toward Critical Theory's openness to a range of intellectual influences. Generally, critical approaches draw attention to the asymmetries of power relations in order to explore possible forms of transformation or emancipation. There is, however, no definitive Critical Theory position, as writers draw upon a plurality of perspectives (Collinson, 2005).

The New Leadership approach

By the 1980s, the field of leadership studies was experiencing a general malaise acknowledged by some of its principal contributors (Mintzberg, 1982; Yukl, 1989). According to Bryman (1996), a general shot in the arm was provided by a group of theories that appeared in the 1980s and that signalled a new way of conceptualizing and researching leadership. Collectively these theories became known as the school of New Leadership (Bryman, 1992). The school revealed a conception of the leader as someone capable of defining organizational reality through the articulation of a vision, which is a reflection of how he or she defines the mission of the organization and the values that underpin it (Parry and Bryman, 2006). Although criticized for repackaging existing theory (Western, 2008), collectively the New Leadership school has developed a resonance among scholars and practitioners alike that has meant that its theoretical underpinnings have come to represent a normative understanding of leadership (Western, 2008).

The theories of the New Leadership approach

During the 1980s, leadership researchers became very interested in the revitalization and transformation of the fortunes of organizations through what was perceived as charismatic leadership. This interest can possibly be attributed to the declining performances of US corporations when compared to increased global competition, particularly from Japan. Yukl (1989) asserts that the interplay between transformational and charismatic processes and the positive and negative effects of those processes is an area of great interest and potential. The New Leadership approach seemed to tie in to an increasing appetite for stories about heroic chief executives and a growing awareness of organizations and their missions. New Leadership can be seen as a cause, symptom and consequence of this self-reflection (Bryman, 1996).

"Transformational" leadership involves influence by a leader on subordinates, resulting in the empowerment of subordinates to influence the transformation of the organization. The resulting processes influence major changes in the attitudes and assumptions of organization members and the building of commitment for the organization's mission, objectives and strategies, recognizable in the outputs of the transformed organization. Transformational leadership is therefore seen as a shared process, involving the actions of leaders throughout the organization and not just those actions of the foremost leader in the hierarchy (Burns, 1978).

"Charismatic" leadership refers to the Weberian perception that a leader possesses some form of divinely inspired gift. Followers not only trust and respect the leader but they also idolize and, to an extent, worship the leader as a hero (Bass, 1985). According to House (1977), the indicators of charismatic leadership include the followers' trust in the correctness of the leader's views, and unquestioning acceptance, affection and obedience. As opposed to transformational leadership, the focus here is on the individual leader.

Both transformational and charismatic theories of leadership are broader in scope than those theories that preceded them, and thus they represent an important step toward the integration of the leadership literature (Yukl, 1989). The major theories in the area of New Leadership are briefly outlined below.

House's charismatic leadership theory (1977)

This theory specifies indicators of charismatic leadership that involve the attitudes and perceptions of followers about the leader. The theory also deals with leader traits that increase the likelihood of the leader's being perceived as charismatic, including a strong need for power, high self-confidence, and assured beliefs. Behaviours of charismatic leaders include impression management, articulation of an appealing vision, communication of high expectations, and expressions of confidence in follower ability. In addition, charismatic leaders set examples for followers through their own behaviour, and can act to arouse follower motives appropriate to the task.

Bass (1985) noted some conceptual limitations to the theory and recommended extending it to include additional traits, behaviours, indicators of charisma and facilitating conditions. He proposed that charismatic leaders were more likely to appear in crises where formal authorities have failed and traditional values and methods have fallen under scrutiny.

Conger and Kanungo's charismatic theory (1987)

The version of charismatic theory proposed by Conger and Kanungo (1987) is based on the assumption that charisma is an attributed phenomenon. Followers attribute charismatic qualities to a leader, based on their observations of the leader's behaviour and outcomes associated with it. Such behaviours are not assumed present in every charismatic leader to the same extent, and the relative importance of each behaviour can vary, dependent upon the situation. The behaviours include the enthusiastic advocacy of a compelling vision differentiated from the status quo and yet still within follower tolerance; making sacrifices of self and risking personal loss in the pursuit of the vision; and undertaking unconventional actions in order to achieve the vision. Traits enhancing the attribution of charisma include self-confidence, impression management skills, high cognitive ability, and the social empathy required to understand the needs and values of followers.

Attributed charisma is more likely for a leader who relies on expert and referent power to influence followers, as opposed to authority and participation. Charismatic leaders are likely to emerge when there is a crisis requiring major change or when followers are dissatisfied with the status quo. However, in the absence of genuine crisis a leader may be able to create dissatisfaction in order to demonstrate expertise in dealing with the problem in unconventional ways.

Burns's theory of transforming leadership (1978)

The theory of "transforming leadership" was developed from skilled observation of a number of political leaders. Burns (1978) described leadership as being a process of evolving inter-relationships in which leaders influence followers and are influenced in turn to modify their behaviour as they meet responsiveness or resistance. Transforming leadership is viewed both as a micro-level influence process between individuals and as a macro-level process of mobilizing power to change structures and institutions. According to Burns, leaders seek to increase followers' consciousness by appealing to their higher ideals and values and not their baser instincts. Followers are thus elevated away from everyday selves to better selves. Transforming leadership can be exhibited by anyone in an organization regardless of position, as it may involve the influencing of peers or superiors as well as subordinates.

Burns contrasts transforming leadership with transactional leadership, in which followers are motivated primarily by appeals to their own self-interest. He also differentiates transforming leadership from influence based on bureaucratic authority which emphasizes power, rules and traditions.

Bass's theory of transformational/transactional leadership (1985)

Bass's approach draws heavily on the work of Burns, but goes much further in two respects (Bass and Avolio, 1990; Bass, 1985). First, as opposed to the opposite ends of a continuum, Bass sees transformational and transactional leadership as separate dimensions. The ideal approach is to demonstrate elements of both forms of leadership. Second, in contrast to Burns's generalized discussion of the two types of leadership, Bass has developed a set of quantifiable indicators for each component.

Transformational leadership consists of four components:

- idealized influence or charisma, the development of vision, in turn promoting pride, respect and trust;
- inspiration, motivating through aspiration toward higher expectations, the modelling of appropriate behaviours, and the use of symbols;
- individualized consideration, the allocation of time to followers, demonstrating respect and giving responsibility;
- intellectual stimulation, continually challenging followers with ideas and approaches.

Transactional leadership consists of two components:

- contingent rewards, the rewards to followers for attainment of tasks and targets;
- management by exception, the taking of action when things are not going to plan.

Research findings on the model have shown charisma and inspiration to be the two components of leader behaviour that are most strongly associated with outcomes such as the performance of subordinates (Bryman, 1996). Charisma, inspiration, individualized consideration and intellectual stimulation interact to influence changes in followers, and the combined effects distinguish between transformational and purely charismatic leaders. Transformational leaders seek to inspire and elevate followers; with charismatic leaders the opposite sometimes occurs (Yukl, 1989).

In later theorizing, the transformational leadership model was developed because of widespread empirical studies, and Full Range Leadership Theory was conceived (Avolio, 1991; Bass, 1999; Bass and Avolio, 1994a). In this model, a distinction can be made between four aspects of transformational leadership, namely idealized influence (what was formerly called charisma), inspirational motivation, intellectual stimulation and individualized consideration. The new model comprises three aspects of transactional leadership rather than two: contingent reward, active management by exception and passive management by exception. The major variation away from the previous model is a classification for those leaders who abstain from the influencing of subordinates. This is referred to as laissez-faire leadership. The Full Range Leadership Theory model is depicted in Figure 2.1.

Idealised influence (charisma): Envisioning a valued future and articulating how to reach it; setting high standards and using self as an example that followers identify with and wish to follow.

Inspirational motivation: Providing simplified and symbolic appeals in support of goals.

Intellectual stimulation: Encouraging followers to address old problems and to be more creative and innovative.

Individualised consideration: Treating each follower individually as having different needs for development and support.

Contingent reward: Providing reward or promise of reward in exchange for meeting standards.

Management by exception: Active or passive; taking corrective action in light of failure to meet standards (correction, negative feedback, reproof, sanctions, disciplinary action).

Laissez-faire: Appearing unconcerned; procrastinating and avoiding issues and decisions.

Figure 2.1 Full Range Leadership Theory (Bass, 1999).

Leadership in the public sector

The foundations of the aforementioned studies have provided the conceptual base for an application to the public sector. Alimo-Metcalfe and Alban-Metcalfe (2004) maintain that they have further developed models in response to criticism that the models of New Leadership lack the complexity to be applicable to the UK public sector (Alimo-Metcalfe and Alban-Metcalfe, 2005). Having extensively researched and collated the views of followers in the UK public sector, they arrived at 14 dimensions that comprise a public sector transformational model (Alimo-Metcalfe and Alban-Metcalfe, 2001 and 2004). This model is differentiated from other transformational models by the "nearness" of the leader to followers; it is built upon the foundation of work concerning social and leader distance (Antonakis and Atwater, 2002; Napier and Ferris, 1993; Shamir, 1995), and as such is very closely related to work concerning self-leadership (Greenleaf and Spears, 2002).

Leading and developing others: a transformational model

Showing genuine concern: Takes genuine interest in staff as individuals; values their contributions; develops their strengths; coaches, mentors; has positive expectations of what staff can achieve

Enabling: Trusts staff to take decisions and initiatives on important matters; delegates effectively; develops staff's potential

Being accessible: Approachable and not status-conscious; prefers face-to-face communication; stays accessible and keeps in touch

Encouraging change: Encourages questioning traditional approaches to the job; encourages new approaches and solutions to problems; encourages strategic thinking

Personal qualities

Being honest and consistent: Honest and consistent in behaviour; more concerned with the good of the organization than personal ambition

Acting with integrity: Open to criticism and disagreement; consults and involves others in decision-making; regards values as integral to the organization

Being decisive, taking appropriate risks: Decisive when required; prepared to take difficult decisions, and risks when appropriate

Inspiring others: Charismatic; exceptional communicator; inspires others to join them

Resolving complex problems: Able to deal with a wide range of complex issues; creative in problem-solving

Leading the organization

Networking and achieving: Provides inspiring communication of the vision of the organization or service to a wide network of internal and external stakeholders; gains the confidence and support of various groups through sensitivity to needs, and by achieving organizational goals

Focusing team effort: Clarifies objectives and boundaries; team-orientated to problem-solving and decision-making, and to identifying values

Building shared vision: Has a clear vision and strategic direction; engages various internal and external stakeholders in developing this; draws others together in achieving the vision

Supporting a developmental culture: Supportive when mistakes are made; encourages critical feedback

Facilitating change sensitively: Sensitive to the impact of change on different parts of the organization; maintains a balance between change and stability

Source: Dimensions of the public sector transformational leadership model,
Alimo-Metcalfe and Alban-Metcalfe, 2004

Despite the assertion of the UK government (Performance and Innovation Unit, 2001) and others (Alimo-Metcalfe and Alban-Metcalfe, 2001, 2004, 2005) of the value of leadership to the UK public sector, studies have demonstrated that the issues related to leadership and performance of the public sector are highly complex and contradictory. In a major study by Blackler (2006), the author demonstrates that the image of empowered, proactive leaders within UK public sector organizations fails to reflect reality. The evidence demonstrates that public sector chief executives had become little more than conduits to a politicized centre. Critical to this is the issue of bureaucratic discretion, which resides with central government, thus denying senior managers the leadership role (Van Wart, 2003). Blackler asserts that the study of leadership within the UK public sector cannot be divorced from a broader study of the institutions of state (Blackler, 2006).

In a study concerning leadership at different levels of organizational hierarchy, Kan and Parry (2004) recorded similar phenomena, in that complex cultural and societal factors combined to repress the leadership capacity of those under study. Fundamental to this repression is the issue of paradox and how individuals respond to paradoxical situations, defined as inconsistencies and contradictions in the workplace. Having identified a paradox, leaders either reconciled or legitimized the paradox in question. Reconciling paradox tended to reflect some of the criteria of sanctioned political activity identified by Zanzi and O'Neill (2001), while legitimizing paradox involved the use of political tactics identified as non-sanctioned in the same study.

Conclusion

In an overview of New Leadership developments, Bryman (1996) warns against exaggerating the differences between it and previous approaches. The New Leadership approach is wedded to an overtly rational model of organizational behaviour, and the approach appears to be associated with a specific quantitative research methodology (Bryman, 1996; Western, 2008; Yukl, 1999). Despite the view of the principal theoretical contributors of the New Leadership school that their approaches are distinct, others assert that the approaches congregate around three thematic principles: a focus on heroic leaders; a preoccupation with leadership at the highest levels of organization; and a focus on individuals as opposed to groups (Jackson and Parry, 2008; Parry and Bryman, 2006). This has led to the suggestion that the theories of New Leadership should be considered collectively, and they have subsequently been referred to as neo-charismatic theories of leadership (Beyer, 1999; House and Aditya, 1997).

Nevertheless, well-intentioned criticisms of the New Leadership school do not appear to have significantly damaged the currency with which it is held (House and Aditya, 1997; Parry and Bryman, 2006). Western (2008) maintains that the dominant normative position of New Leadership theory is maintained by two strong fundamental urges. The first is that changing social, political and economic conditions appear to predicate the intervention of a heroic leader in order to resolve the "wicked problems" evident in the contemporary social world (Grint, 2005a). The second urge is a requirement to keep the leadership development industry afloat, supported on the one hand by individual leaders being required to demonstrate their leadership impact immediately, and promoted on the other by consultancies, training companies and business schools marketing New Leadership as a form of easily assimilable commodity (Mintzberg, 2004).

A critique of leadership studies

The following three sections detail concerns related to progress within leadership studies. The first two have roots in Joseph Rost's (1993) seminal study, *Leadership for the Twenty-First Century*. Principal among Rost's concerns is the lack of definition within studies that have been undertaken, and their concentration on an historical view of leadership that purports to demonstrate progress in the understanding of leadership. The third section below gives an account of concerns about the research methodologies used in leadership studies.

Definition

One of Rost's criticisms relates to lack of definition within leadership studies (Rost, 1993). While a general definition of leadership is not a concern from a Critical Theory perspective, a lack of rigour, as identified by Rost and exemplified in many scholarly works, serves to illustrate this weakness in understanding the phenomenon.

Rost maintains that a lack of definition as to what constitutes leadership is the root cause for the lack of progress in leadership studies. If you cannot define it, how can you study it? Noting this definitional confusion, Yukl states that "the numerous definitions of leadership that have been proposed appear to have little in common with each other" (Yukl, 1989). The plethora of definitions and the volume of scholarly works that do not even define the area of study, "leadership", frustrate the possibilities of progress being made. It seems likely that the New Leadership school may be ultimately undermined by the fact that the majority of its contributors have placed no emphasis on the nature of leadership.

To complicate the matter further, there are a number of problematic differences beyond the definitions that have been presented. Yukl attempts an integrating conceptual framework in order to assist the understanding of prior theorizing. Rost, on the other hand, attempts to demolish the old ideas and replace them with a new model. These two perspectives offer two distinct platforms of understanding (Rickards and Clark, 2006). Nevertheless, there would appear to be some common ground between the platforms, as both see leadership as an influencing process founded upon a reciprocal relationship.

Other commentators have more recently developed a wider scope of views on the problem of defining leadership that could be appreciated as a third platform of understanding. Definitions in general provide clues as to what one is trying to address, but they are less helpful than is conventionally understood. Language is too ambiguous and meaning too context-dependent for abstract definitions to work effectively, as the definer seldom manages to control meaning particularly well (Alvesson, 1996), leading Grint to ask if leadership is an "essentially contested concept" (Grint, 2005b p. 17). Grint outlines four possibilities for defining leadership. The first is leadership as a person; is it "who" leaders are that makes them leaders? Second, leadership can be appreciated as results; is it "what" leaders achieve that makes them leaders? Third, leadership may be seen as a position; is it "where" leaders operate that makes them leaders? Finally, leadership can be seen as a process; is it "how" things are done that makes leaders?

Deconstructionists would claim that a half-conscious metaphorical structuring of a focal object gives an imaginative, rather than analytically clear-cut, meaning to the words (Calás and Smircich, 1991; Morgan, 1997). The same definition could therefore be informed by different metaphors and consequently different associated meanings. Alvesson (1996) illustrates this by drawing on an example from a study related to organizational culture. People may embrace a similar definition of organizational culture as a set of meanings, ideas, values and symbolisms shared by a group. This may also be accompanied by a high diversity of thinking, due to a metaphor for culture being one of a compass used for providing direction. Is culture a sacred cow protecting certain basic assumptions, or a frozen reality where meanings, ideas and values fix the reality and subordinate members to it? (Alvesson, 1993). Definition is only a limited part of how language and cognition work.

Given the variety of existent phenomena that leadership studies may address, the idiosyncrasies of the researchers, and the ambiguities of language, ways of thinking and doing research will not be standardized, even if a particular definition is seen to dominate. This illustrates that leadership, both as a term and as an object of study in relation to a distinct group of phenomena, is difficult to conceptualize in a uniform manner. Two problems occur here and are interrelated: the social worlds that are of interest to leadership researchers do not lend themselves to neat taxonomical classifications; and language has limitations in fixing goals and purposes through the use of definitions (Alvesson, 1996).

An historic view of leadership studies

A second major criticism of leadership studies concerns the attempts to portray the leadership literature as a historical narrative. There are generally two strategies used in employing this device, both of which give the impression of progress having been made in findings. The first illustrates the various epochs of leadership research developed over time, and the second focuses on the dominant research methodology utilized in leadership research.

In the first instance, it is relatively commonplace for researchers to provide an historic summary of leadership studies, split into apparent dominant schools of research; examples are House and Aditya (1997), Bryman (1996) and Yukl (1989). The story as told from this perspective is that "great man" theory proved unsupportable by the 1930s, and a new approach to studying leadership was pioneered by social psychologists. This line of enquiry was halted when it became evident that the findings were not transferable to large groups or organizations. Trait analysis was quashed by the efforts of Stoghill (1948), who by the 1950s had concluded that the trait studies were inconclusive and contradictory. He and others at Ohio State University therefore pioneered a behavioural appreciation of leadership, but were unable to isolate key behavioural patterns that made much difference. Situational researchers attempted to discover what behaviours were best in certain situations, but the research foundered on the sheer complexity of the models and the countless variability of situations to be studied. By the 1980s researchers were strongly repudiating situational models to conclude that leadership is about personal primacy and doing the right thing to achieve excellence, which forms the core of the New Leadership school (Rost, 1993).

The second strategy, considering the leadership story from a methodological perspective, is dominated by an experimental scientific approach taken from management studies and social psychology. Research in this context has been predominantly conducted within an exemplar scientific experimental methodology, experimenting and refuting theory until a new combination is discovered that holds promise (Rost, 1993). The point of this is that scientific exploration is a time-honoured process of theoretical discovery, illustrated by Edison's tale of repeated failure until the right discovery is made possible. Leadership researchers are continuing this practice, attempting to find the right mix of variables that constitute a general theory of leadership. Illustrated with reference to the heroic stance of the New Leadership school, researchers looked at excellent organizations and CEOs to determine lists of trait behaviours, group facilitation strategies and culture-shaping practices for potential leaders. While New Leadership may serve as a watershed in leadership development, much of the acknowledged developments in leadership understanding are merely repackaged theories from the past (Western, 2008).

Accordingly, there are two primary criticisms of the kinds of summaries that suggest that progress in understanding is being made (Rost, 1993). The first of these relates to the common practice of repeating the summary. As with other things that are frequently repeated, people start to acknowledge the content as facts. Like other myths, this summary of the movement of leadership research may be what we want to hear, but is not representative of what really happened (Gemmill and Oakley, 1992). There is no Kuhnian paradigm shift in relation to the development of understanding; rather, the theories and models are a mishmash of what has gone before (Rost, 1993).

The belief that distinct epochs of leadership study have produced commensurate increases in understanding is therefore misleading. There remain a great many theorists currently using traits as an explanation of leadership (Hough, 1992; Lord *et al.*, 1986; Strang and Kuhnert, 2009), and new trait models such as the five factor model of leadership are currently being developed (Digman, 1990). Furthermore, the great man/woman theory is alive as much today as yesterday: Bill Gates is our Henry Ford, Bill Clinton is our Theodore Roosevelt, and Nelson Mandela is our Mohandas Ghandi.

Second, in communicating that progress is being made, the narrative serves to produce a feeling of well-being, a sense that all is well in the study and practice of leadership that ultimately serves to foster a self-serving contentment. This message is very comforting for those that believe that leadership is of paramount importance in the survival and growth of our organizations, societies and the world (Rost, 1993 p. 23). A more critical appraisal, however, may lead to the suggestion supported by Rost that a realization of the two conforming narratives has simply brought about theoretical congruence.

The above critique of the historical view of methodology is an important factor and can be developed beyond the historical to incorporate the actual research method employed, and it is this that is considered in the next section of this chapter.

Research method

As in many other fields of management studies, leadership research has been dominated by a tradition of quantitative research drawn from psychology in which quantitative variables are related to various outcomes (Parry and Bryman, 2006; Rost, 1993; Western, 2008). The assumptions of the aforementioned positivistic and neo-positivistic tradition underpin an emphasis on rules and procedures for the securing of objectivity in practice and results (Alvesson, 1996). This methodology argues that well-conducted studies should, through the process of verification and falsification, lead to growing support for more and more accurate theories with greater explanatory and predictive capacity (Alvesson and Deetz, 2006a). While some researchers are optimistic about current research (House and Aditya, 1997), many are critical of progress made to date (Alvesson, 1996; Mintzberg, 1982; Parry, 1998; Rost, 1993; Western, 2008; Yukl, 1999), to the extent that a number of scholars have called for a profound adjustment to methodology (Alvesson, 1996; Bryman, 1996; Knights and Willmott, 1992; Parry, 1998; Smircich and Morgan, 1982).

Criticism concerning methodology appears to stem from the practical methods employed, which have been dominated by the static correlational analysis of data drawn from survey questionnaires (Yukl, 1999). The majority of these surveys ask subordinates to rate retrospectively how frequently a leader displayed a form of behaviour over a period that may extend for several months or years. Frequency ratings on individual behaviours are a poor method for measuring behaviours embedded in complex social situations, relying as they do on simplistic two-factor models (Yukl, 1999).

Researchers have therefore been employing methods that are designed to reduce the phenomenon into ever more simplistic models in attempts to "get it right" (Alvesson and Deetz, 2006a). These studies are neither designed nor evaluated by their capacity to challenge an assumption or to provide alternatives, let alone consider multiple ways of conceptualizing leadership. The research method underpins the core assumptions concerning leadership, weakening its conceptual capacity, leaving the primary level of analysis of the leader–follower dyad, and underestimating therefore the importance of other external factors that may effect the leadership process (Yukl, 1999). A requirement for the measurement of the leadership relationship under such assumptions is that the leadership dyad remains stable. This results in an essential "fixing" of the phenomenon, thus narrowing the conceptual alternatives that may be available to the object under scrutiny (Alvesson and Deetz, 2006b).

There is a very real possibility that such research may result in the reproduction and reinforcement of the "leader category" as well as contributing to the institutionalization of leadership (Alvesson and Sköldberg, 2005). The ideas expressed in research about the nature of leadership not only reflect "object" conditions, they also constitute them. If "heroic", "charismatic" or any such label applicable to leadership receives sufficient attention, then it acquires a certain importance in social circumstances. A consequence therefore is that scholars of leadership become predisposed toward asymmetrical power relationships and assign actors to either a leader or a follower classification.

Thus the research method employed may have a real tendency to reduce and simplify the phenomenon, which results in a conceptually fixed object of study. Researchers reproduce and reinforce conventions as a response to expectation and institutionalized forms of power, thus providing an ideological alibi, but they thereby limit the possibilities of alternative interpretations and analyses of leadership (Alvesson, 1996).

Conclusions

The previous three sections have highlighted factors that have retarded the development of knowledge and understanding related to leadership. The first factor is a lack of definition, the second concerns the typical use of historical narrative, and the third is the fixing of research methodology that is typically conventional within organization studies. The combined effect of these three factors is to promote an orthodoxy that ostensibly supports progression in understanding but has reduced the complexity of the phenomenon, thus prejudicing understanding and eliminating the possibility of conceptual alternatives.

An introduction to following

There are few points that leadership scholars agree upon, but one of them may be that, in order for a leader to exist, followers are required. The essence of leadership therefore is followership; there can be no leader without followers (Kellerman, 2008 p. 239). As noted above by Grint, leadership may be an essentially contested concept, and so rather unsurprisingly, the theorizing of the role and value of followers is contested in equal measure.

At one end of the spectrum, the role of followers has been underplayed if not ignored. One of the most likely reasons of this is the dominant trend of New Leadership research. This has typically focused on top leadership teams in order to develop highly focused leader-centric models, which consequently view leadership as a top-down process between leader and subordinate (Yukl, 1989). A number of contributors to New Leadership theory concur with this view, maintaining that leaders are set apart by their ability to mobilize followers and bring about elevated performance from them (Bass, 1985, 1998; Bass and Avolio, 1990, 1994a; Yukl, 2002). Later developments such as Full Range Leadership Theory continue to assert this, stating that the transformational leader focuses on the material needs of the follower, and is able to build on the follower's self-concept and self-worth to mould a self-concept that reflects the leader's own self-concept and mission (Bass, 2000). The relationship between leaders and followers is therefore essentially a linear, one-way relationship. The follower is, in effect, a blank slate upon which the leader writes the script (Jackson and Parry, 2008).

Alternatively, at the opposite end of the spectrum sit a number of contributors who maintain that followers have a vital role to play in the leadership process. Followers have traditionally been presented both individually and collectively as passive objects to be moulded, influenced and coerced by the leader. As an alternative to this traditional approach, and influenced by post-structuralist analysis, the currency of followers has become more elevated as the dualist approach is challenged (Western, 2008). Consequently, some contributors have challenged the notion of followers as docile and have sought to state their individual and collective value (Chaleff, 2003; Collinson, 2006; Kellerman, 2008; Kelley, 1992, 2004; Lundin and Lancaster, 1990; Potter *et al.*, 2001; Raelin, 2004; Rosenau, 2004; Seteroff, 2003). Not surprisingly, the value and the role of followers are stated in many ways. The three most prevalent of these are discussed below: first, followers as moderators of leadership; second, followers as substitutes for leadership; and finally, followers as constructors of leadership (Jackson and Parry, 2008)[1]

Followers as moderators of leadership

This perspective of following locates followers in their mainly passive role as receivers of leadership influence, but acknowledges, at least, that the leader's influence may have to be differentiated depending on the follower(s) being addressed. Here the view sits comfortably with contingency theories of leadership (Fiedler, 1967; House, 1971), but is also relevant when considering aspects of neo-charismatic models such as Bass's Full Range Leadership Theory model. This perspective recognizes that the approach of the leader may have to be moderated in order to appeal to the follower. Those leaders designated as transformational "diagnose the needs of their followers and then elevate those needs to initiate and promote development" (Bass and Avolio, 1994b p. 552). This, along with the transformational criterion of "individualized consideration", requires that there is some modification of approach to the individual follower. Furthermore, this perspective relates to the criterion of "idealized influence" or charisma, particularly if charisma is acknowledged as being a socially derived construct (Bryman, 1992), as charismatic appeal and social contagion may require moderated approaches dependent upon the follower or group of followers. This consideration was given some credence in a study of manager career development, where derailment was attributed to lack of interpersonal skills (Dansereau, 1995).

In earlier models, Bass observed transformational behaviours being held as superior to transactional behaviours. Within the Full Range Leadership model, however, the value of transactional behaviours has become appreciated as critical to the overall leadership approach. The best leaders employ both transformational and transactional behaviours dependent upon the follower (Rickards and

Clark, 2006). Within this, the negotiation of transactional benefits between the leader and follower demands a modified approach to leadership appropriate to the follower.

The division between transformational and transactional behaviours may be less clear-cut than New Leadership scholars would assert. Rost is very critical of leadership scholars asserting the presence of differences between leadership and management without clarifying what those differences comprise. Much of leadership theorizing is indistinct and weak in definition, and consequently the two terms are conflated. He suggests therefore that much of what has been supposed to be leadership is, in fact, effective general management (Rost, 1993).

Followers as substitutes for leadership

The theory of followers as substitutes for leadership, developed by Kerr and Jermier (1978), maintains that a variety of organizational, group, task and individual factors are important in providing guidance and good feelings for employees. Leadership behaviour, as classically understood, can be important but should be examined in the context of other factors, some of which can be substituted for or can neutralize the leader's influence (Kerr and Jermier, 1978). Included among these variables identified as potential substitutes for leadership are four subordinate characteristics (ability, experience, training and knowledge; need for independence; professional orientation; and indifference to organizational rewards); three task characteristics (task feedback; routine, methodologically invariant tasks; intrinsically satisfying tasks); and six organizational characteristics (organizational formalization; organizational inflexibility; group cohesiveness; amount of advisory/staff support; rewards outside the leader's control; and the degree of spatial distance between supervisors and subordinates) (Kerr and Jermier, 1978).

Unlike the transformational approach to leadership, which assumes that the leader's transformational behaviour is the key to improving leadership effectiveness, the "substitutes for leadership" approach assumes that the real key to leadership effectiveness is to identify those important situational or contextual variables that may be "substituting" for the leader's behaviour, so that the leader can adapt his or her behaviour accordingly. If the leader's influence is being substituted for, the question of whether leadership is actually occurring must be considered, as the leader's activities may be deemed largely irrelevant (Jackson and Parry, 2008).

The theory has been developed primarily with the aim of de-emphasizing the role of the nominated leader and enhancing the agency of followers (Jackson and Parry, 2008). Empirical studies have failed to substantiate the substitution theory to any satisfactory degree, but recent theorizing by the original authors has reinvigorated interest in the concept (Dionne *et al.*, 2005; Jermier and Kerr, 1997), leading to the suggestion that the construct may have the ability to show how followers, through their own activities, effectively moderate or construct leadership. The specific activities of followers in this construct, however, remain untheorized (Jackson and Parry, 2008).

Followers as constructors of leadership

> In whatever direction a ship moves, the flow of waves it cuts will always be notice-
> able ahead of it.... When the ship moves in one direction there is one and the same
> wave ahead of it; when it turns frequently the wave ahead of it also turns fre-
> quently. But wherever it may turn there always will be the wave anticipating its
> movement. Whatever happens it appears that just that event was foreseen and
> decreed. Wherever the ship may go, the rush of water which neither directs nor
> increases its movement foams ahead of it, and at a distance seems not merely to
> move of itself but to govern the ship's movement also.
>
> Tolstoy (1869/1991 p. 1289)

In this group of theories, the scholars involved have made the activities of followers as constructors of leadership their primary area of focus. Rost (1993)
affirms the importance of followers within the leadership relationship but maintains that followers do not engage in "followership". Their actions should instead
be appreciated as part of the leadership process, acting in tandem with leaders.
The view of followers constructing leadership is raised by Grint (1997), who
uses Tolstoy's metaphor of a ship's bow wave (reproduced above; taken from
Grint, 1997 p. 1) to suggest that leaders are mere figureheads propelled by events
and people beyond their control. The researchers are primarily concerned with
the thoughts of followers and how their thoughts construct and represent leaders;
leadership is fundamentally in the eye of the follower.

Romance

A concern that leadership scholars had become overly preoccupied with leader-
centric views of leadership led to the perception that leadership research was
perpetuating the hype and unrealistic expectation that is routinely placed upon
leaders. This concern became the central focus of Meindl and colleagues. Their
archival studies supported an attributional perspective in which leadership is
romanticized (Meindl *et al.*, 1985). This suggests that there is a strong belief,
bordering on faith, in the importance of leadership to the functioning, effectively
or otherwise, of organized systems (Meindl and Ehrlich, 1987). In the absence of
direct and unambiguous information concerning the organization, followers
would ascribe control of and responsibility for events to leaders that could be
plausibly linked with them (Meindl *et al.*, 1985). In effect, leadership acted as a
simplified, biased but attractive way to explain organizational performance, particularly in extreme cases (Jackson and Parry, 2008).

Meindl describes the romance of leadership as a social construction; followers
construct an opinion concerning a leader by interacting with other followers,
facilitating a process referred to as social contagion, not dissimilar to the spread
of a socially constrained virus spread from follower to follower until everyone
becomes infected. Social contagion highlights the interpersonal processes and

group dynamics that underpin the widespread dissemination of charismatic effects among followers and subordinates (Jackson and Parry, 2008).

Social identity theory

Within social identity theory, leadership is confirmed as primarily a social process in which leaders are able to persuade others to embrace new values, attitudes and goals, and to exert additional effort in the achievement of those goals (Hogg, 2001). The theory proposes that the extent to which an individual is accepted as a leader depends upon how "prototypical" (or representative) the individual is of the group (Hogg, 2001). Other contributors state that prototypicality may not be the sole basis for establishing leadership, considering alternative task-related schemas and stereotypes of leader behaviour (Lord and Brown, 2001; van Kippenberg *et al.*, 2004). A leader may be likely to attract a follower who shares a similar background and beliefs, but also the reverse process is possible, whereby the leader is selected and supported by followers because the leader is like the group in terms of characteristics, beliefs, aspirations and values (Jackson and Parry, 2008). In the absence of a leader prototypical of the group, group members will use demographic information to generate an impression (stereotype) of the person involved (van Kippenberg *et al.* 2006).

Haslam and Platow (2001) maintain that leadership and identity are mutually interdependent features of social group life. Leadership is dependent on group members sharing a social identity, where leaders play a fundamental part in the construction of that identity. While the main focus of this work is on the leader's identity, there is some complementary interest in the way that leaders influence followers' identity as an indirect means of increasing commitment (Chemers, 2003). Reicher *et al.* (2005) claim that traditional leadership models are often seen as a form of zero-sum game, and that leader agency can only be achieved at the expense of follower agency. In line with social identity theory, the writers argue that the agencies of leaders and followers are interdependent to the extent that they rely upon each other to create the condition where mutual influence is possible; the actions of both leaders and followers are therefore dependent upon each other.

Despite acknowledging many contributors to the field, Reicher *et al.* (2005) maintain that the extent of social identity theory is deficient in four areas. First, theories need to be reconsidered in order to incorporate Weber's earlier work on charisma and thus to support the work of transformational theorists. Second, the impact of leaders on followers must be addressed in the context of their involvement in a joint relationship. Third, models need to be developed in order to account for how leaders actively shape identities and how followers respond to these attempts. And finally, the authors suggest that the balance between autonomy and constraint in leadership is a dynamic process that unfolds over time.

Collinson (2006) has gone some way to reducing the gaps identified by Reicher and colleagues. He maintains that studies of leadership need to develop a broader and deeper understanding of followers' identities, and rejects the idea that identities comprise a singular homogeneous grouping, as people's lives are inextricably interwoven with the social world around them (Layder, 1994). Collinson's post-structuralist approach suggests that followers' identities may be much more complex and differentiated than previously conceptualized. Individuals are best understood as social selves whose actions have to be understood within their own complex conditions, processes and consequences. While some of these co-existing identities may be mutually reinforcing, others may be in tension, mutually contradictory and even incompatible. Organizations not only produce products and services, but, in important symbolic and material ways, they also produce people capable of differing responses to leadership (Collinson, 2006).

Critical approaches to leadership

The following section reviews leadership literature that has been written from a Critical Theory perspective. It is based upon the Critical Theory requirement of seeking to challenge the conception of leadership as an asymmetrical relationship, in order to establish an emancipatory objective. Traditional formulations of leadership as a relationship embedded in a social setting rarely take into account the complexity of the social practice of leadership. Such accounts share a reluctance to take an adequate account of context and, specifically, of the interplay of power and subjectivity in the dynamics of the relationship (Knights and Willmott, 1992). Despite an increase in the variety of approaches, including Marxist, neo-Marxist, poststructural, feminist and postcolonial approaches, the field of critical organization studies has evolved around, and remains rooted to, an implicit binary opposition that privileges either organizational control processes or employee resistance to such mechanisms of control (Mumby, 2005). The following studies go some way toward remedying this, considering as they do a complex environment comprising the interplay of various concepts such as identity, power, resistances, politics, and ambiguity. The first section below deals with identity, power and resistances; the second with the impact of politics; and the third with the effects of ambiguity on relationships within organizations.

Identity, power and resistances

Alvesson and Willmott (2002) argue that identity regulation is now a central feature of organizational control in post-bureaucratic organizations. Collinson (2006), drawing on Foucauldian analysis, points to the way that workplace surveillance systems such as human resources initiatives and technology developments can discipline employees by actively constructing followers' conformist selves, a position which dominates much of the followership literature. Very few studies have examined follower resistance.

Collinson's work shows that organizations confer multiple identities and meanings upon people. Equally, however, they can generate considerable employee insecurity and anxiety (Collinson, 2003). Subsequently leaders are frequently surprised by the reactions of followers (Collinson, 2005), and followers are frequently adept and cunning at responding to leaders, whether it is in supporting, conforming with or resisting them (Collinson, 2003, 2006; Kellerman, 2008). Collinson's perspective suggests that as a result of routinized surveillance, heightened self-consciousness and the audit culture it produces, followers can become increasingly skilled manipulators of self and information (Collinson, 1999).

Chaleff (2003) is one of the few writers on followers to consider the possibility of followers' oppositional identity, observing that honest feedback from followers to leaders is frequently absent in organizations. Chaleff recommends that courageous followers should challenge leaders' views and decisions, a position that shares some similarities with Collinson's (1994) own examination of "resistance through persistence". Further developments along this line of thinking suggest that workplace resistance is not only a primary means through which employees may express discontent, but is also a way for followers to construct alternative, more positive identities to those provided or prescribed by the organization. This focus on followers' oppositional, resistant selves suggests that identity construction in organizations may be shaped by differentiation as much as identification (Collinson, 2006).

Iedema and colleagues (2006) extend the concept of worker suppression, framed in terms of disciplinary practices of surveillance and subsequent compliance or resistance responses. They suggest that people are unlikely to simply obey or reject organizationally defined and aligned conduct. To regard workers as being caught between being determined by surveillance or being forced into resistance is to miss some central facets of contemporary workplace dynamics. These facets, collectively referred to as observance, are to do with workers enacting a social-organizational form of reflection, which enables compliance and resistance to coexist together. This mobilization is achieved through any number of organizational initiatives, one of which is the recasting of professionalism, an "ideational" control strategy regarded by some as a particularly insidious source of influence capable of manipulating identity (Hodgson, 2005).

Zoller and Fairhurst (2007), with reference to Foucault, state that just as leadership cannot be captured as simple categories of behaviour, power should not be viewed simplistically either. From such a perspective, a form of leadership, classed as resistance leadership, emerges, incorporating evolving relationships *among resistors* as well as between resistors and their targets, always within particular social and historical contexts.

Leadership concepts help us to see mutual influence between individuals and groups, and groups-in-formation. Yet there is still much to learn, because a complete view of resistance leadership views the construct from all sides: those in and out of power as well as those on the rise, and taking in issues of justice, ethics and moral accountability at every turn, providing alternative perspectives and thereby influencing understanding. Leadership concepts will not explain all aspects of resistance, and analysts must take care to avoid the romanticization of resistance leadership to which both actors and analysts may fall prey (Zoller and Fairhurst, 2007).

Political influences

Within leadership studies there is an acknowledgement that the interaction between leaders and followers cannot occur in a vacuum. Contingency theorists assert that leadership exists in context and have theorized variables that impact upon leadership behaviour (Fiedler, 1967; Hersey and Blanchard, 1984; House, 1971). While the effectiveness of the aforementioned theories has been brought into question, it is acknowledged that their contribution to leadership studies has at least provoked better theory (House and Aditya, 1997). In attempting to understand organizations and interactions between people, Morgan portrays the organization as a political system, but warns that classification of an organization as political is potentially problematic (Morgan, 1997). The levels and types of political activity within the organization are a consequence of the kind of political rule inherent within a system. Morgan provides a taxonomy of possible modes of political rule in organizations, suggesting the very real possibility that political rule underpinned by bureaucracy can be appreciated as a particular form of normalized social domination (after Weber cited in Morgan, 1997 p. 304).

Common varieties of political rule found in organizations

Autocracy: absolute power held by an individual or small group, supported by control of critical resources, ownership rights, tradition, charisma and other claims to personal privilege.

Bureaucracy: rule exercised through the use of the written word, providing rational authority under the "rule of law".

Technocracy: rule exercised through the use of knowledge, expert power and ability to solve relevant problems.

Co-determination: rule by opposing parties who combine in the joint management of mutual interests, each party drawing on a specific power base.

Representative democracy: rule through the election of officers mandated to act on behalf of the electorate; office held as long as support of electorate maintained.

Direct democracy: everyone having an equal right to rule and being involved in the decision-making; encourages self-organization as a key mode of organizing.

House and Aditya (1997 p. 455) claim that most observers of organizations would admit that politics and political behaviour occur within organizations and that such behaviour can have profound effects. Despite this, the authors are amazed to find that notwithstanding the extensive study of power and influence, and of the processes in organizations, there is no political theory of leadership. Several authors have offered definitions of political behaviour, which in essence describe political behaviour as that which is driven by self-interest and is not explicitly condoned or condemned by organizational policy or norms. Thus defined, political behaviour is neither inherently good nor evil, and neither detrimental nor functional for organizational performance (Porter *et al.*, 1981).

Pfeffer (1981) has described the conditions that give rise to, and enhance, the exercise of political behaviour. Mintzberg has further described many of the countervailing political forces that exist in organizations, leading him to theorize that political activity occurs when people think differently and want to behave differently. In order to resolve the tensions between individuals, recourse to political behaviour, often defined as games, is regularly manifested in those organizations defined as a political arena (Mintzberg, 1985). The ability to thrive in such an arena is referred to by Ferris and colleagues as a critical skill in organizational survival (Ferris *et al.*, 2007).

Ammeter *et al.* (2002), in moving toward the development of a political theory of leadership, acknowledge these games, but assert that such behaviour does not always need to be seen as damaging. Political activity performed by leaders can be seen as a neutral, and inherently necessary, component of organizational functioning (Pfeffer, 1981), giving rise to the reduction or elimination of organizational ambiguity (Bolman and Deal, 1991; Ferris and Judge, 1991). Political activity should be perceived as valuable to the constructive process of developing shared meeting (Ammeter *et al.*, 2002), in turn seen as critical to the establishment of leadership (Smircich and Morgan, 1982). This is problematic, as leaders must adopt political behaviours that align with the established political norms, because their behaviours must match the situational assessments of their followers.

The use of external expertise has been identified as a potentially negative political tactic (Fairholm, 1993). This position was endorsed in a study of sanctioned and non-sanctioned political behaviours by Zanzi and O'Neill (2001), where the use of experts can be ambiguously perceived as both sanctioned and non-sanctioned behaviour depending on the manner and circumstances. Other potentially ambiguous behaviours are reactive behaviours that may be classified as impression management, and behaviours used in order to avoid action, most often for self-serving purposes, as identified by Ashforth and Lee (1990). There is a wide array of situations where the use of non-sanctioned tactics and potentially unethical behaviour may prove advantageous to the leader, to followers, or to the organization as a whole (Zanzi and O'Neill, 2001). An example of this might be the senior leadership of an organization exploiting the ambiguity of a situation to increase their own power or to protect power sources, a process referred to as "institutionalization" (Yukl, 2002 p. 351).

Ambiguity

Critical scholars have shown concern over the lack of appreciation of organizational ambiguity in leadership theory. Much of the problem here derives from the research paradigm under which most leadership studies are conducted. The positivistic approaches of management science render it incapable of studying the complex and ambiguous dimensions of leadership processes and practice (Alvesson, 1996; Knights and Willmott, 1992; Morgan, 1997). In order to achieve something that appears to be objective, variations are reduced, standardization is sought, and overt simplification prevails. The arbitrariness, emotionality and uncertainty of social life is suppressed to fit procedures that give the impression of objectivity. The standardization of social phenomena risks a basic distortion of social reality, not in the sense of reporting "reality" incorrectly, but in terms of representing certainty and order at the expense of openness and ambiguity (Alvesson and Sköldberg, 2005).

A number of contributors agree that while ambiguity is important in organizational life, it need not always have a detrimental effect. Eisenberg (2007) sees management communication as the strategic use of symbols, in which the communicator's goals are neither unitary nor consistent. He therefore advocates "a shift in emphasis away from an overly ideological adherence to clarity toward a more contingent, strategic orientation". This perspective sees organizational communication as the process through which organization occurs and not something that occurs within organizations.

In striking a balance between being understood, not offending, and maintaining self-image, individuals adopt different strategies, one of which may be to use ambiguity, which in this context is seen as a process that promotes "unified diversity" (Eisenberg, 2007 p. 7). *Strategic ambiguity* fosters the existence of multiple viewpoints, thereby allowing varied interpretations to exist among a population who contend that they are attending to the same message.

Eisenberg suggests that to make organizational activity meaningful to members, leaders should use language that is "abstract, evangelical, and even poetic". It therefore becomes a political necessity to engage in strategic ambiguity so that different constituent groups may apply different interpretations to the message or symbol. Thus leaders use ambiguity strategically to guard against the acceptance of a standard way of viewing organizational reality (Eisenberg, 2007).

Further developing the concept of strategic ambiguity, Giroux (2006) assembles a number of themes that are related to each other by a central concern for collective action and the role of ambiguity. The author characterizes *pragmatic ambiguity* as admitting more than one course of action, so that a practical solution to the difficulties of divergent interpretation may be found, thereby resolving organizational paralysis.

The term pragmatic ambiguity may more accurately reflect the crux of the matter, in that equivocal accounts allow for differing courses of action while also maintaining a semblance of unity. This process may be seen as both the result and resource of a management approach. The very activities of organizing require alliances to be made, within which differences are negotiated and compromised; pragmatic ambiguity should be appreciated as a practice – strategic or otherwise – borne out of and sustained by discursive activities (Giroux, 2006).

In a study by Alvesson and Sveningsson (2003a), the authors specifically consider the impact of ambiguity upon the understanding and practice of leadership within a knowledge-intensive organizational context. The authors maintain that organizational context renders the organization under study as particularly susceptible to modern conceptualizations of leadership, comprising as it does uncertain, long-term and complex work processes underpinned by an apparent lack of need for close supervision. The conclusions of the study are surprising and provocative.

The study makes four related conclusions. First, managers' ideas around leadership seem to be vague, disconnected and not easily applicable to work. Managers are caught between leadership discourses, practical constraints, and administrative demands. Second, contemporary ideas about leadership have little impact on organizational practice. Third, managers make sense of their work situations from different moral positions: self-location in the "good" position of leadership does not restrict people from practicing a "bad" form of micromanagement. Finally, managers, despite the apparent contradictions, separate the position of good leadership from bad management to the extent that they sustain a leadership ideal seemingly at odds with much of managerial work. This serves to undermine the essence of leadership itself, thereby reducing its importance. This constitutes the "ugly" aspect of leadership – a position underpinned by the ambiguity inherent in leadership construction and the working context (Alvesson and Sveningsson, 2003a).

It remains to be seen how ambiguity affects the dynamics of the leader–follower relationship and whether this behaviour deviates from that outlined in more traditional leadership studies. With particular reference to the studies of Eisenberg (2007) and Giroux (2006), the use of ambiguity, strategically or otherwise, in support of agency in this context remains to explored and illustrated.

Critical Theory and leadership

Critical organization studies have yet to embrace research that addresses leadership as a significant concept. One reason for this reluctance may be the conflation of leadership with the study of leadership, which is largely quantitative and managerially focused. As a result, leadership may be equated with the managerial role itself, so that only those in organizationally sanctioned roles count as leaders. A second factor may be a tendency to view leadership as a form of domination, an aggregation of leadership with other "mechanisms of domination" such as culture and structure (Hardy and Clegg, 2006). This view may lead critical scholars to devalue leadership, given preferences for understanding deep structures of power over relational approaches (Zoller and Fairhurst, 2007).

A foundation of the present study is to utilize a broad understanding of the literature as a vital resource when reflecting upon and interpreting the empirical materials. Furthermore, the study aims to widen the scope of voices included in the interpretations and not therefore to limit them (Alvesson and Sköldberg, 2005). Generally, Critical Theory approaches to leadership studies have thrown doubt upon the normative understanding of leadership and its value in organizational life (Bresnen, 1995; Grint, 2005a). It is evident therefore that some studies will provide a more salient anchor point for interpretation than others, given the political-ideological continuum that is particularly relevant to Critical Theory examination. It is to these studies that attention is now turned.

Positioned slightly outside the approaches outlined below is a study by Calás and Smircich (1991), who use feminist deconstructionist methodologies to juxtapose "leadership" and "seduction" functions to expose the rhetorical and cultural conditions that support organizational leadership. This perspective is centred on the seductive effects of academic organizational writings, from which the authors conclude that as a form of seduction, there is nothing profound about leadership. This poststructuralist analysis is claimed to be of particular value when innovations in theory and research are expected, but not forthcoming. Researchers and theorists of leadership may be *saying/doing* about leadership very different things from what actual managers are *saying/doing* about it, but one and the other constantly reproduce strong manifestations of the homosocial order by repeating seduction as truth. Calás and Smircich (1991) conclude by asserting that this process of legitimizing fixes structural relations of power within broader social systems. While Calás and Smircich provide evidence of an alternative conceptualization of leadership, the present study deals lightly with the implications of their findings and considers mainly the structural relations of power between leaders and followers and the extent to which they are fixed in practice.

A seminal paper in leadership studies by Smircich and Morgan (1982) states that successful acts of organization are often seen to rest in the synchrony between the initiation of action and the appeal for direction; between the actions of leaders and the receptivity and responsiveness of followers. They focus therefore on the way meaning in organizational settings is created, sustained and changed, as this provides a way of understanding the fundamental nature of leadership as a social process. The key challenge for the leader is to manage meaning in a way that orientates other individuals to the achievement of desirable ends.

Smircich and Morgan's analysis draws attention to the role of power as a defining feature of the leadership process, characterized by the way that the leader's sense-making activities assume a priority over the sense-making activities of others. Situations of formal leadership institutionalize this pattern into a system of rights and obligations, where the leader has the prerogative to define reality, and the led accept the definition as a frame of reference through which to orient their own activity. Leadership is therefore a power-based reality construction process, an unintended consequence of which may be a condition referred to as "trained inaction". Building upon this analysis, the present study will further consider aspects of power within the leader–follower relationship and the extent of the perceived asymmetry of the power relationship between the two.

Developing further the restrictive capacity of leadership, Gemmill and Oakley (1992) utilize a Jungian approach to speculate that leadership as a social myth represents a regressive wish to return to a protected environment absolved of consciousness, mindfulness and responsibility. This expression of infantilization is born out of an actual unitive experience of a symbiotic environment and comprises therefore the ultimate form of de-skilling and learned helplessness.

Members of social systems may behave as alienated robots, paralysed by an environment in which nothing appears fixed. Work processes are imbued with meaning by each individual and therefore have no objective meaning of their own. Subsequently individuals are locked into a dependency upon a leader myth that helps to rationalize and make safe individual fears. Leaders and followers therefore act in well-defined and limited roles that reflect and consequently reinforce existing norms and values (Gemmill and Oakley, 1992). This study exposes the capacities of followers to interpret meaning inherent in the workplace. It is beyond the scope of the present study to consider fully the findings of Gemmill and Oakley's paper, given the variations in approach employed. However, aspects of the study that include compliance with norms and values and the utilization of power structures will be further considered.

In analysing the socially constructed nature of leadership in practice, Knights and Willmott (1992) consider further the effect of power on the leadership relationship. A critical reflection on leadership qualities demonstrates that power is relational and involves an interdependence between more and less advantaged groups. Instead of assuming an underlying consensus between leaders and followers reinforced by effective leadership to generate a "committed polity", it is more plausible to understand the achievement of consent from followers as precarious and often achieved through the exercise of power.

Knights and Willmott point to the limitation that results from conceptualizing power as a possession, in that it distracts attention from the interdependence of social relations and the socially constructed nature of reality. The phenomenological dimension of power is important, since the meanings which secure and sustain power relations have to be negotiated and can never be assumed to meet with acceptance merely because they are issued from leaders. Furthermore, negotiations have to be continually repeated, as in practice power does not exist independent of its exercise. The importance of this insight is that it positions leadership as a dynamic social practice. In considering leadership as a practice between leaders and followers, the present study will further consider the conceptualization of interdependence to include the possibilities (in practice) of an interdependence of power relations between constituent groups by reflecting upon the structure of agency and related behaviours.

Bresnen (1995) challenges the mainstream understanding of leadership theory by exploring in depth the nature of leadership as a socially attributed and constructed phenomenon. Assuming that "managers" act as "leaders" creates definitional problems, which in turn lead to leadership processes being amalgamated within the wider power and authority structures inherent in leader–follower relations. Furthermore, approaches that emphasize the socially constructed nature of leadership often tend toward a deterministic view of the impact of common conceptions of leadership and underplay the role of agency in negotiating, reinforcing and otherwise influencing leadership as a social construction.

From the accounts of practicing managers, the present study highlights basic similarities but also many more differences in the way the concept of leadership is interpreted and articulated by practitioners. The interpretive approach is posited therefore to bridge the apparent gap in understanding between mainstream theory and research and other alternative, critical platforms, by providing a more "grounded" perspective. This study utilizes an interpretive approach, albeit through a Critical Theory lens, to examine the construction of leadership as a social influence process and to outline areas that may bridge from the traditional to more critical approaches to leadership conceptualization.

Alvesson and Sveningsson (2003b) choose to centre their analysis on organizational contexts typified by high levels of ambiguity, complexity and the educational attainment of workers. While it may be probable that leadership in normalized terms could be observed, the general conclusions of the study indicate that it is difficult to say anything concerning the existence of leadership in the vast majority of organizational situations. The study details two breakdowns in leadership construction, but does not dismiss the possibility of others occurring in different contextual situations.

The observed breakdowns lead the authors to propose three specific findings for their study. The first concerns the value of leadership, given the vague and contradictory notions about leadership as stated by practitioners. The second concerns the fragility of leadership as a position relative to practice. Finally the study draws attention to methodological problems and points toward the requirement for a more open and questioning approach. This leads to the assertion that leadership requires critical study and should not therefore be taken for granted.

In drawing conclusions from interpretations of empirical materials, the present study will utilize a Critical Theory approach to examine breakdowns in leadership (Alvesson and Sveningsson, 2003b) and particularly those related to dominant management ideologies. Unpacking of these structures exposes to scrutiny constructs such as power (Gemmill and Oakley, 1992; Knights and Willmott, 1992; Smircich and Morgan, 1982), complexity and ambiguity (Alvesson and Sveningsson, 2003a; Eisenberg, 2007; Giroux, 2006) and organizational context (Alvesson and Sveningsson, 2003b). This study builds upon these works to demonstrate how the dynamics of the relationship between leader and follower are influenced by the aforementioned constructs and are bridged by political considerations, an additional construct that is implicit in much critical management research but rarely dealt with satisfactorily in leadership studies (House and Aditya, 1997).

Conclusions

The final section of this chapter will briefly summarize the main arguments presented in each of the sections above. Using these arguments, a framework will be presented that sets up the research question and establishes a basis for the study.

The first section introduced Critical Theory and a critical approach to organization studies, establishing the emancipatory credentials of the approach as opposed to the orthodox privileging of the management-leader perspective. Following this, the principal theories of the New Leadership school were presented; it was argued that this school has come to represent the normative conceptualization of leadership. Criticisms of this school were made from three distinct angles. The summation of these criticisms is that the progress of leadership understanding has been retarded by the assumption that progress has been made, an assumption underpinned by lack of conceptualization concerning the nature of leadership, a reliance on the use of historical narrative, and a conservative research methodology.

The second section of this chapter outlined theories that challenge the leader-centric position of leadership studies by focusing on a follower perspective. These theories were broken into three distinct conceptions of the role of the follower as moderator of, substitute for, or constructor of the leader–follower relationship.

The third section of the chapter presented literature supporting a Critical Theory perspective of leadership. This perspective challenges the asymmetrical, conceptual orthodoxy of normative leadership derived from the functionalist research paradigm. It moves the leader–follower relationship beyond the purely dyadic and establishes the necessity of appreciating leadership from a holistic perspective. It introduces the factors of power, identity, resistance, politics and ambiguity. These factors have been largely ignored by a leadership conceptualization underpinned by neo-positivistic assumptions. The final part of this section outlined the small number of leadership studies conducted from a Critical Theory perspective.

The application of a Critical Theory approach to leadership demands that we look beyond the management and leadership literature that draws too heavily on the insider view of leadership. This insider view comprises a normative understanding of leadership and is built on rationalistic and functionalist ideas from management theory (Alvesson, 1996; Western, 2008). The New Leadership approach noted by Bryman (1996) produced an initial jolt to the impetus of leadership studies. However, it remains dominated by a predominantly functionalist perspective and research methodology that, as a result, privileges management knowledge presented as science, obscuring the political and power aspects of organizations.

The present study will utilize a Critical Theory methodology in order to develop a framework of the dynamics of the leader–follower relationship. The organization of this study has been informed by the literature presented in the preceding sections of this chapter and has established a number of criteria for the conduct of the study.

A Critical Theory methodology establishes different parameters for the study of leadership, as opposed to the neo-positivistic assumptions of the traditional research methodology. In conducting this study through a Critical Theory lens, the authors respond to the call for a radical reorientation in leadership studies (Alvesson, 1996; Calás and Smircich, 1991; Grint, 2005b; Rost, 1993; Smircich and Morgan, 1982; Watkins, 1989).

This study makes no judgement upon the objective truth of any of the literature outlined above. It acknowledges the literature and seeks to utilize it in making interpretations concerning the dynamics of the leader–follower relationship as detailed in the materials collected during fieldwork.

This study defines leadership as an influence relationship between leaders and followers. It recognizes that the relationship is more complex than that presented within the normative literature. It establishes the principle of observing the relationship between leaders and followers from a holistic perspective and acknowledges that contextual factors such as power, politics and ambiguity are important when making interpretational analysis concerning the dynamics of the relationship.

In deliberately viewing the leader–follower relationship through a Critical Theory lens, the study seeks to challenge traditional conceptual notions of leadership and leader–follower relations by drawing attention to the stereotype of power relations theorized to exist between the two groups. In establishing this challenge, the study confirms its emancipatory intent.

3　The public sector in context

Drip, drip, drip. Day after day an insidious poison is fed into the nation's veins, spreading anger and cynicism about everything in the public sector. Nothing works, billions are wasted, public servants of every kind are pointless jobsworths feathering their nests and twiddling their thumbs.

Toynbee (2009 p. 29)

Introduction

International calls for improved leadership have been widespread, not least in respect of public sector organizations. What this improved public sector leadership may look like is open to considerable debate, and notions of the leadership phenomenon have been criticized for the normative conceptualizations on which they depend (Alvesson, 1996; Alvesson and Spicer, 2011; Collinson, 2006; Rost, 1993; Watkins, 1989; Western, 2008). To counteract these perceived deficiencies, this book moves beyond a normative appreciation of leadership to set the leader–follower relationship in its national and institutional context. Interpretations based upon a localized study offset the reductionist tendencies of dominant methodologies and allow for a wider and deeper appreciation of the leadership phenomenon (Alvesson and Willmott, 2001; Bryman, 1996).

To develop a broader understanding of the leadership environment, it is necessary to consider wider contextual factors. A Critical Theory perspective places value on political issues related to power, control and ambiguity (Alvesson and Willmott, 2001). No less important, however, are the historical antecedents that can supply a deeper situational understanding of the dynamic organizational context within which the leader–follower relationships are played out.

This chapter therefore is broken down into three sections. The first section sets out dominant trends in global public sector reform and examines their consequences. The second section outlines the UK's history of legislative reform targeted at the public sector and local government in particular. The third section outlines how reform has affected public sector working life in four specific ways: the move from markets to hierarchies; New Public Management and the importation of private sector practices; the challenges to public service ethos; and ambiguity in the public sector. The chapter concludes by asserting that many interpretive spaces in UK public sector organizations are affected by global trends in public sector reform and successive governments' attempts at reform, with the consequence that the notion of a managerially functionalist and normative style of leadership has come to dominate.

Global public sector reform

A pattern of public sector reform has been noted by a number of prominent authors. Barzelay (2001) has outlined a number of key case studies of public sector reform across North America and Western Europe. In each study, the traditional method of public administration has been challenged by the attempted reforms of executive government and a number of similarities have been noted. It has been proposed that traditional "outmoded" forms of organizing public administration have become displaced by a paradigm shift in public sector management, referred to in the literature as New Public Management (NPM) (Common, 1998; Hood, 1995; Rhodes, 1991). In essence, NPM is grounded in two fundamental philosophies: "managerialism" and "economic rationalism" (Parker and Guthrie, 1993).

Generally scholars have mediated an agreement that the principal mechanism for change is market based – involving either quasi-markets or the contracting out or privatizing of services that were previously undertaken by the state (Christensen and Lægreid, 2007; Dent *et al.*, 2004; Dunleavy *et al.*, 2005; Pollitt, 2002). Scholars have also noted the importance of generic management practices (Hood, 1996; Peters, 2010), specifically human resource management practices based on the assumption that the clarification of goals and performance objectives improves performance. At the core of this lies the belief that performance can be enhanced by articulating goals and accentuating management accountability for achievement, based on indicators to assess the achievement of goals and using budget as an incentive (Boyne and Chen, 2007; Lee *et al.*, 2009; Noordegraaf and Abma, 2003). However, as services are restructured, the ownership of the services does not change, while the form of the ownership structure may alter as government withdraws from the production of goods and services in major areas of public sector activity, leaving behind complex arrangements of production and measurement (James, 2004).

Global trends in reshaping public sector institutions have tended to both mimic and follow trends in industrial organization. It is the contention of a number of contributors that the mirroring of private sector practices has served as a leitmotif for reform (du Gay, 2006). Since the mid-1990s, there has been a move away from the consolidation of large corporate structures requiring devolved administration and many layers of management, towards smaller more flexible organizations. Firms have been radically downsized, and levels of management have been stripped out to make flatter, less hierarchical organizations (Hassard *et al.* 2009). As a consequence, power has shifted from professional managers (insiders) to investors in charge (outsiders). These moves are characterized by a shift from "management" to "leadership". Hierarchies, order, paternalism and stability are replaced by flexibility, networks, speed and frequent shifts of strategy and position (Boltansky and Chiapello, 2005). Boltansky and Chiapello call this the "third spirit of capitalism", where organizations are led by high profile CEOs who must convince via "visions and values", and leadership is said to be about coaching staff towards acting upon visions rather than micro-managing performance. However, rapid progress in information technology has enabled ever more detailed measurement and monitoring of performance against business goals and targets. Hassard *et al.* (2009) argue that this amounts to a new organizational ideology that moves beyond scientific management, rationalism, strategic planning and management, towards flatter organizations with fewer levels of middle management, shorter job tenures and much wider and more demanding work roles for managers. Companies, no longer dominated by insiders, have to be more sensitive to the needs of customers and reorientate their businesses accordingly. It is maintained here that the ensuing public sector reforms have mirrored in practice what has been observed in the private sector.

The reforms to which we refer have been associated with the NPM movement and have been generally acknowledged as being conceptualized in the UK under the Thatcher administration, with 1979 proving to be a watershed for the public sector. It is from this point that a profound and intensive programme of reform of public service provision and personnel was initiated (Ackroyd *et al.*, 2007), a programme which over 40 years later shows no sign of relenting. Dimensions of NPM as outlined by Pollitt (2002) and ensuing from this date are as follows:

- disaggregation of previously monolithic units in the public sector into purchaser and provider functions, and the introduction of contracting standards;
- performance management and target setting, especially for professional services;
- emphasis on output controls linked to resource allocation, including reduction and control of costs, doing more with less, and controlling labour union demands;
- hands-on professional management with an emphasis on private sector management style and greater flexibility (Hunter, 1996).

It has been argued that NPM offers a thin veil for work intensification and a means of extracting more work for less money (Cooke, 2006). NPM has several inherent contradictions, such as the argument that managers are said to have been freed to manage while political control of public organizations has increased; or that staff are said to be empowered and motivated while their work is intensified and relative pay reduced; or, not least, that bureaucracy is said to have been reduced while audit and measurement increases. These contradictions serve to fuel the debate concerning the extent to which NPM and associated reforms have acceded to global proportions.

There is now a substantial branch industry in defining how NPM should be conceptualized and how it has changed, in particular as it has evolved through the New Zealand, Australian, UK, and latterly European public administration systems. The conclusion is that "NPM is a slippery label" (Manning, 2000; Savoie, 1995). Different conceptualizations of NPM all stress different things. For Barzelay, it "is primarily concerned with the systematic analysis and management of public management policy. This policy-domain relates to all government-wide, centrally managed institutional rules and routines affecting the public management process" (Barzelay, 2001 p. 156). Rival conceptions characterize NPM in terms of specific policy principles, of "trait" policy interventions seen as typical, or as an overall "paradigm" for reforming government institutions. Among these accounts, NPM is variously described. Sometimes it is represented as copying the business managerialism of an older order (Pollitt, 1993), or in terms of unusually strong customer service orientation. At other times, NPM is defined in terms of internal organizational cultures and the use of a repertoire of more individualistic, less hierarchical organizational control mechanisms (Aucoin, 1996; Hood, 1998). Some conceptions additionally seem to assimilate NPM into strongly normative concepts, as in Aucoin's (1990) discussion of "the well performing organization."

The question remains, however, as to the extent to which the reforming spirit was captured and employed, not only throughout the UK, but also throughout the rest of the world. It has been stated that a mélange of influences drawn from consultants, practitioners, politicians and academics has contributed to the public sector reform programme, referred to in places as an "industry of NPM" (Hood and Peters, 2004). The description of a movement collectively inspired by such varied sources suggests that the reforming agenda is not a minor or insignificant movement but has a scope of "industrial" proportions. Sahlin-Andersson (2001) refers to the observation of similar reform attempts in Australia, New Zealand, Norway and Sweden – four countries on opposite sides of the globe – as evidence that NPM is a global trend. While this may prove to be an adequate starting point, a small number of albeit geographically distant countries may not be sufficient to assert a movement of global proportions. While other contributors may agree with the sentiment expressed by Sahlin-Anderson, they too have relied upon other observations to make their case. Within these general conclusions drawn from a "casual empiricism" (Hood and Peters, 2004), points of difference are made that may prove contradictory to the thesis of NPM as a global movement.

Reinventing Government by Osborne and Gaebler (1992) is often cited as the work that sets out a prescription for NPM reform. The authors maintain that the progress of reform is not only desirable but inevitable, as governments around the world recognize the benefits that reform can bring to the nation in terms of efficiency and effectiveness, but also in terms of macroeconomic prosperity and growth. It is worth noting that while Osbourne and Gaebler's work is often criticized in terms of its prescriptive content, less frequent are criticisms of the book's intent, specifically the need for and benefit of reform. Given the reach of this work, copies sold and extent of readership, the lack of alternative views as to the need for and value of reform are somewhat surprising. Nevertheless, the view that NPM reforms have obtained a global extent has reached a resounding degree of acceptance. Pollitt (2002) observes that many academics from Europe, North America and Australasia share the view that NPM reforms have obtained a global reach and confirms that this view is generally held to be the dominant opinion of public administration researchers. Pal (2007) confirms this view and asserts that the progenitors of the reform movement in Western Europe and Australasia have provided the blueprint for the global spread and impact of NPM reforms.

Adding impetus to the originating administrations' examples, momentum was continued by international and global bodies such as the OECD, the EU and the World Bank, organizations that have been primarily responsible for the spread of reform through and over international boundaries. Consequently, numerous studies have been published detailing NPM-type reform in countries that are outside of the traditionally supportive population or that have shown a resistance to public sector reform. Examples of this type include, but are certainly not limited to, studies on Mongolia (Yadamsuren, 2006; Damiran and Pratt, 2006), Turkey (Ateş, 2004), Japan (Muramatsu and Matsunami, 2003; Kudo, 2003; Yamamoto, 2003), south-east Asia (Common, 2001; Samaratunge *et al.*, 2008), India (Chakraverti, 2004), Malaysia (Bin Sarat, 2009) and Kyrgyzstan (Baimyrzaeva, 2011). This has led Kettl (2005 p. 1) to suggest that, "since the 1980s, a global reform movement in public management has been vigorously underway".

There should be little doubt remaining, therefore, that the period under scrutiny has witnessed an apparently unending wave of public management reforms, specifically in the developed world. There does remain, however, considerable debate concerning the distribution and direction of this activity. The work of Osborne and Gaebler (1992) and the insistence on the inevitability of world-wide public sector reform as a global convergence comprises one view; however others maintain that the "convergence" is not as extensive as stated but that only a partial convergence is occurring (Jones, 1993; Flynn and Strehl, 1996). Others argue that even within north-west Europe the convergence has been exaggerated. Still others maintain that the convergence view of public sector reform is not just a carefully crafted myth but actually comprises two co-joined myths (Goldfinch and Wallis, 2010). The first myth, of world-wide global reform converging around a set of NPM principles, is challenged by a second myth of convergence around a differing set of post-NPM principles. These are identified as being synonymous with a second movement referred to in variety of post-NPM headings such as New Managerialism (Clarke and Newman, 1994), Public Value (Wallis and McLoughlin, 2009), Whole Government (Christensen and Lægreid, 2007) and e-government (Dunleavy *et al.*, 2005).

First, the arguments in support of the convergence view have a particular effect of driving and legitimating the reform movement. What is acceptable and contained within the reforms is driven by the myth of the inevitability of convergence. This further corroborates the convergence myth as policy reformers acquire the status of "insiders", with the commensurate levels of power to access the resources necessary to make additional reform. Those who stand opposed comprise an "outsider group" who are effectively marginalized, appearing recalcitrant against reform and in possession of alternative agendas. Post-NPM convergence allows the analysis of previous reforms but also the diagnosis and solution of perceived reform deficiencies. Post-NPM implies therefore the existence of NPM as a convergence to be transcended. Second, a post-NPM view of convergence has an understated and beguiling creditability. As the new reforms have never been tried and cannot be demonstrated to have "failed", they are able to present a series of potential solutions to problems deemed intractable by the previous but diminishing belief system. Third, the new convergence myth attempts to demonize what has gone before: NPM has failed (Dunleavy *et al.*, 2005) and should therefore be abandoned, while a new set of solutions is drawn from a disparate set of post-NPM prescriptions (Goldfinch and Wallis, 2010).

Peters (2010) maintains that the path of reform following the influences of market-based reform has had considerable impact upon the management of public sector organizations. He acknowledges the dominant pattern of reform, but broadly classifies the reform movement differently from contemporaries, while still maintaining that a period of reform has been followed with a post-reform movement. In the first instance, a period of "liberation management" typified by "allowing managers to manage" has been transcended by a second period, whether managerialist or participatory, distinct from the earlier period in its focus on performance management and "making managers manage" – utilizing the private sector as the exemplar model for what comprises a "good manager" Peters (2010).

The first wave of reform made assumptions that managers will perform better if they are not dominated by political considerations and traditional bureaucracies. The monopolistic structure of the public sector needed to be removed in order to promote competition through quasi-markets, which in turn have the effect of driving down costs and increasing efficiency. Implicit in this argument is that the monopolies of government are underpinned by hierarchy, and a solution to eradicating this is to provide greater involvement in the administration process at all levels. The first round of reform promoted greater managerial freedom, while the second emphasized new forms of constraint. The need to produce measurable outputs comprises a different form of constraint through the tools that are used to measure and judge performance; this puts additional pressures on managers to produce and justify their actions in complex circumstances. It is claimed that the first wave created the capacity for further reform by increasing the pressure upon managers to produce high-quality services at reduced cost. While the first wave may have fragmented public services, the second wave was designed to put them back together again (Peters, 2010).

This has led Dunleavy *et al.* (2005) to claim that the NPM movement has largely stalled or is actively being reversed in some countries, giving rise to a crisis in New Public Management. This is compounded by an intellectual crisis of similar proportions, as debates are polarized by political sciences on the one hand and organization studies and management sciences on the other (Boyne, 1996). This is most observable in the "agentification" of public service, where large-scale bureaucracies have been broken up into smaller, ostensibly independent bodies and given the responsibilities for services previously undertaken by the central administration. As an example, in New Zealand, a population of some 3.5 million people is served by over 300 separate agencies, 40 small ministries, and local and health services (Dunleavy *et al.*, 2005). Subsequent reforms therefore have sought to enhance the workings of public services by combining them through a legislative framework.

It is not our intention to focus on the debates concerning the type and classification of reform. We acknowledge the complexity of defining the boundaries between one movement and the next, particularly as second-wave reforms may coincide with movements to a "third way" of public sector restructuring and operating (Dent, 2005). We are in broad agreement with those that see these newer structures as representing a whole string of specific interventions that are related to and have continuously expanded the NPM movement, keeping it moving and vibrant (Dunleavy *et al.*, 2005). Though the various terms – New Public Management, managerialism, entrepreneurial government – may vary, they point to the same phenomenon. This is the replacement of traditional bureaucracy by a new model based on markets. "Improving public management, reducing budgets, privatization of public enterprise seem universal" (Hughes, 1998 p. 4). The various journeys undertaken by reforming administrations are unique but may possess elements of important commonality (Common, 1998).

History of legislative reform

This section sets out the history of public sector reform undertaken since the Conservative administration under Margaret Thatcher gained control of the UK parliament in the late 1970s. Here it is established that reform was imposed upon a public sector by a managerialist executive government whose primary assumption was that the public sector was inefficient in comparison to private sector enterprise. This historical narrative of the reform of UK public services is integral to the present organizational context of UK local authorities and provides an essential backdrop to the understanding of the dynamics of the relationship between leaders and followers.

Background

The structure of local government within the UK was established by the Local Government Act of 1972, which was introduced into Parliament as the Local Government Bill and debated in 51 sittings from 25 November 1971 to 20 March 1972. The Act abolished the previous local government structure, and created a two-tier system of counties and districts. (Some civil parish councils were maintained in England, giving rise to a three-tier system.) The majority of provisions established by the Act came into force at midnight on 1 April 1974. In England, there were 46 counties and 296 districts.

Political opinion had always favoured, in principle, the establishment of unitary authorities, and the 1972 Act was considered a political fudge. The

Labour Party's statement of policy in 1982 states: "There is an irrational split of functions between the two tiers compounded by a confusing overlap of responsibilities.... We favour the creation in England and Wales of unitary authorities (Labour Party, 1982 p. 220). In 1991, Michael Heseltine announced that the Conservative government would review local structures and in particular would consider the implementation of unitary authorities, defined as "any authority which is the sole principal council for its local government area" (Local Government Changes for England Regulations, 1994 section 3). A general review of local government including the formation of unitary authorities was carrried in the House as the 1992 Local Government Act. The finalization of the principles of the Act came out of the Cooksey Commission in September 1995, which finally established the structures of local government in the UK in 1996.

A brief historical account of reform, 1979–1997

It has been argued that public sector reform in the UK began in 1976 when the International Monetary Fund imposed stringent conditions on government spending in exchange for stabilizing sterling against foreign currencies. Hence, the practice of imposing spending limits was well established before the Conservative defeat of Labour in the 1979 General Elections (Barzelay, 2001).

According to Barzelay's (2001) reading of Colin Campbell and Graham Wilson's case study of public sector reform in the UK, entitled *The End of Whitehall: Death of a Paradigm* (Campbell and Wilson, 1995), Thatcher's use of spending limits to restrain public sector wages and involvement in negotiations should be viewed as significant. Ultimately these negotiations produced wage settlements that curtailed cash spending limits more than had previously been thought possible. The government's stance in this appears to have been of considerable significance in controlling the growth of public expenditure. According to the authors, it was Thatcher's personal interventions, which were more in line with managerialism, that were most significant. Her strategy involved the statement of objectives and aligning activities toward achievement as opposed to the consensus coordination of the past. Thatcher also held her cabinet colleagues responsible for making a mark on their own departments.

> Mrs Thatcher is an extraordinary mixture of recklessness and caution. When she is in her reckless mood, she is in effect a permanent revolutionary, deeply dissatisfied with the government's record, and convinced that, but for her unceasing vigilance, the whole country would instantly slide into sloth and chaos. In this mood, she is almost Maoist in her suspicion of established institutions, seeing them as mere encrustations of temporizing and vested interest, and above all as obstacles to change, change, change. At such moments, Permanent Secretaries, Governors of the B.B.C. – and her ministerial colleagues – are perhaps fortunate that the British system denies her the power to send them off to work in the fields.
>
> (Anderson, 1986)

According to Fry (1988), the initiation of public sector reform had been under-way since the introduction of "accountable management" in the late 1960s. The introduction of a computerized system involving a network of 120 cost centres, each controlled by a manager with budgetary responsibility for running costs, made financial management a fact. Departments became better equipped to review their activities, set objectives and establish priorities.

However, it was the Financial Management Initiative, launched in 1982 in the White Paper *Efficiency and Effectiveness in the Civil Service* (Cabinet Office, 1982), that raised questions concerning ministerial accountability, which accord-ing to Fry "is the economic liberal gospel as applied to the Civil Service" (Fry, 1988 p. 5). In practice, the initiative involved relatively junior civil servants accepting responsibility for their own budgets. According to the White Paper, the initiative was designed:

> To promote in each department and organisation a system in which manag-ers at all levels have:
>
> A clear view of the objectives, and means to assess and, wherever possible, measure outputs or performance in relation to those objectives;
> Well defined responsibility for making the best use of their resources, including a critical scrutiny of output and value for money; and
> The information (particularly about costs), the training and the access to expert advice that they need to exercise their responsibilities effectively.
>
> (Cabinet Office, 1982 paragraph 13)

Further reforms included the National Audit Act (National Audit Act, 1983), which established the Comptroller, the Auditor General and the staff of the National Audit Office as officers of the House of Commons, giving them powers to examine the efficiency and effectiveness of government departments. As a consequence, one of the Thatcher government's first acts was to appoint Sir Derek (later Lord) Rayner from Marks and Spencer to the Efficiency Unit estab-lished by the Treasury, to advise it on the promotion of efficiency and the elimi-nation of waste in government departments. Following Rayner, Sir Ralph Ibbs, as advisor to the Prime Minister, published *Improving Management in Govern-ment: the Next Steps* (Efficiency Unit, 1988), later known as the Ibbs report, stressing the acceleration of finding better value for money.

Alongside public sector reform, the Thatcher government embarked upon a programme of compulsory competitive tendering initiated by the Local Govern-ment Planning and Land Act of 1980 and culminating in the Local Government Act of 1988. This was a further attempt to bring greater efficiency to local gov-ernment and health services utilizing competition and internal markets, by opening up public sector services to private sector competition. Existing public services were tendered alongside private sector alternatives, and service con-tracts were subsequently organized. Public organizations became influenced by monetarist economic policies that signified the widespread introduction of "free market" influences on public services.

Labour's reforms, 1997–2010

Following the election of the "New Labour" government under Tony Blair, the government continued the reforming policy of the public sector set out under the March 1999 White Paper *Modernising Government* (Cabinet Office, 1999), in which further reforms were established. Ian McCartney, the Secretary of State for the Cabinet Office, presented the progress report following publication of the White Paper:

> Good government need not be big government. Rather, it is about working together in ways that haven't happened before. Central government working in partnership with town halls, unions and the private and voluntary sectors to deliver the best possible services.... It is not about dogma, it's about what works. This applies to joined-up government too.
>
> (Cabinet Office, 2000 pp. 2–3)

Central to Blair's agenda of modernizing government was the idea of pursuing a "third way" between the markets of the free economy and the hierarchical traditions of public administration (Kirkpatrick, 1999). Central to this analysis is the sustained hostility displayed by ministers over the years to public servants, the climax of which was the refusal of the Conservative government to rescue the Royal Institute of Public Administration (RIPA) from bankruptcy in the mid-1980s.

An extension of this view is the belief that public sector business can be improved by applying the methods of private business in order to increase the economy, efficiency and effectiveness of public services. A method for attempting this was through the employment of business people as efficiency advisors or heads of public service agencies (Elcock, 2005). Although the Blairite philosophy of following a "third way" was presented, through government rhetoric such as the *Modernising Government* White Paper (Cabinet Office, 1999), as a radical alternative to markets and hierarchy, others saw the adoption of the third way as reinforcing the conceptual superiority of the private sector (Pollitt, 1993). The "third way" principle is based on a belief drawn from the private sector that suggests that inter-firm networks founded upon mutually supportive relationships are a source of advantage for public organizations (Kirkpatrick, 1999). Commensurate with this policy change and associated with this era of reform, the executive administration's advocacy of leadership becomes plain, as expressed by Tony Blair:

> Leadership is a key factor in any large organisation. This is especially true in the public sector where leaders are being asked to deliver more modern, efficient and dynamic services at a time of great social and technological change. I value the tremendous job being done by leaders in our hospitals and schools, local authorities and elsewhere. But I want to see more being

done to develop and support effective leadership across the public sector as a whole.

(Cabinet Office, 2001)

Coalition government; reforms from 2010

The general elections of May 2010 failed to deliver a majority government, and following a period of intense negotiation between the Conservative and Liberal parties, a coalition government was formed under Prime Minister David Cameron. The context for the election was critical, given the "credit crunch crisis" and the bailout of the UK banking system, which led to the nationalization or part-nationalization of some of the UK's high-street banks. The net result of the previous administration's spending plans, as claimed by the election victors after forming a government, was an apparent fiscal deficit of such proportions that immediate corrective action to balance the UK's public finances became the priority of the new administration.

> This is an urgent priority to secure economic stability at a time of continuing uncertainty in the global economy and put Britain's public services and welfare system on a sustainable long term footing. The Coalition Government inherited one of the most challenging fiscal positions in the world.
>
> (HM Treasury Spending Review, 2010 p. 5)

While it remains a corollary that UK public services, as opposed to the international banking system, were held up as responsible for the fiscal deficits, it is the public sector that has borne the brunt of the administration's attempts to balance the fiscal accounts of the UK. Approximately 67 per cent of the deficit was to be recovered through reductions in spending on UK public services, and 33 per cent from increased tax revenues resulting from growth in the UK economy. Obviously, such extensive cuts in public service signalled more than an extensive round of job cuts:

> You can't have room for innovation and the pressure for excellence without having some real discipline and some fear on the part of the providers that things may go wrong if they don't live up to the aims that society as a whole is demanding of them.... If you have diversity of provision and personal choice and power, some providers will be better and some worse. Inevitably, some will not, whether it's because they can't attract the patient or the pupil, for example, or because they can't get results and hence can't get paid ... Some will not survive. It is an inevitable and intended consequence of what we are talking about.
>
> (Oliver Letwin, Minister of State, Cabinet Office, 31 July 2011)

The initiation of additional public sector reforms signposted a continuation of a form of flexible mass production in which workers and managers would be subject to the progressive intensification of labour in the context of a the UK's relative economic decline, described as a "high-output low-commitment economy" (Hoggett, 1996): "The Spending Review is underpinned by a radical programme of public service reform, changing the way services are delivered by redistributing power away from central government and enabling sustainable, long term improvements in services" (HM Treasury Spending Review, 2010 p. 8).

Principal among the proposed reforms of the Coalition government are those that restructure the National Health Service and the Welfare State. These reforms have been criticized for their severity and their challenge to the existing arrangements of public sector workers, and not least for apparent encroachments of the private sector into the public sphere, some of which have been resisted, such as attempts to privatize areas of the UK's public forests. At this writing, the indications are that the Coalition governments's modernization agenda will continue:

> Every year without modernization the costs of our public services escalate. Demand rises, the chains of commands can grow, costs may go up, inefficiencies become more entrenched.... Pretending that there is some "easy option" of sticking with the status quo and hoping that a little bit of extra money will smooth over the challenges is a complete fiction.
>
> (David Cameron, Prime Minister, 17 January 2011)

The government expressed the intention to widen the scope of "third way" administration by inviting greater consumer involvement in public sector policy through the e-petition initiative (available at http://epetitions.direct.gov.uk/), and by joining up government services through inclusion of the private sector, charities and consumer groups under the "Big Society" banner.

This section has outlined the history of UK public sector reform since the late 1970s. Reform has sought to remove the perceived inefficiencies inherent within the public sector, but reform has also challenged the nature of work for many public sector employees. New Labour's "Modernising Government" agenda challenged the notion of the public sector itself, a process that looks set to continue under the Cameron administration. The following sections of this chapter will deal with the impact of public sector reform on those that work within the public sector, in order to provide a deeper contextual understanding of the environment within which relationships between leaders and followers are conducted.

Impact of reform

Common to NPM is the call for the adoption of the organizational designs and practices that are perceived to be transforming private business, driven by a technocratic imperative, communication and technological advances, and a narrow view of the state and the public sector generally (Elcock, 2005). Furthermore, the authors support the view not only that NPM or New Managerialism reforms have slavishly copied similar activities of the private sector (du Gay, 2006), but also that the mirroring of practices in the private sector are linked by the ideological foundation of managerialism. The characteristics of New Managerialism in public organizations include the erasure of bureaucratic rule-following procedures; emphasizing the primacy of management above all other activities; monitoring employee performance (and encouraging self-monitoring); the primacy of financial and other targets; devising means of publicly auditing quality of service delivery; and the development of quasi-markets for services. New configurations of public services stress the pursuit of efficiency and effectiveness in service delivery (Farrell and Morris, 2003), and labour-force restructuring is advocated to enable more teamwork and flexibility. Finally, New Managerialism is associated with new kinds of imposed external accountability, including the widespread use of performance indicators and league tables, target setting, benchmarking and performance management (Deem and Brehony, 2005) – characteristics which are mirrored in commercial enterprises (see Boltansky and Chiapello, 2005; Hassard *et al.*, 2009).

Despite the various debates concerning the definition, characteristics and timescales of the public sector movement since the early 1980s, it is our contention that waves of reform broadly described as belonging to either New Public Management or New Managerialism share similar political and ideological underpinnings. One of the principal themes of this book is the need to analyze complex social phenomena in their proper context; the ignorance of managerialist ideology would only invoke justified criticism of our final analysis. Enteman (1993) argues that in the recent world, context managerialism is the ideological principle on which the economic, social and political order of advanced industrial societies is actually based. Managerialism is an ideology created by managers, generally for managers, which has evolved in a vacuum following the breakdown of capitalism, socialism and democracy, and it sees society neither as a collection of individuals nor as a unified whole. The ideology of managerialism is therefore an ideology of the powerful, as it possesses the capacity to constrain democracy but lacks the moral dimension to moderate its dominion over the less powerful.

Generally, the political and ideological nuance of the reform movement has been underplayed (Deem and Brehony, 2005), The main reason for this appears to be the traditional association of this ideology with the New Right and the observation that many political denominations other than the New Right have taken up the reforming banner. The manner through which proponents of New Managerial reforms have sought to establish a regime of managerial discipline and control within various areas of the public sector has led New Managerialism to be considered as a general ideology, which legitimizes and seeks to extend the rights to manage (Clarke *et al.*, 2000). This view is supported by Kirkpatrick *et al.* (2005), who point to professional work in the public sector being colonized by a management ideology and subject to more rational methods of top-down control and surveillances. From an alternative perspective, O'Reilly and Reed (2011) point to recurring ideological discourses within the public sector, maintaining that the ideologies of professionalism and managerialism have contributed to the emerging doctrine of "leaderism", which compensates for the failure of earlier discourses to articulate innovative and visionary models for public services. While still being aligned with New Managerialism and NPM in its adherence to transformational models of leadership, this account nonetheless incorporates a powerful change narrative that includes service users (O'Reilly and Reed, 2010).

Locke and Spender (2011) associate managerialism and its affiliated values not with the alleged "commercial brilliance" of post-war management and the corporate movement but more with the failures of that world, of which the recent banking and financial crisis is the latest and most potent example. Additionally, the authors attribute the rise and supremacy of the managerial ideology with the practices of management being reinforced by a compliant media and the teachings of the world's best business schools. The managerialist movement within public sector organization has slavishly followed this progression in what has been described as a colonization of managerial values: "At best a management re-tread and at worst syncretic vulgarism" (Berg *et al.*, 2004 p. 166).

Statements such as this not only point out the ideological underpinnings of managerialism within the public sector but also guide us to the view that the implementation of such ideologies may have been misplaced, and consideration should therefore be given to the performance of the reformed administrations against their initial ideological objectives. The underlying assumption that the modernization of public services was both welcomed and beneficial can be brought under more critical scrutiny. Decisions to reform were undertaken in a very short time-frame with little consideration of what the public sector routinely achieved or of the implications, intended and unintended, of the reforms (Kirkpatrick *et al.*, 2005). As the New Managerialist reform programme was driven by a need for economic rationalism on the one hand and management restructuring of organizations and practices on the other (Parker and Guthrie, 1993), it is therefore these domains that should provide an adequate base for challenging the assertions as to the need for and successes of that reform programme.

Central to the justification for undertaking widespread reform was mounting economic and international pressure: a reformed public sector would return benefits in terms of economic prosperity through an increase in macroeconomic activity. In this case, however, this claim can be demonstrated to be false, or tenuous at best, as the relationship between public sector reform and macroeconomic performance is less than convincing:

> Confronting our findings with the hypothesis formulated by the OECD as to the relationship between macroeconomic performance (economic growth, productivity and unemployment), on the one hand, and the regulation regime (bureaucratic governance by rule and its alternatives) on the other, the OECD hypothesis has to be strikingly refuted: all the countries with bureaucratic governance by rule exhibit with respect to almost all the dimensions a markedly better macroeconomic performance than the other countries.
>
> (Naschold, 1995 p. 39)

While we acknowledge the analytical complexities of making judgments that link the macroeconomic performance of a country to its reforming practices, the point remains that consideration of macroeconomic factors tells us nothing conclusively concerning the relationship between reform and economic growth. Three countries that were reluctant, initially at least, to enter into the radical reform evident in much of the rest of developed world were Germany, Japan and the United States, and yet these three enjoyed relatively prosperous levels of growth in the two decades before the 2008 banking collapse. It should also be noted that some of the poorest-performing administrative systems have been the slowest to reform. In Europe, for instance, Italy, Greece and the European Union itself have all proved reluctant to reform during the peak of the NPM era.

A central mantra of the NPM movement was a reduction in bureaucracy through decreased emphasis on process controls. It was surmised that this would provide for a larger discretionary space within which managers could seek to add service value. However, a general shift in this direction has been frequently questioned by detailed studies (Hoggett, 1996; Hood *et al.*, 1999; Jones and Thompson, 1999; Pollitt *et al.*, 1999). As a result of the fragmentation of the public sector apparatus, additional regulation by the UK government during the NPM era seems to have grown substantially. The apparently deregulatory "let managers manage" rhetoric was combined with a very marked increase in the resources, staffing and organizational numbers of arm's-length regulators of the public sector (Light, 1993). Such studies point to the unintentional production of additional bureaucratic activity of a style more rule-based and process-driven than the systems they were initially designed to replace. Further examples of this type are the implementation of measures to promote broader strategic thinking by public servants, which produced a middle-level bureaucratic paper chase, as in the case of the US Paperwork Reduction Act (Margetts, 1999), and attempts to downsize public bureaucracies that expand the state into the private sector, such as the £700 million bailout of part of the UK rail network in July 2009. Furthermore, in a cross-national study, Maor (1999) showed that despite the intention of reform to depoliticize service provision, the main effect was to make civil servants more responsive to politicians. Politicians increasingly intervened in managers' operations and imposed additional reporting structures in order to avoid what would could be construed as a loss of control over the implementation process. Similar findings have been made in analysis of other administrative systems, most notably Blackler (2006) in his study of the chief executives of the UK's National Health Service.

A second principal theme of the NPM reforms was the attainment of service and cost efficiencies through reform. While many of the claims of efficiency gains are probably perfectly reasonable and accurate, it would be prudent not to take all assertions at face value. As in the cases mentioned above, the constraint of bureaucracy has been misplaced, leading not only to increases in regulation but also to a commensurate increase in cost and the subsequent reduction of efficiency:

claims that that empirical studies find "consistently" and "without exception" that contracting out is more efficient than municipal supply are demonstrably untrue. Even taken at face value, only around half of the studies discussed in the paper (a review of contracting out in US local government) is associated with lower spending and higher efficiency.

(Boyne, 1998 p. 482)

While there is some evidence of new management policies being effective in reshaping services, a survey conducted by the UK Social Services Inspectorate concluded that "most councils do not fully understand costs and struggle to forecast future activity and expenditure" (Social Services Inspectorate, 1998). Many reform initiatives take on characteristics of a "triumph of hope over experience" (Hood and Peters, 2004), as improvements are anticipated despite previous experiences. For example, the use of information technology is based upon the recurring belief that new systems can produce a dramatic fall in government operating costs while improving service quality. Visions of administrative reforms of this type appear to be particularly vulnerable to "inflexible technology" syndrome, where solutions are developed on a larger scale than required in a way that is contrary to more incremental styles of learning and development (Collingridge, 1992; Margetts, 1999).

Further studies have cast doubt on ubiquitous claims of efficiency gain. A study of the Inspectors-General in the US suggests that an effort to reduce regulatory compliance costs on business produced a willingness to impose ever-increasing levels of regulation on executive agencies and their employees (Light, 1993). Other studies demonstrate that this may not be an isolated case. Talbot (1996, 1997) shows that performance-monitoring systems used in the UK's "Next Steps" scheme showed that measurements of efficiency were patchy and volatile. A study by Ter Bogt (1999) failed to find good evidence of efficiency improvements in a set of recently "autonomized" Dutch organizations. Embarrassing performances may be quietly forgotten or realigned indicators put in their place (Pollitt, 2000). Sometimes organizations may even cheat (Hencke, 1998). A study of five European national audit offices showed that even audit institutions, when they conduct performance audits, were able to construct and apply true efficiency measures in only a minority of their cases and consequently fall back on assessing good management practice (Pollitt *et al.*, 1999).

A further popular theme of the NPM reform agenda is that benefits are to be accrued from partnerships with the private sector (PPP). However, a review of PPP schemes (Flinders, 2005) concluded that they represent something of a Faustian bargain in that forms of PPP may deliver efficiency gains and service improvements in some policy areas but may also involve substantial political and democratic costs. The BBC reported in September 2011 that the short-term benefits of the UK's PFI (Private Finance Initiative) system, the government strategy of utilizing private sector money to finance public sector capital works, may be outweighed by a number of long-term cost problems. Of the 800 PFI contracts in operation with a capital value of £64 billion, the associated repayments to private contractors over the next 50 years will equate to some £276 billion, prompting promises to revisit the schemes by George Osbourne, Chancellor of the Exchequer.

We have drawn attention to the problem of uncovering cost savings through reform and measuring those savings aligned with a downsizing of the public sector; it still needs to be acknowledged, however, that the full-costs side effects remain obscure. Turning to focus on the impact of management restructuring and particularly that associated with the second wave of reform, the picture remains equally unconvincing, as Kirkpatrick *et al.* (2005) most pointedly conclude by asserting that the effectiveness of management reform has proven to be inversely proportional to the amount of resources spent upon it. The authors refer to the continued management reform within the National Health Service of the United Kingdom as but one example of this kind of paradoxical occurrence.

In reforms geared toward making cost savings and reducing the size of the administrative apparatus, one should be mindful that the services and features of public life not measured may have subsequently been rendered poorer, and groups of workers and members of the public may have suffered degenerating conditions. Rarely is the full balance sheet of public service provision made available for scrutiny (Pollitt, 2000). As an example, while NPM or New Managerialism reform has proved to be influential in the United States, data collated from the Government Performance Project of 2000 shows results that are contrary and disappointing and prompts the conclusion that the stated objectives for the Managing for Results programme of reform fell somewhat short of expectations (Moynihan, 2006).

Possibly one of the most critical and underreported areas is the full-cost impact that decades of reform has had upon workers in public sector organizations (Pollitt, 2000; Ackroyd *et al.*, 2007). Efforts to induce change have been ongoing for many years, and the human and financial costs have been extraordinary. One can point to the restrictive policies for controlling and monitoring practice, intensification of work in many areas, rising levels of stress, staff demoralization, employee turnover, and the costs of reversing some of the more damaging elements of the reform programme (Kirkpatrick *et al.* 2005). Furthermore, one can point to the demand for ever-increased productivity under increasing levels of control and the impacts that these demands have had on stress and associated illnesses (Berg *et al.* 2004).

The oppressive nature of management controls within the public sector produces a paradox caused by reform, between an unregulated private sector and a regulated public sector. This generates a type of flexible mass production, in which workers are subject to several inherent contradictions as mentioned above: political control of public organizations increases while managers are said to have been freed to manage; work becomes more intensive and relative pay decreases while staff are said to be empowered and motivated; and audit and measurement increases while bureaucracy is said to be reduced. Consequently, it has been argued that NPM offers a thin veil for work intensification and a means of extracting more work for less money (Cooke, 2006), leading to a high-output, low-commitment economy in which the value of trust has been eradicated from the experiences of contemporary workers (Hoggett, 1996).

Attempts to reform public services and the work of their professionals have not been as uncontested as many would assume. In much of the literature, it is assumed that management reform has either transformed or is transforming public and professional work toward more corporate and managerial modes of organizing (Ackroyd *et al.*, 2007; Kirkpatrick and Ackroyd, 2003). Additional accounts point to professional work being colonized by a management ideology and subject to more rational methods of top-down control and surveillances, in which change is accomplished through a new breed of "commercialized professional". This view of unequivocal and completely accomplished change may be challenged on two fronts. First, the dominant view fails to consider the robust nature of the institutions in question. The public sector should not be seen as a passive instrument of policy, and it should not be assumed that policy reforms as deemed necessary by political leaders were immediately translated into new patterns of activity as dictated by the policy-makers. Kirkpartick *et al.* (2005) present a comprehensive analysis and review of the literature as it pertains to the reforms of the UK, noting how professional groups have interpreted and responded to reform by drawing attention to wider costs and the unintended results of the reform process.

Underpinning much of this is the resilience of much of the traditions and ethos of public sector work. Orr and Vince (2007) have described 14 separate traditions that counter the argument that local government comprises a homogeneous organizational entity; rather, it possesses a cacophony of voices, interests and assumptions about how best to organize, prioritize and mobilize action (Orr and Vince, 2007). Additionally, a generic public sector ethos (PSE) has been identified as a common denominator held between professional groups that work within the public sector (Pratchett and Wingfield, 1996). Despite recurrent attempts to impose a New Managerialist ideology, framed by a new language (Deem and Brehony, 2007), it has been shown that these reforms can be appreciated to be at odds with the public sector ethos and have therefore sparked a clash of cultures (Brown, 1998). The study by Pratchett and Wingfield (1996) concludes that PSE is a political institution in its own right, based on the assertion that the value and beliefs expressed among a wider population of professions and functions have become institutionalized to form a coherent but tacitly articulated culture. The PSE appears to possess great durability and resilience and has an appeal that helps workers deal with the complexity and ambiguity of a confused political and organizational existence (Pratchett and Wingfield, 1996; Kirkpatrick *et al.*, 2005). The capacity of these groups to capture and minimize disturbance to their own activities should not be underestimated (Ackroyd, 1996; Collinson, 1994).

The uneven application of reform leads to the suggestion that elements of reform have been presented as a series of inconsistent, sometimes competing and irreconcilable demands that in effect appear contradictory. This contributes to the overall ambiguity of the designated path to change, which in turn may have greatly problematized attempts to translate policy objectives into meaningful actions (Pollitt, 2000; Kirkpatrick *et al.*, 2005). This effect may be compounded in that public sector organizations may inherently possess higher degrees of ambiguity as a result of having more ambiguous goals than other types of organization (Lee *et al.*, 2009). In studying the relationship between organizational ambiguity and public management, Pandey and Wright (2006) conclude that political influence can have an impact on organizational goal and role ambiguity. Structural mechanisms that are designed to control or direct employee behaviour appear to hinder performance when goals are complex, not agreed, or poorly communicated. This finding may shed light on the potential distinctions between public and private organizations, in that public organizations are likely to experience external agencies with considerable influence over resources, decision-making and organizational goals (Pandey and Wright, 2006).

The effects of ambiguity on organization functioning has occupied critical scholars, leading to the suggestion that in ambiguous situations, individual actors look to their institutions to help interpret the course of action to be undertaken (Noordegraaf and Abma, 2003). Subsequent behaviour therefore can be appreciated as being in accordance with the norms and conventions that are conditioned by both the formal and the informal institution (Pratchett and Wingfield, 1996). Contrast this logic of appropriateness affiliated with traditional public administration with the logic of consequence that pervades much of New Public Management. Ambiguity underscores the equivocal nature of social reality, but it remains nearly impossible to give an unequivocal account of ambiguous conditions; yet there is a strong case for a reliance on circumstantial evidence in supporting the relevance and importance of ambiguity (Noordegraaf and Abma, 2003). It is the contention of Noordegraaf and Abma among others that public managers handle the interpretive spaces created by ambiguity with a reliance on institutional tradition, ethos and expectation, as opposed to resorting to normative managerial practices of reducing the interpretive space through the application of increasing amounts of data and analysis.

From the late 1970s onwards, public institutions and their underpinning structures have come under extensive and sustained forces of reform. It has become common for politicians and the media to project the image that public services are in crisis (Kirkpatrick *et al.*, 2005). The development of NPM reforms over time has given rise to the emergence and observation of paradox (see Hood and Peters, 2004; Christensen and Lægreid, 2001; Hesse *et al.*, 2003; Hood, 1998; Suleiman, 2003) that presents additional challenge and complexity in the continued reform of public services. Wildavsky (1988) argued that the need to confront the surprising or unexpected promotes resilience and learning in social institutions, and while we would acknowledge this endeavour, we have critically questioned the validity of the reform movement and its rationalist underpinnings to public services and the people involved in their operation and coordination. Observations of the reform movement suggest that the development of new management practices and associated values has been painfully slow. The potency of established value systems (such as PSE and tradition) that inform practice should not be discounted among senior professionals, who sit supposedly at the vanguard of the reform movement.

The extent of real change, however, is questionable, as deep changes in the hearts and minds of public sector worker may encounter more entrenchment and resistance then initially appreciated (Laughlin, 1991). It has been suggested that the interplay of forces instigated by reform is likely to have inflated the impact of organizational ambiguity, a factor underplayed by researchers of organizations (Alvesson and Sköldberg, 2005). Further, it has been argued that the reforms of executive government have undermined the traditions of public administration both ideologically and practically, leading to a widespread belief that public servants were less estimable than successful businessmen (Greenaway, 1995). New Public Management and its derivative reform movements are far from a doctrine beyond question (Kirkpatrick *et al.* 2005).

Conclusion

This chapter does not attempt to unravel the complexities of the definitions, phases and classification of the public sector reform movement referred to as the New Public Management. It is accepted that there are differences between administrations defined by geography and time. Similarly, it is accepted that there have occurred broad differences in the type of reform that over time have come to be referred to under new and distinct headings. This gives rise to the possibility that one epoch of reform may have been transcended by a new period of reform which signals the end of the previous period and all the initiatives that have taken place therein. It is further acknowledged that the school of research into public administration contains many debates and as many questions as there are answers, as scholars throughout the world attempt to make sense of a 40-year phenomenon that shows no sign of relenting. We are content that these debates should be furthered by others more expert in their fields, and we maintain that this does not diminish our argument or propositions in the slightest.

It is sufficient for us to maintain that reform of the public sector is a global occurrence, ongoing and escalating. The continuance and tenacity of reform as progressed by executive governments has changed the nature of governing throughout the world. Those countries that have been at the forefront of reform are being joined by a steady progression of others that have hitherto been resistant or reluctant to enter into the reform movement. The formal rational-legal bureaucracies that traditionally served as the basis for administration have been replaced, or are being replaced, with managerialist systems that strongly resemble the systems of the private sector. However, we do not believe that using the private sector as exemplary models for reform will necessarily bring about the changes as designed and intended. The private sector itself wrestles with problems of economic slowdown and other issues defined as inherent within a "third spirit of capitalism" (Boltansky and Chiapello, 2005), and an imposition of managerialist ideologies and models from one to other is unlikely to promise much more than an uncertain future and continued phases of reform. It is little surprise that both private and public sector models of operating have coalesced upon leadership as part of the solution to a world of seemingly intractable problems.

4   Methodological considerations

This chapter demonstrates the methodological issues that were considered and resolved in order to undertake this study. First, the section on the emergence of aims shows how the scope of the study was finalized after contact with some of the respondents under study. The chapter next outlines the underpinnings of the Critical Theory method before describing the variants of a critical ethnographic approach. After establishing the soundness of the method, the chapter outlines the various criteria of the research design, discussing what considerations were made to ensure the validity of the research findings.

Emergence of the aims

The aim of this study was to utilize a Critical Theory qualitative methodology to examine empirical material so as to make interpretations concerning the dynamics of the leader–follower relationships within a large unitary local authority based in northern England. The objectives of this study have been laid out in an earlier chapter, but in practice the scope of the study emerged after contact with respondents shaped the focus of the enquiry. Early conversations with officers and elected members of the authority were surprising, in that initial attempts to gain insights into the leadership process lacked focus, as conversations drifted toward structural elements of the organization. These structural elements appeared to shape peoples' expectations of leader and follower behaviours significantly, but were contrary to those represented by a traditional understanding of leadership. This suggested that a reductionist study of the dyadic relationship, as would be conducted within a functionalist methodology, would not be appropriate for dealing with the inherent complexities of the leadership process within the organization. It was these initial insights that served to shape and focus the inquiry, necessitating a more critical interpretation of the empirical materials collected.

The research on which this book is based commenced with a plan of study drawn up in the summer of 2007. A lengthy programme of ethnographic fieldwork and interview-based research was undertaken in the years that followed. In order to achieve the aims of the research, a major requirement was for the leader–follower relationship to be explored in depth and in context. Subsequent interviews were conducted in order to clarify issues and assist with interpretation. The research was brought to a conclusion with the drafting of a research report in 2010 and a book manuscript in 2011 and 2012.

The authority under study had recently been restructured to comprise four directorate (service-providing) departments, supported at the centre by an administrative Corporate Services Directorate. In addition to these, there was a smaller department comprising the Chief Executive's Unit. The initial plan of study was to spend time engaged in observation of all the constituent parts of the authority. Due to the size and complexity of the various departments and the researcher's desire to explore issues developed through interpretation, the initial research plan was revised so that time was spent within three of the principal departments.

Access was negotiated with each departmental director individually, following a letter of introduction written and circulated by the elected member of the ruling political party and leader of the council. The researcher was then invited to attend a meeting of the officers' executive committee, referred to as the Corporate Management Team, and presented the research design and a broad statement concerning the aims and focus of the study to the most senior heads of service within the authority. The researcher was given free and full access during the course of the study, the only limitation being that members of the authority were granted full confidentiality. Should issues of confidentiality have arisen during observation, it was agreed that the researcher would retire from the room until the item under discussion was completed. In practice, however, this never happened.

The field notes of each observed activity were written up long-hand in a journal and were based on the notes taken during the time of the observation. During the writing of field notes and during periods of reflection, preliminary interpretations were made. These informed subsequent observations and areas of focus for interviews. Thus the study can be perceived as an iterative process, with the collation of empirical material being informed by what had occurred in earlier activities, and by observations and interview responses. The intention of the research process was to follow themes as they occurred, in order to uncover leader–follower dynamics as they unfolded. Kuhn (1990) is critical of the tendency of researchers to impose a planned sequence of discovery so that, within the final writing, discoveries are presented as occurring in a series of logically coherent steps, when in reality the process was far more chaotic. The above description of the research process presents a "clean" version of the process as it actually happened. In reality, opportunities for observation and interviews were missed due to conflicting work and time requirements. Furthermore, the authority, in their desire to help, made invitations to attend work activities so that it became practically impossible to observe the workplace "naturally" or without a chaperone. Finally, comments made by actors aroused interest due to the resonance they triggered with prior experiences and understandings; further consideration of these may have prejudiced the taking into full account issues with more pertinence to a Critical Theory approach.

Critical Theory methodology

It is the contention of this study that the field of leadership studies has been dominated by the research methodologies drawn from management science and psychology (Rost, 1993; Western, 2008), which are typified by neo-positivistic and normative assumptions with an emphasis on rules and procedures for the securing of objectivity in practice and results (Alvesson and Deetz, 2006a). As a result, the mainstream accounts of leadership studies can be criticized in a number of ways. Principal among them is that the repeated use of a similar methodology has resulted in a coalescing of theory, to the extent that there still remain significant gaps in the understanding of the phenomenon (Parry, 1998): "the yield of knowledge is much less than would be expected from the immense literature on leadership" (Yukl, 1989 p. 279). Other authors, Alvesson in particular, are more scathing about the results of nearly 60 years of research in leadership studies.

> If the philosophical assumptions and rules for method were sound, then one or a set of empirically well-supported theories, explaining leadership phenomena and providing valuable advice for practitioners, would have been produced. But this is not the case and rather than calling for five thousand more studies according to the logic "more of (almost) the same" – the time has come for radical re-thinking.
>
> (Alvesson, 1996 p. 457)

The traditional research method and its shortcomings have been recognized by a number of influential scholars, who have made calls for the adoption of alternative research methodologies to broaden understanding related to leadership phenomena (Alvesson, 1996; Alvesson and Deetz, 2006a; Alvesson and Sköldberg, 2005; Bryman, 1996; Knights and Willmott, 1992; Smircich and Morgan, 1982). These authors have drawn particular critical attention to forms of abstract empiricism based on the use of quantitative methods and are not advocating a wholesale shift toward an abstract empiricism based on qualitative methods. The choice of research method is not limited to a choice between quantitative or qualitative approaches; this would represent an oversimplified dichotomization, as the choice and adequacy of any method embodies a variety of assumptions regarding the nature of and attainment of knowledge, as well as assumptions regarding the object under investigation (Morgan and Smircich, 1980). While the debate over method is not exclusively concerned with a polarization of methodological options, Alvesson and Sköldberg (2005), among others, maintain that much of what comprises qualitative method in practice is underpinned by the neo-positivistic foundations which it ostensibly opposes. There is a move toward general support for qualitative method, and its adoption would more adequately represent the depth and complexity of the leadership phenomenon than alternatives.

Burrell and Morgan (1979) draw upon diverse traditions of social organizational analysis to identify four fundamentally different lenses through which social and organizational realities can be interpreted. Taking direction from Alvesson and Willmott (2001), the four paradigms may be differentiated by assumptions that are made about science and society. The first assumption relates to objectivist and subjectivist philosophies of science. Objective philosophies assume an existence "out there" that can be captured by the application of "scientific" methods. The reality of the social world is assumed to be similar to, if not exactly the same as, the natural world, and thus social phenomena can be observed and measured using equivalent methods, typically the careful construction of objective instruments such as questionnaires designed to provide comparative information about the variables under study.

Subjectivist philosophies of science assume that social phenomena are fundamentally different from natural phenomena, and that measurement of social phenomena by objective instruments is not possible. The social world is understood to be continuously constructed, reproduced and transformed through inter-subjective processes. Only through attention to the meanings of the processes is reality made "objectively" real to its members and an adequate appreciation of the social world made. Typically, this methodology requires a close involvement with those under study, to discover how the meanings of concepts are formulated and interpreted and how these meaning alter over time.

The second assumption of Burrell and Morgan's framework relates to theories of regulation at one end of a spectrum and theories of radical change at the other end. Theories of regulation assume that modern societies are characterized more by order than conflict. Evidence of order is interpreted as reflective of a fundamental equilibrium and consensus among members. Disorder is treated as a temporary and necessary means of re-establishing equilibrium. Consensus is a broad assumption, and attention is given to how cohesiveness and functional adaptation is achieved. Social order is assumed to be because of an accord between the constituent elements of organization and society, and attention is given to how the mechanisms of order can be maintained and strengthened.

Theories of radical change, in contrast, assume that social relations are conditioned by contradictory pressures for transformation rather than by forces of integration and continuity. Evidence of consensus is associated with forms of social domination that impose order, either through direct repression or through a repressive form of tolerance in which dissenting voices are tolerated or marginalized. The appearance of order therefore is because of mass subordination and/or insidious forms of socialization. From this perspective, the reproduction and transformation of prevailing institutions and routines is understood to depend upon institutionalized inequalities or injustices. When diverse sources of tension combine and prove resistant to suppression or accommodation, major expression of revolt and radical change may occur. The above dimensions combine to inform four distinct paradigms, in which each defines fundamentally different perspectives for the analysis of social phenomena, as shown in Figure 4.1. Which paradigm to adopt in research depends on answers to questions that relate directly to the nature of society (Kelemen and Rumens, 2008).

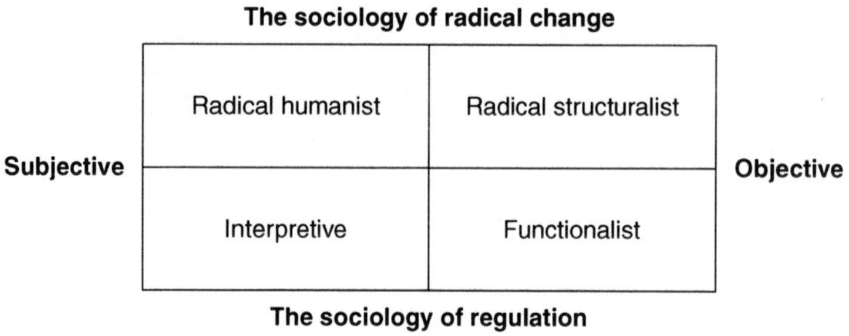

The sociology of radical change

Radical humanist	Radical structuralist
Interpretive	Functionalist

Subjective ... **Objective**

The sociology of regulation

Figure 4.1 Four paradigms for the analysis of social theory (Burrell and Morgan, 1979 p. 22).

An outline of Burrell and Morgan's social research model

The four paradigms are classified as functionalist, interpretive, radical humanist and radical structuralist. These views reflect the major traditions in social thought and embrace a number of distinct yet related modes of theorizing. The functionalist paradigm is based on reality assumptions generating positivist and systems-oriented explanations of social life. The assumptions of the interpretive paradigm are shaped by phenomenology and a concern to understand how reality is socially constructed. The radical humanist paradigm builds on assumptions that have supported Critical Theory and expresses a concern to reveal the power dimension underlying our social constructions (Alvesson and Deetz, 2006a). The radical structuralist paradigm has given rise to various Weberian and Marxian analyses of social life concerned with understanding the modes of domination embedded in social structures and the contradictions that generate social change. The interplay of the four sociological paradigms, and their associated theoretical perspectives, are shown in Figure 4.2.

Contributors to leadership studies have asserted that much of the research on leadership has been conducted within the functionalist paradigm (Alvesson and Deetz, 2006a; Collinson, 2006; Kelemen and Rumens, 2008; Parry, 1998; Watkins, 1989; Western, 2008) and that this methodological myopia has resulted in a low return in knowledge (Alvesson, 1996; Bryman, 1996), due to the narrow conceptualization of leadership itself (Rost, 1993). The following sections discuss first the functionalist paradigm, and then the radical humanist paradigm within which Critical Theory is located.

The functionalist paradigm

This paradigm combines an objectivist philosophy of science with a regulation theory of society, and is identified as the dominant research paradigm in social science; it tends to be "highly pragmatic in orientation", "problem oriented in

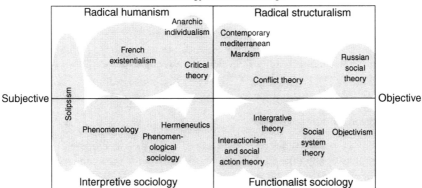

The sociology of radical change

Radical humanism	Radical structuralism

Anarchic individualism

French existentialism

Critical theory

Contemporary mediterranean Marxism

Russian social theory

Conflict theory

Subjective — Solipsism — Objective

Phenomenology

Hermeneutics

Phenomenological sociology

Intergrative theory

Interactionism and social action theory

Social system theory

Objectivism

Interpretive sociology

Functionalist sociology

The sociology of regulation

Figure 4.2 Interplay of the four sociological research paradigms (Burrell and Morgan, 1979 p. 29).

approach", and "firmly committed to a philosophy of social engineering as a basis of social change" (Burrell and Morgan, 1979 p. 26). Empirical observations are presented as data or facts, from which unequivocal statements of "reality" may be derived. It is then possible to gain a reasonable basis for empirically grounded conclusions as a step toward generalizations and theory building (Alvesson and Sköldberg, 2005). Alvesson and Willmott (2001) note how knowledge that is based upon assumptions of this kind has dominated management textbooks and the teaching of the major business schools. The authors suggest that part of the reasoning behind the dominance of the functionalist paradigm could be attributed to the widespread preference for functionalist metaphors that reify the operation of systems and privilege their survival (Alvesson and Willmott, 2001).

Historically, studies of management have tended to treat concepts such as leadership as if meaning were self-evident and as if workplace processes were largely determined by an abstract logic irrespective of human volition and thought (Collinson, 2003). Academics within leadership studies have stated that many of the problems associated with leadership research are a consequence of the research paradigm involved (Alvesson, 1996). There has been a continued focus on superior-subordinate relationships, to the exclusion of other leader functions and organizational and environmental factors that significantly affect leader practice. Leadership research has been primarily concerned with generic leadership functions, to the exclusion of specific behavioural manifestations of these functions. Furthermore, the diverse styles or mannerisms in which leader behaviours are enacted have been largely ignored. The result is that much of our understanding about leadership is not easily operationalized in practical settings (House and Aditya, 1997).

Although functionalism remains highly influential in leadership studies, it has been heavily criticized in social theory for interpreting conflict purely in terms of its contribution to social order and for aligning with the interests of the powerful (Burrell and Morgan, 1979). By also discounting agents' reasons for their actions, functionalism has a tendency to derogate the subject. Within leadership studies this is particularly evident in the recurrent neglect of followers (Collinson, 2005).

The radical humanist paradigm

The radical humanist paradigm is concerned with the development of a sociology of radical change from a subjectivist standpoint; it views the world from a perspective that tends to be nominalist, anti-positivist, voluntarist and idiographic. The radical humanist paradigm understands social order as a product of coercion, rather than consent, and supports a view of society overthrowing or transcending the limitations of existing social arrangements. It can, therefore, be appreciated as a brand of social theorizing designed to provide a critique of the status quo. It tends to see society as anti-human, and seeks to articulate ways in which human beings can transcend those limitations which tie them to existing social patterns and constraints, thereby enabling their full potential. The radical humanist paradigm in essence is based upon an inversion of the basis of the functionalist paradigm (Burrell and Morgan, 1979), and is the one that is adopted within this study.

Critical Theory has probably been the most influential of a number of approaches that may exist in the radical humanist paradigm (Alvesson and Willmott, 2001). Positioned in the least subjective area and adjacent to radical structuralism, it nonetheless contrasts strongly with the unmediated materialism of radical structuralism. Critical Theory places greater emphasis on the role of ideas in the formation and reproduction of society. For the radical humanist, therefore, the potential for change resides in the human capacity to be creative and self-determining in ways which could fundamentally challenge the reproduction of dominant structures and the status quo.

Through critiques of existing social structures, radical humanism makes an appeal to all those oppressed within, and alienated from, modern institutions. The mission is first to raise awareness of how "normality" is oppressive, and then to facilitate the liberation of individuals from oppressive states of mental incarceration. Radical humanists see all individuals as victims of systemic oppression – an oppression so taken for granted that it has inevitably become appreciated as part of "life". Radical humanists would assert that when such life experiences are subject to critical reflection, this could inspire opposition to forces of control.

Within the radical humanist paradigm, Critical Theory is best viewed as a key resource for advancing ideas and practices that share a commitment to the construction of a more rational society (Alvesson and Willmott, 2001). Critical Theory has consistently stressed the Weberian view that the key to the understanding of human interaction is through the meaning and ideologies by which institutions are changed. In management and organization studies, an ideological extension of Taylorism can be appreciated as a mode of technocratic thinking, in that managers are presented as impartial experts whose authority is legitimized by the possession of particular specialist knowledge that leads to successive increases in efficiency – the pursuit of which becomes a new ideology; a new form of control.

In studying leadership, the study itself may mean reproducing and reaffirming the "leader" category's interests and positions as well as contributing to the institutionalism of leadership as such. Ideas expressed in research about the nature of leadership do not only reflect "objective" conditions; they also constitute them. If "strong" leadership receives a high degree of focus, it also acquires an elevated importance in social practice. Both leaders and non-leaders come to believe that leadership is essential to successful operations and act accordingly. Leadership becomes therefore an ideal for a variety of social relations. Consequently the practice of an idealized form of leadership may mean strengthening and legitimizing asymmetric social relations (Alvesson and Sköldberg, 2005).

Critical methodology

Within Critical Theory approaches, there is no definitive or broadly agreed procedure for research practice. This has led to criticisms of critical studies, stating that it is an ivory-tower approach that has little to say to managers and practitioners and that fails to connect the outputs of research to organizational problems facing people in organizations.

While is has been suggested that the research outcomes of critical approaches to management research are not value-free (Kelemen and Rumens, 2008), Critical Theory scholars may counter by pointing to the emancipatory value at the core of such methods. Critical management research aims to reduce the limitations on thinking about, feeling about and relating to established practices, values and institutions. Ideals such as "defamiliarization" – making the well-known, natural and self-evident into something strange, arbitrary and possible to redo and undo – and "dissensus" – disruptions of consensus and of seemingly harmonious, robust meanings – may comprise overall objectives. Each of these goals may in turn be linked to Critical Theory's core optimistic goals of facilitating emancipation (Alvesson and Deetz, 2006a).

It is the contention here that we live in a world ruled by ideologies and practices of managerialism and as such are justified in referring to the "managerialization" of the world. (Alvesson and Deetz, 2006a). In this light, the point of all learning and reflection is to change and develop our understandings in order to reduce illusion. Learning, as the reduction of illusion and ignorance can help reduce the authority of hitherto unacknowledged constraints, dogmas and falsehoods (Sayer, 2000). While this may appear obvious on one level, it is often ignored, as one is socialized into the ways of thinking associated with the conventional view of knowledge as a mirror or external representation of the world. Critical management research is therefore important as an antidote to this, as

Critical Theory and other associated research platforms offer very powerful stimuli for rethinking about contemporary society and its institutions (Alvesson and Deetz, 2006a). An implication is that as researchers attempt to uncover emancipatory change in their work, they stimulate similar changes in others.

Critical Theory does not simply replace research on what *is* with a criticism of what *is*, plus a view of what might *be* from the perspective of emancipation; it also notes that people within a society possess a capacity that remains dormant, and consequently acknowledges that unrealized capacity may become active, leading to lasting change. If learning is not to change people's understanding of the world and themselves in it, it remains only for the edification of the elite. With this in mind it should be noted that the emancipatory intentions of this study, in common with others (Kelemen and Rumens, 2008), while valid, remain less grand.

It is also acknowledged that there may be a cost to emancipation, and the associated costs should not be glibly glossed over, as the price to be paid for liberation from dominant ideologies may be high. For example, the outcome of increased freedoms and creativity at work – which are likely priorities emerging from critical reflection and emancipatory change – may be reduced wages and consumption (Alvesson and Willmott, 2001). Emancipation involves a trade-off between certain gains and certain losses. People may have reasons for refusing emancipatory invitations, including both the fear of failure and the fear of the successful emancipatory change. These fears may only be dealt with if they are addressed openly and not dismissed as "irrationality". Furthermore, the dynamics and dialectics of an emancipatory project mean that there is the possibility that an idea or intended practice could be subverted in its practical application, so that critique and liberation from the old dogma would simply be replaced by a new dogma (Alvesson and Willmott, 2001)

A focus for this study is how emancipation may be achieved through stimulation of debate and disturbance, informing a more democratic and empowered workplace and working practices. In this case, the research outcomes should have something to say to actors – managers and other employees – that is relevant to their situation. This calls for appreciation of the work situation and of the contingencies and constraints of their work practices.

The literature on Critical Theory and methodology is sparse, and apart from general guidance in line with the emancipatory aims outlined above, it has seldom had anything concrete to say about practical methodology (Alvesson and Sköldberg, 2005). The shortage of empirical studies is, to a minor extent, a consequence of the lack of methodologies for critical management research (Alvesson and Deetz, 2006a). Nevertheless, such studies do exist; without intending to cover all the possibilities, attention will be drawn to three versions of empirical research that are feasible from a critical emancipatory perspective.

Critical ethnography

Generally, critical approaches do not prioritize empirical studies; those that do are closely related to conventional inductive or interpretive ethnography. A critical element may be possible, but this tends to be limited in extent (Alvesson and Sköldberg, 2005). Researchers work in a broadly traditional way while trying to consider themes and questions in the context of domination versus emancipation, and interpret these in light of Critical Theory. Thomas (1993) suggests that a critical ethnography accentuates the repressive aspects of a culture. It chooses its subject (focus) in terms of injustices, and is inclined to scepticism with regard to data and interviews. It adopts a defamiliarizing role in its interpretations (avoiding established paths emphasizing the non-natural or strange). It considers language in relation to power and reflects upon the process itself, both in the researchers' involvement and in the broader relevance of the research. Thomas contends that through such a process, critical ethnography can counteract the focus on professional technique and authority that characterizes the majority of empirical studies in the social sciences.

A fundamental part of a critical ethnography is the constant use of negation – attempting to see things not as natural or rational but as exotic and arbitrary – an expression of action and thinking within fixed conformist patterns (Alvesson and Deetz, 2006a; Alvesson and Sköldberg, 2005). Critical Theory interpretation can involve considerable reflection, and it is difficult to integrate extensive empirical materials into such reflections (Kelemen and Rumens, 2008). In a critical ethnography, therefore, a possibility is to select from the main body of the material parts that appear to be particularly pertinent to the emancipatory intent of the study. In practical terms, this would mean that despite the fieldwork being as comprehensive as in a conventional ethnography, the compilation of the empirical material and descriptions of objects could be reduced, and more time therefore devoted to interpretive reflection (Alvesson and Deetz, 2006a; Alvesson and Sköldberg, 2005). The shaping of text with a critical ethnography would be the same as a conventional ethnography, with the focus on empirical descriptions but with interpretations of a more critical nature (Thomas, 1993).

Focused critical ethnography – "close reading"

A variant of full-scale ethnography is to go further in concentrating the empirical focus as outlined above. In a focused critical ethnography, it is a question of making a fairly qualified interpretation of a more limited level of material on the basis of a relatively extensive basic knowledge of the object of study (Alvesson and Sköldberg, 2005). This research strategy could be to pick out something from the broader empirical context which illuminates the theme in question and is amenable to critical interpretation, and focus on that. This methodological strategy has been referred to as an intensive critical interpretation or "close reading" (Alvesson and Sköldberg, 2005). The important point here is that the researcher, by way of conducting the fieldwork, has gained a qualified understanding of the context within which the phenomenon occurs. This understanding with a theoretical framework guides the empirical focus. A limited part of the empirical material is subject to a close reading and careful critical-interpretive focus. Critical empirical studies within organization studies have concentrated upon the study of specific situations in which dominating actors have sought to define reality for their subordinates within an organization (Alvesson and Sveningsson, 2003b; Collinson, 2003; Knights and Willmott, 1992).

Theoretical methodology

A third variant of critical research is for the researcher to work primarily on a theoretical level; using, synthesizing and interpreting existing studies while adding smaller empirical studies of their own. The researcher uses a small proportion of the empirical material collected; the remainder is not subject to such intensive analysis as in the variants above.

Methodology of this study

Within the present study, a critical ethnography based upon the conditions cited by Thomas (1993) was conducted over a 16-month period, and empirical materials were collected in the form of documents, field notes and interviews. In the conduct of the ethnography, a qualified understanding of the context, enhanced by the first author's working relationship with the organization under study, was obtained. Reflection on the materials allowed themes to emerge, and these informed the focus of the fieldwork and the subsequent collection of further empirical materials. Further concentration of the empirical material informed by a "close reading" elicited interpretations on *illustrative* examples of the object of study, which are presented in Chapters 5–10. A focus on the research design and the process of reflection is provided in the following sections.

Research design

This study concerns the dynamics of the leader–follower relationship within a large unitary local authority in northern England, here known as A Big Council or ABC. In studying leaders and followers undergoing their normal work activities, a Critical Theory methodology was utilized to uncover and interpret the dynamics of the relationship.

Local authorities have undergone extensive pressure from governments to reform their service provision. This external pressure has created a movement of change within local authorities and the public sector, referred to as the New Public Management (Rhodes, 1991). It is the contention of this study that local authorities are subject to extreme pressures, rendering the work context highly complex and ambiguous. Normative understandings of leadership as produced by extensive research studies conducted within the functional paradigm have failed to uncover knowledge that either illuminates leadership processes or offers constructive advice to leaders and followers (Alvesson, 1996).

This study offers insights into the ways in which leaders and followers operate within local authority environments. In its conclusions, the study seeks to supply understanding into leadership that goes beyond normative conceptualizations, thus stimulating dialogues and discourses concerning the concepts of leading and following. This may provide an emancipatory consideration of the roles individuals undertake within organizations. As an example, leaders and followers within normative understandings are perceived as a superordinate and subordinate dyad. Leadership is something that happens to followers who, through some form of social influence process, undergo a realignment in line with the leader's aspirations, which in turn increases identification with the leader and the organization; this enhances the followers' motivations and commitment to the leader's vision and, ultimately, raises organizational performance (Bass, 1999). This interpretation does not take into account the complexity and ambiguities related to the interplay of dynamics in the organizational context, such as power and politics. An examinatino of these dynamics may support the view that followers are not a homogeneous mass, but are vitally important in the construction of, and the perceived successes of, leaders and leadership (Collinson, 2005, 2006; Grint, 2005a; Knights and Willmott, 1992).

This study was conducted using a variant of a critical ethnography informed by the principles outlined by Thomas (1993), but moderated as a response to the complexity of the interpretations involved (Alvesson and Sköldberg, 2005). As a consequence, the research methodology utilized in this study may be referred to as a close reading or intensive critical interpretation (Alvesson and Sköldberg, 2005).

The leader of the council wrote an introductory letter to colleagues throughout the authority in support of the study. In response to this letter, preliminary conversations were established at which the terms of access were agreed, and initial insights informing the scope of the study became evident. For example, a member of the political leadership, a leader of one of the opposition parties, had served for many years as a local councillor and had been leader of the council in previous administrations. During conversations, the councillor voiced opinion concerning the frustrations of being a councillor, complaining of a lack of focus and the rise of "technocracy" within the authority.

The research design was initially undertaken as a critical ethnography. Thomas (1993) cites the following points to consider in undertaking a critical study: ontology, selecting a topic, method, interpretation and analysis of data, discourse, and reflection on the whole research process. Each of these points is considered in turn here in order to illustrate and summarize the research design.

Ontology

Critical Theory studies begin from the premise that the structure and content of social life oppresses individuals within that culture or society. Critical Theory approaches to social research therefore generally advocate the emancipation of groups marginalized within society (Thomas, 1993). Critical management research aims to follow the spirit of Critical Theory research but focuses on management phenomena (Alvesson and Deetz, 2006b). Within management studies, this may relate to the asymmetrical power relations within organizations or to the perceived superiority of management insights, knowledge and practice. Assumptions such as these have become entrenched and reinforced by functionalist research practices, which are open to challenge by Critical Theory scholars operating from the radical humanist standpoint.

Selecting a topic

Factors pertinent to management studies are equally applicable to leadership studies taken as a branch of management studies. In addition, leadership in practice has been elevated in importance because of the apparent popularity of adopting neo-charismatic models to supersede management practices. The results derived from mainstream research on such models show followers as not only requiring leaders but also actively searching for them. In addition, leaders themselves are exposed to heightened expectations from recruiters and employers, who stipulate the need for heroic levels of performance.

The focus of this study is to examine and interpret the dynamic of the relationship between leaders and followers in their normal work environment. Functionalist literature maintains that the relationship between the two is a social influence process, though this process is not well understood (Parry, 1998). While this may be so, these theoretical conceptualizations of leaders and followers do not take into account the interplay of power and politics within the work environment, nor do they take into account the ambiguities and complexities of the work context.

This study is built upon a wide-ranging body of existing literature, and the conclusions drawn from it are to be utilized as guidelines, as opposed to truths to be either confirmed or refuted. Acknowledging that research is value-laden (Kelemen and Rumens, 2008), a guarded stance must be incorporated to ensure that data is not gathered in order to prove a point. This study has argued that much of leadership research has not considered the full complexity of the object of study. Consequently, a research topic has been chosen that is deliberately open-ended, allowing for the possibility of a change of perspective during data collection, reflection and interpretation.

Method

The technique by which data is collected is not a neutral process; how it is collected can dramatically shape the critical potential of a project (Thomas, 1993).

Data sources

This study is concerned with the dynamics of the relationship between leader and followers. Steps have been made, therefore, to observe leaders and followers in their normal workplace engaging in their usual work practices.

Initial conversations with members of the organization informed thematic concepts to be focused upon during the course of the extended observation. Subsequently, informal interviews were undertaken with members of the work force, during observation and during breaks and work-related social occasions. Documents related to the activities observed were also collected, and interviews were set up involving the principal actors in the scenarios observed. A summary of the data sources is provided in Figure 4.3.

City Development Department (126 hours)

Field observations, plus:

Interview 1 – Director Trent
Interview 2 – Chief Officer Soar
Interview 3 – Chief Officer Idle
Interview 4 – Head of Service, Cultural Events
Interview 5 – Chief Officer Leen
Interview 6 – Chief Officer Maun
Interview 7 – Chief Officer Poulter
Interview 8 – Chief Officer Erewash

Housing and Neighbourhoods Department (24 hours)

Field observations, plus:

Interview 9 – Chief Officer Welland

Children's Services (31 hours)

Field observations, plus:

Interview 10 – Head of Service
Interview 11 – Chief Officer Manifold
Interview 12 – Area Manager

Central Services (including Chief Executive's Unit) (90 hours)

Field observations, plus:

Interview 13 – Chief Officer Penk
Interview 14 – Head of Service, Admin
Interview 15 – Head of Service, Diversity
Interview 16 – Head of Strategic Human Resources
Interview 17 – Chief Executive
Interview 18 – Senior Officer
Interview 19 – Assistant Chief Executive

General observations (54 hours)

Figure 4.3 Data sources for study of the leader–follower relationship at ABC, showing research hours.

Accuracy of evidence

While it has been asserted that the accuracy of evidence is not a critical factor in methods which are alternatives to quantifiable studies (Glaser and Strauss, 1967), observational and reporting rigour has been maintained through the scrutiny of data in this study. Thomas (1993) warns against the imposition of research values through the use of leading questions. While attempts have been made to negate this effect in collecting data, on occasion interviewees were deliberately provoked in order to elicit a response. Where this occurred, further questioning and conversation concerning the point made was undertaken in order to clarify the interviewee's intention and meaning where possible. Where deliberate prompting has occurred, it has been noted in the presentation of the empirical material.

Data collection

In order to complete a critical study, the researcher must be aware of inconsistencies or contradictory statements, or occurrences that are made and witnessed. Such anomalies when pursued may lead to surprising insights and information. Consequently, rather than using a structured questionnaire, this study used a short list of four or five areas "to be covered" based upon previous fieldwork, which served as a guide for the interviews undertaken. Informal interviews allowed the interviewees to talk freely, with minimal prompting from the researcher.

Conceptualization

Following the initial collection of empirical materials, areas of thematic focus began to emerge as greater understanding of the work context began to be understood. Periods of conceptualizing and interpretation were scheduled through the interview and observation process. As the fieldwork progressed ad hoc, opportunities for further observation and interview became available, and so the period of conceptualizing, in such cases, may necessarily have been curtailed or postponed. On such occasions, time away from the fieldwork allowed for clarification of thoughts and decisions concerning further themes for future exploration.

Interpretation and analysis

The interpretation of data requires a defamiliarization process in which the observations are translated into something new. Defamiliarization is a process of distancing oneself from the empirical material collected. According to Thomas (1993), a critical ethnography resembles literary criticism in that the researcher seeks non-literal meanings in the data-texts.

In order to interpret the data fully, the researchers used a process of "funnelling" the empirical material. This involved an iterative process of visiting various observed scenarios and associated field notes in order to arrive at those scenarios utilized for interpretation. This probably required a process of familiarization, as distinct from and before the process of defamiliarization. The illustrative potential of scenarios that were concerned specifically with the interactions of leaders and followers, the leadership topic, or meetings related to particular leader–follower realtionships were prioritized.

After choosing specific illustrative scenarios, the researchers collated the documentation, including field notes, other supporting documentary evidence, and recorded transcripts of interviews pertaining to the scenario. Much of the empirical material collected was discarded at this stage, but familiarity with the material did impinge upon the interpretive process. Continual iterative interpretation allowed the framing of the familiar in a different perspective.

Interpretations were explored primarily within the research team, and subsequently in ad hoc conversations with members of the organization. The first author was invited to a "wrap up" meeting with members of the Chief Executive's Unit in which the research interpretations were discussed, in order that misinterpretations and blind spots were covered adequately.

During this questioning process, the research position used in the study became a minor obstacle, but was also illuminating. As the members of the Chief Executive's Unit were senior managers and designated leaders within the organization, they were resistant to issues related to the asymmetries of power, the positioning of themselves as followers and the political bias of relationships, despite evidence to the contrary (Hales, 2002). However, after initial reluctance, issues related to the principal dynamics of the leader–follower relationship were acknowledged.

Discourse

Linguistic exchange, and therefore all interaction, entails a form of symbolic domination, in that pre-naming shapes cognition and discourse. This especially includes the "authority" of scholars and academics. The critical ethnographer's goal is to examine both the language of our data and the language with which researchers speak, so as to identify characteristics of the culture that provide access toward the unblocking of alternative metaphors and meanings.

Reflection

Ethnography requires the researcher to adopt the position of an active creator as opposed to that of a passive recorder of narratives or events. All ethnography requires systematic intellectual or personal involvement with the subjects, regardless of whether reliance is upon artefacts or full immersion with the subjects themselves. Reflection refers to the act of rigorously examining how this involvement affects the data gathering, analysis and subsequent presentation to an audience. Through reflection – an act of continuously rethinking about the study – attempts were made to become more self-aware, to guard against the possibility of either gaining disproportionate empathy with the subjects, nor becoming disillusioned with the subjects or the study.

In undertaking reflection, a strategy of maintaining sympathy for the subjects under scrutiny was followed. Simultaneously, focusing on the areas of enquiry along with the actors ensured that the problem of distortion was reduced (Thomas, 1993). The problem of elevating and reinforcing leadership is replaced with an analysis of the dynamics of an influence relationship that may be considered as leadership.

Presentation of the material

The chosen illustrations are presented as compact case studies, utilizing studies already published as examples (Alvesson and Willmott, 2002; Collinson, 1999; Knights and Willmott, 1992). In total, the empirical material comprises six separate illustrations. They are referred to thus:

- The challenge to leadership and the dynamic of ambiguity.
- The limitations to leadership and the dynamic of the environment.
- The negotiation of leadership and the dynamic of resource acquisition.
- The balance within leadership and the dynamic of symbiosis.
- The negotiation of leadership and the dynamic of politics.
- The agency of followers and the dynamic of game playing.

There is no chronological order to the scenarios as they are presented here, but a scenario may appear before another if its inclusion serves to assist in the understanding of the following scenario. Each illustration can be said to demonstrate daily life, as there is no suggestion that the scenarios as described here are not typical of day-to-day life of the organization under study.

Criteria for empirical research

The findings here are drawn from qualitative data sources. The criteria for establishing the soundness of qualitative findings differ fundamentally from those used to assess findings drawn from quantitative sources. This section outlines the processes involved in ensuring that a credible study was achieved within accepted standards.

The views advanced by critical theorist scholars have gone beyond the truth criterion – where theory is confirmed by empirical evidence reflecting "objective reality out there" – as the ultimate yardstick for science (Alvesson and Sköldberg, 2005; Denzin and Lincoln, 1994). By emphasizing the researchers' active construction of a reality – through perception, cognition and the handling of language as well as through social interaction with those involved in the research – a fundamental critique of the traditional empirical epistemology emerges. To this is added the historical and changeable nature of social phenomena: what might be "true" in one context may not necessarily be "true" in another. The concept of generality can be appreciated as a semantic issue within qualitative studies

(Alvesson and Sköldberg, 2005). Generality is not an issue confined to lower or higher levels of proof, as in reality there are not just two levels but an arbitrary number of them. The production of generality has not been a principal objective of this study, as the aims are to make interpretations concerning the leader–follower relation within the organization under study; nevertheless, the findings of the study may have the capacity to inform aspects of leader–follower relationships in similar settings (Alvesson and Deetz, 2006a).

From the perspective of Critical Theory it is important to note the way dominant institutions and ideologies are uncritically taken for granted and reproduced in research. Researchers have a tendency to take for granted phenomena in a society to which they belong and thus pass on its fundamental values. Critical Theory encourages a much more reflective emphasis than mainstream social science research. Within this reflective capacity lie the principal criteria for credible research from a Critical Theory perspective, namely the promotion of reflection on, and emancipation from, frozen social and ideational patterns. Critical research should have something to say to actors – leaders and followers – that is of relevance to their particular situation (Alvesson and Deetz, 2006a).

The critical-political dimension in research can be attributed, more or less, to a variety of factors ranging from the object of study to preference. Other knowledge interests have their parts to play in social science, and consequently an exclusive emancipatory cognitive interest may not be a requirement for all research (Alvesson and Sköldberg, 2005). Researchers should acknowledge that they are working in the political-ideological continuum. The tensions between the reinforcement and reproduction of social order and the challenge to the same order should be made clear in the research context, and researchers should avoid pandering to established thinking and dominating interests.

Alvesson and Sköldeberg (2005) assert that success criteria for qualitative research remain problematic, as the very definition of "meaningful research" makes it impossible to lay down any rules – simple or ambiguous – for the evaluation of the research. Nevertheless, this study is required to display a level of proficiency and rigour, and has utilized the following strategies to support the success of the research (Alvesson and Sköldberg, 2005 p. 276).

- In analysing the empirical material, the researcher attempted to consider alternative "arguments" to move beyond a "functional fit" for the material. The arguments were discussed with actors within the organization at the end of the fieldwork and informally with other actors at various times during the course of the fieldwork. Confirming and contradictory reactions to the arguments were proactively sought (Alvesson and Sköldberg, 2005; Golden-Biddle and Locke, 1993).
- The study used an iterative process of data collection, meaning that the collection of material was informed by what had gone before. After an intervention, a period of reflection was undertaken to clarify thought processes and to allow for conceptualization before embarking on the next intervention (Denzin and Lincoln, 1994).

- In order to make transparent the probable impact the researcher may have made on the study, personal information related to experience within organizations and the organization under study, and to some of the actors involved, has been declared. In instances where the researcher has deliberately "provoked" a response, this has been declared. Inevitably this declaration has forced an examination of the shared assumption held between the researcher and the participants of the study (Golden-Biddle and Locke, 1993).
- The researcher took an open attitude to the vital importance of the interpretive dimension to social phenomena.
- The researcher undertook critical reflection regarding the political and ideological contexts of and issues in research.
- The researcher maintained an awareness of the ambiguity of language and its limited capacity to convey knowledge of a purely empirical reality.
- Following the period of the fieldwork, the empirical material was reduced to enable a close reading to be conducted; this required that the illustrations were valid examples of themes identified during the research. Further interpretation was embarked upon in the development of "argument" in order to develop a "richness of points" (Alvesson and Sköldberg, 2005).
- The implication for theory development based upon an understanding of the literature under review is made in the interpretive and concluding chapters of the study.

Limitations of the study

The goal of this section is to examine the limitations of this study and the research method, in order to substantiate the significance of the study's specific contributions to knowledge concerning the dynamics of the leader–follower relationship.

From a methodological perspective, there are potential limitations in the study. The treatment of the various dynamics in a necessarily linear fashion may be considered a limitation, as some of the links and interrelatedness between them are lost. The structure of the presentation of the various dynamics may be construed as being artificial, but the authors consider this to be the most easily understood method of presentation without building in levels of additional meaning that is not intended.

A further limitation may be in the selection of and the interpretations of the empirical material. With reference to selection, there is the potential to suggest that materials selected as illustrations were chosen from the body of the empirical material because they demonstrate a preconceived finding of the study. Clearly, other interpretations based on the entire body of material collected are possible, and yet six illustrations have been selected. The authors consider those chosen to represent scenarios that are typical of the events that occur within the organization. Reflection upon the entire body of material was made to ensure this. It is contended within Critical Theory studies that empirical evidence is not a primary factor of the research and that the materials are surpassed by the depth of critical interpretation that the researcher produces (Alvesson and Sköldberg, 2005).

Additionally, the authors have chosen to include a wide variety of materials in support of the illustrations. As suggested above, limitations may be created by associating certain statements with certain illustrations to make connections that do not exist. Moreover, the values of critical reflection act as a counter to the potential limitation, as does the stance we take in conducting Critical Theory studies in attempting to uncover deeper social structures inherent in human interaction and language. The iterative technique of observation-interview-reflection ensures that a critical appreciation of the overall process is undertaken (Thomas, 1993).

A potential limitation is also present in the interpretations made. It is potentially valid to suggest that the authors may have drawn interpretations to match their ontological stance, and that other interpretations could be made. From a critical standpoint, additional possible interpretations are to be welcomed if they seek to uncover further social structures to provoke debate concerning the phenomenon of leadership. Critical theorists do not express their findings as factual statements concerning an objective reality "out there", and are more concerned about addressing issues of imbalance and injustice (Alvesson and Sköldberg, 2005; Denzin and Lincoln, 1994), thereby maintaining an element of sympathy for the subjects, and focusing on the area of enquiry so as to reduce potential distortion (Thomas, 1993).

A further potential limitation to the study could be one that is inherent within the research design. A variation of a critical ethnography referred to as "close reading" was used in this study, followed by a reflective interpretation of the material collected. Criticism can be made of this method, as it falls short of a full ethnography. In defence of the method, thousands of studies have been undertaken utilizing positivist and neo-positivistic methods to produce a body of knowledge that is questioned by those inside the school of research. Alternative methods have been called for (Alvesson, 1996; Bryman, 1996; Grint, 2005b; Morgan and Smircich, 1980; Thomas, 1993), and this is an attempt to utilize a qualitative method to produce a deeper and more contextually relevant and critical interpretation of the phenomenon under study. To an extent, this is borne out by the findings of the study, which were subject to scrutiny by the host organization before being written up. Furthermore, critical scholars have not produced a codification of critical research method; the process of reflection upon deeper issues such as power and the process itself may be seen as countering accusations of limitation in design (Alvesson and Sköldberg, 2005).

And finally, the findings may be considered limited in their lack of generality. It was not the intention of the study to produce findings that were general across organizations, and it is recognized that these findings may be entirely limited to the organization under study. In response to a criticism for this lack of generality, a critical researcher would point to the semantic nature of the concept of generality within qualitative studies, to demonstrate that generality is not an issue confined to lower or higher levels of proof, as there are not two levels of proof but an arbitrary number of them (Alvesson and Sköldberg, 2005). Only the production of more studies will demonstrate the external validity of the findings achieved. The aim here is to eradicate the problem of elevating and reinforcing a normative understanding of leadership and to replace it with an interpretive analysis of the dynamics of an influence relationship that may be considered to be leadership. This has the capacity to inform aspects of the leader–follower relationship in other organizational settings (Alvesson and Deetz, 2006a).

Conclusion

This chapter has described the research process of collecting and interpreting data and has outlined how the findings will be presented in the final chapters. The chapter has shown how research aims emerged in response to initial conversations. The epistemological and methodological foundations for the study were examined, and the research design was described, including data collection, interpretation and presentation. The chapter continued with an examination of criteria for research of this type. Finally, an examination of the method made explicit the potential limitations of the study.

Part II
Field research

Data illustrations and interpretations

Introduction to Chapters 5–10

The present study concerns a large unitary local authority in the north of England, here referred to as A Big Council (ABC; see Figure I.1). At the time of study the ABC was under a coalition administration of an unusual mix, referred to locally as the "rainbow coalition", comprising 99 elected members. The leadership of the coalition passed at six-monthly intervals between the leaders of the two main political parties of the coalition. The aim of the present study was to examine the influence relationships between leaders and followers in a public sector organization and how these relationships inform social influence processes.

One of the criticisms of the normative models of leadership that have dominated the leadership research school since the mid-1980s is that they employ reductionist methodologies, leading to the oversimplification of the phenomenon being observed (Alvesson, 1996; Alvesson and Deetz, 2006a; Western, 2008). The resulting leader-centric theories see leadership as a concept that exists

Location	Northern England		
Structure	Unitary local authority		Children's Services
Format of administration	Coalition		City Development
Elected membership	99 councillors	Directorates	Adult Social Services
Wards	33		Corporate Services
Size	40,000 acres		Neighbourhood and Renewal
Population	840,000		
Combined gross expenditure on services	£2.4 billion		

Figure I.1 ABC: description and directorates.

devoid of context, and other members of the relationship (followers) as blank slates upon which the leader writes the script (Jackson and Parry, 2008).

In order to combat this oversimplification, each illustration of ABC's activities is considered separately and, in each chapter, the illustration is coupled with interpretations drawn from it. Each of the next six chapters is structured in the same way.

Each chapter comprises four parts. First, background material is provided to allow for a holistic appreciation of the illustration itself which, in turn, assists in a deeper and broader appreciation of the leadership phenomenon. Second, statements in support of the illustration, drawn primarily from interviews, are presented. These are presented as "leader voices" and "follower voices"; this provides an opportunity to give space to a wider "congregation of voices" depending on the role played in the leader–follower relationship. Leader voices come from members of a particular group that possess leadership responsibilities in its myriad forms. Follower voices mainly come from the population in receipt of the leadership activities. Third, the illustration is presented. Each of these comprises events witnessed during the fieldwork and is reproduced here from field notes and supporting materials collected at the time. It is the contention here that these illustrations are typical, or are at least not atypical, of regular occurrences within the organization. Finally, the fourth part comprises interpretations of the empirical material, leading to the identification of the dynamic(s) of the leader–follower relationship.

It should be noted that in making a choice of the materials to be presented, it is possible that the authors favoured some material and prejudiced other material. In funnelling and choosing the relevant supporting data from the total empirical materials collected, the authors might be said to have used functionalist methods, effectively, to reduce and simplify the evidence presented. Furthermore, it must be recognized that within the categorization there is the distinct possibility that the population of the two constituent groups may ebb and flow, as a leader in one situation may play the role of follower in another.

The authors consider that this style of presentation assists in the understanding of the data for the following three reasons. First, this style is primarily a presentational tool and has been employed to portray complex organizational data. The authors do not assert that the influence of any of this is limited to the section or illustration to which it has been associated in the body of the text. The additional supporting information given in this section could, and in all likelihood will, influence all of the illustrations given in these chapters, and is therefore integral to the richer appreciation of the leader–follower relationship as a dynamic one. Against traditional research practice of limiting voices (categorizing and synthesizing), it is the intention here to widen the range of voices heard and to seek variation in the empirical material (observation and interview) collected during the course of the fieldwork, allowing for more ambitious interpretation (Alvesson and Sköldberg, 2005). Second, the empirical materials are not presented en masse before the interpretations, as it is the intention to make a connection between the data and the interpretation. To divorce the data from the interpretation would only serve to promote additional abstraction of the material and make the process of cross-referencing material to interpretation laborious, complex and ineffectual. Finally, the data is presented in this way as it assists in the provocation of interpretations pertaining to the empirical work. In the book's final chapter, subsequent to the six illustrations, the various interpretations and dynamics are brought together in order to permit a holistic appreciation, drawn from a Critical Theory perspective, of the dynamics of the leader–follower relationship.

The six illustrations outlined are as follows:

- **Chapter 5 – The challenge to leadership and the dynamic of ambiguity:** this chapter concerns an organizational seminar arranged to introduce the methodology of an international consulting company (ICC) and its relationship between leadership, culture and performance. The seminar was intended to form the bedrock of the ABC's stated objective of developing leadership capacity within the organization.
- **Chapter 6 – The limitations to leadership and the dynamic of the environment:** this chapter deals with a meeting about the auditing of the legal and regulatory framework within which the ABC operates.
- **Chapter 7 – The negotiation of leadership and the dynamic of resource acquisition:** this chapter concerns a meeting of the corporate leadership team (CLT). The CLT is the main executive body of the organization outside of the political structure. It comprises the chief executive, the Deputy and assistant chief executives, and all the directors.
- **Chapter 8 – The balance within leadership and the dynamic of symbiosis:** this chapter presents a composite illustration made up of a number of observations concerning the Responsibility, Accountability Communication and Information (RACI) matrix and the response to it by chief officers (followers).
- **Chapter 9 – The negotiation of leadership and the dynamic of politics:** this chapter focuses on a Senior Management Team meeting. The director chairs the meeting, with chief officers of the directorate in attendance.
- **Chapter 10 – The agency of followers and the dynamic of game playing:** this illustration presents meetings between elected politicians and senior managers of the ABC.

5 The challenge to leadership and the dynamic of ambiguity

... raised the issue of leadership, it's on the agenda, we're talking about it all the time, we've put in some training and some developmental work to try and explore that more.... In the corporate context we're looking at embedding leadership into appraisals and that sort of thing, but I'm not sure if we are going to do anything differently.

Chief Officer Idle, City Development

"From Good to Great"[1]

In the following section, an illustration related to the authority's aspiration to develop the leadership capacity of the organization focuses on the leadership seminar "From Good to Great". In the second section, interpretations of the empirical materials are provided. The interpretations suggest that the ABC, despite efforts to the contrary, holds an ambiguous position in relation to the identities and roles of leaders and followers. It is concluded that ambiguity is a significant dynamic in the leader–follower relationship.

Background

Before the "From Good to Great" seminar, the ABC had invested considerable amounts of time and money into leadership development through the Leadership in the City Programmes, which became known internally as the LCP1 and LCP2 programmes. The LCP1 Initiative was based upon the work of Beverly Alimo-Metcalfe and the public sector transformational leadership model (Alimo-Metcalfe and Alban-Metcalfe, 2001). Aimed at senior-ranking officers, it was universally received as being a worthwhile investment of time and resource. The LCP1 comprised a programme of training interventions, including some oriented toward "outward bound"-style activities of the type made famous by the military and subsequently endorsed by the world of management development. Following LCP1, the organization became aware of a need for wider leadership skills within other supervisory levels of the organization and therefore commissioned LCP2, which had at its core the ethos of dispersed leadership models, in which everyone has the opportunity to be a leader.

Following an introductory conference, the various departments were allowed to continue leadership development with a minimum of formal control, but all the activity was badged as belonging to the LCP2 programme of development. Initial reaction to the LCP2 programme was very favourable, but the enthusiasm of the first stages eventually withered. The amounts of energy required to maintain the vitality of a self-sustaining programme such as LCP2 had been underestimated, as had the amount of time required: development activities were seen as encroaching on "work" time. LCP2, despite being well intentioned, well received and seen as valuable to the delegates, eventually degenerated into a lifeless husk of its envisaged self.

As a continuation of ABC's leadership development programme, the organization commissioned an international consulting company (here known as the ICC) to run a training and awareness day, which became known as "From Good to Great". The intention was to engage with the organization in order to implement its model for leadership, cultural and performance development. The ICC had previously been commissioned to run a couple of smaller interventions within operational units of the ABC. Because of these interventions, the two unit heads involved had become confirmed supporters of the ICC programme. They had persistently sought support from members of the corporate leadership team (CLT) for the ICC programme, and the ABC eventually committed the organization to it.

Not only can the "From Good to Great" initiative be appreciated as a natural continuation of leadership training that had occurred throughout the authority, it is also a consequence of the ABC's aspirations to restructure, to generate a more strategic focus and to deal with both internal and external issues.

Much of the motivation for the "From Good to Great" intervention was expressed by one of the architects of the programme: "A lot of the senior managers were saying that 'LCP2 was great, but it was a while ago and can we get some of that back', and that's what Good to Great was about" (Senior Officer Admin, Chief Executive's Unit). It would be useful at this juncture to explore what leadership meant and comprised to members of the ABC organization.

Leader voices

Due to the exposure of individuals to leadership development programmes, either directly through interventions or through less formal methods, the organization had developed a reasonably consistent concept of what leadership meant. A comment from a senior member of the management was typical in many ways of a number of comments collected.

> Leadership brings in woolly concepts like inspiring; and it should be about setting clear objectives and helping people deliver the objectives but not managing the process. The corporate view is that leadership is setting the broad objective and helping people to get there, and I think there has been a very consistent approach.
>
> (Chief Officer Leen, City Development)

The individuals at the corporate centre of the authority seemed more likely to interpret leadership as motivating beyond the pragmatic toward meeting the expectations of wider communities, and the business and media communities in particular.

> We needed to do something radically different from what we had operated previously. In terms of the early discussions I took in some presentations that were very frank with the CLT which was saying, do you realize that this is how we are viewed, do you realize that there is a view within the city that the city council lacks effective leadership.
>
> (Assistant chief executive, Chief Executive's Unit)

While this perspective exists, it is possibly a reflection of the individual style of this chief executive, which was very different from the more media-savvy chief executives of unitary authorities of other neighbouring cities. The ABC leadership was regularly under scrutiny, primarily in the media and also at events and functions throughout the city. Such scrutiny was usually accompanied by exhortations for a more charismatic and vigorous leadership approach. The contention of the business community, in particular, was that the city lost out through not exhibiting a leadership platform typified by the transformational leadership approach. Despite this, however, the personal leadership style of the chief executive, in particular, was one that was welcomed by the vast majority of the ABC workforce.

> You're not a bruiser, [name of chief executive], you're more intellectual.
>
> (Director Wheelock, Children's Services)

A further probable contributing factor was the perception of the most senior officers of the ABC concerning the elected members of the authority.

> Few of our politicians want to be true leaders. Their aspirations are limited to community needs and Ward based needs, so we don't have any politician in a high profile position who has any aspiration to do something on the national stage.
>
> (Assistant chief executive, Chief Executive's Unit)

It was noticeable that during the "From Good To Great" conference none of the elected membership were present. This was explained as follows:

> – That was probably due to lack of invitation.
> – Would they have come if you'd invited them?
> – Eventually.
>
> (Assistant chief executive, Chief Executive's Unit)

The ABC took the considered view that in order to accommodate this gap, ABC officers needed to ascend in order to fill the city leadership role. The

ABC required that strategic directors demonstrate more leadership in order to comply with corporate assessments that had been made, identifying lack of vision and strategy. Furthermore, lower members of the hierarchy need to grow their leadership potential in order to deliver satisfactory outcomes within the complex environment within which the ABC exists. Finally, the "From Good to Great" workshop exhorted managers to resolve cultural differences through leadership interventions. Considering the multiplicity of messages concerning leadership that were aimed at the participants, the potential for an ambiguous appreciation of leadership is self-evident. This ambiguity of expectation is heightened by a lack of clarity, both in describing the task at hand or the "wicked problems" to be resolved, and in expressing the methodology through which resolution might be achieved. This ambiguity is typified by the following statement:

> More and more we are meeting people whose behaviour says that the direction of travel is the right way to go ... once that behaviour is seen, they are providing leadership, direction of which way to go. Head teachers are seeing that integration is the way to go, they are taking on a broader role beyond the education sphere ... let's provide really effective services that are joined up but let's position ourselves so that we're at the centre of it so we can drive it as well as being driven by it.
>
> (Area Manager, Children's Services)

Follower voices

Among the initiatives of the office of the assistant chief executive was the attempt to develop a "One Council" ethos. This notion, as taken from the corporate strategic plan (ABC, 2008 p. 11), stresses the importance of the ABC being perceived as, and acting as, a "coherent whole". Followers frequently voiced concerns about the ABC's strategic plan and the practical meaning of "One Council".

> What's the vision of the council, and I'm still not sure what our vision is ... I'm not clear what One Council means and what's our role, I'm not clear about that – I'm feeling uncomfortable about the change programme.
>
> (Chief Officer Erewash, City Development)

Furthermore, not only had some openly questioned the validity of the ICC's approach to the management of change within the ABC, but others had started to question the legitimacy of leadership development as central to the whole change initiative and the development of the organization itself.

> There's a philosophy behind the leadership thing that says that everyone can become a great leader and I don't believe that.
>
> (Chief Officer Leen, City Development)

Behind an awareness of the possible limitations of leadership, others, particularly those at lower levels of the organization, were showing a great reluctance to acknowledge their own roles as followers.

One manager said that there was "more of a problem with the definition of follower". Nevertheless there was an uncomfortable block, a difficulty in assimilating the idea of following and being a follower. Certainly the concept of the dual nature of a management role and the possibility of being both leader and follower did not seem to be entertained widely, if at all, as shown by the following three fairly typical comments:

> I may lead my team, but I don't follow.
> (Head of Service, Cultural Events, City Development)

> I don't follow leaders. I have to find the tactic to get what I think is right ... I'm not following leaders anymore.
> (Head of Service, Housing and Neighbourhoods)

> I wouldn't consider myself a follower ... that doesn't mean I'm a natural leader either ... I would accept that I'm a supporter, if I'm on board then I am a great supporter.
> (Chief Officer Maun, City Development)

The exception was within the Human Resource function, where the follower role was appreciated:

> The notion of a follower and following is much maligned within this authority, general management is not valued either, technical skills are valued and people play up to this.
> (Head of Strategic Human Resources, Central Services)

More critically, when pressed, members of the ABC would express their general concern relating to developments within the organization. Occasionally this would surface as a more deep-rooted cynicism.

> Management is about adhering to rule and procedures, it's OK but it's not about leading and inspiring people ... so we bring in consultants to tell us what leadership is ... I don't need to be sold this stuff.
> (Chief Officer Maun, City Development)

> It's a fad, isn't it ... part of it says that it's a fad, what we need round here is a bit of common sense, get on with things and stop navel gazing.... Increasingly I see things and I think it's just bollocks ... people are hiding behind jargon, concepts, potted theory.
> (Chief Officer Leen, City Development)

I think a lot of stuff that's being pumped out now is kind of Harvard Business School type stuff, a lot of the stuff coming out is the next Emperor's New Clothes.

(Chief Officer Idle, City Development)

There was evidence of cynicism regarding leadership and the possibility of real change occurring:

... raised the issue of leadership, it's on the agenda, we're talking about it all the time, we've put in some training and some developmental work to try and explore that more.... In the corporate context we're looking at embedding leadership into appraisals and that sort of thing, but I'm not sure if we are going to do anything differently.

We're all about leadership now, it's the new buzz word, it's not changed what I do on a day-to-day basis, I've been re-badged.

I go out for a drink with pals and one of them works for an engineering company and they are subject to this stuff but they usually get it before we do, and one day about three years ago we were laughing about "the elephant in the room".... And then one day when we first started talking about From Good to Great he actually came with a picture of an elephant, and I thought, we've been laughing about this for years in the pub, we're not even up to date with the Harvard Business School stuff.

(Chief Officer Poulter, City Development)

The illustration

"From Good to Great" took place in a venue hired specifically for the seminar and was a stylish corporate event, with all the typically associated paraphernalia of internal communication and corporate professionalism. The main conference hall was set out to accommodate approximately 1,500 ABC delegates, comprising the most senior officers of the authority. All were invited to sit in informal groups around circular tables holding 10 to 12 delegates, but there was ample room to spread out. Prior to the conference, each delegate had received a personal invitation to the event from the chief executive, and on registration each received a branded information pack concerning the day ahead.

The day was structured into two sections. The first consisted of presentations by the directors expressing their personal support and outlining the issues to be faced and the journey ahead. These presentations were very value-laden and visionary – "We must build brilliance; release the magic and switch on to the potential" – but they were not explicit, comprising mostly positive expressions and good intention; they were noticeably very well received. The senior leadership were building a context to demonstrate how "From Good to Great" was structurally essential to embedding the "One Council" ethos. Nevertheless, after

45 minutes a number of the delegates were becoming restless and were starting to lose their sense of engagement. The impression was that they had heard much of this before. There was an overwhelming sense that what had been presented was well-intentioned but perhaps a bit too real, too daunting – impossible? Scheduled to speak after the directors was the chief executive, but the deputy chief executive took his place, concluding the introductory remarks and handing on to the main speaker. The late change in speaker did not noticeably perturb the audience, but every member of the senior leadership team except the chief executive had made a full endorsement of what was to follow.

The second section of the day consisted of a very accomplished presentation from a senior consultant of the International Consulting Company (ICC), presented with style and panache rather like a leading business guru, and full of easy sound bites – "Best practice comes from variance" – and humour – "How many of you were kids?" The speaker was concerned with demonstrating how to create a collective belief in the organization so that everyone can make a difference, through a causal link between culture, leadership and performance. Effectively, the speaker made it impossible for the audience not to believe the presentation and, therefore, not to fully endorse the programme as outlined. The speaker stated that there are two types of organizational culture: defensive and constructive. Constructive cultures are typified by growth: "I can't sing, but I can sing better". The assertion was, therefore, that if one is not part of a constructive culture and does not support the outlined prescriptive programme, then one must inhabit the defensive culture and therefore one represents a problem! It was a very skilful presentation, endorsing the ICC's methods and rationale and ultimately asking each delegate to decide which culture they identified with.

During the course of the day, opinion was canvassed concerning the "From Good to Great" seminar; almost exclusively, delegates were very supportive. Only one very senior officer had the courage to express his own very critical interpretation. This officer is well known to the researcher, as we have served together on boards throughout the city, and perhaps the familiarity between us allowed him to voice his opinions. However, it would also have been somewhat surprising not to have heard some form of well-reasoned critique of the initiative.

Given the almost universal acceptance of the seminar, the concluding remarks were surprising. According to the agenda, the conclusion was to be made by the chief executive, who duly addressed the delegates. First, he apologized for not being present for the whole of the day, as "other" duties had taken him away. Following a brief period of thanking the main speakers and summarizing the presentations of the senior colleagues, he began to talk more openly about the challenges the organization faced. Rather than fully endorsing the ICC and their programme, he rather remarkably distanced himself from the event by raising questions about to approach. From the audience, this submission was greeted with lots of outward shows of agreement. It seems that delegates needed permission to allow themselves a more challenging disposition and to be more openly critical of the ICC and the day in general, and the chief executive's remarks permitted this. This position became more openly evident in observations and interviews conducted in the following days.

Ambiguity

This illustration will be broadly interpreted with reference to the literature discussed in Chapter 2. Interpretations are made concerning the meaning of leadership to the ABC, the perceived value of following, and the problem of fixing identities in a leadership relationship. The discussion concludes by asserting that, due to the fluidity in identity, ambiguity is a significant dynamic in the leader–follower relationship.

As reported in the previous section, the ABC had been engaged in a comprehensive leadership development programme for some time. During the fieldwork, this development programme culminated in the "From Good to Great" seminar, designed to promote leadership awareness and skills. This was to involve the adoption and distribution of the methodologies of an international consulting company referred to within this study as the ICC. It should be made clear from the outset that the development of exemplary leaders and leadership processes within the ABC was believed to be vital to the attainment of the ABC's business plans and had therefore been formally expressed in all the corporate planning literature.

What is immediately striking about the ABC's attitude to leadership is the initial, almost universal, acceptance of leadership as a vital commodity to be developed within the ABC community. Interviews with senior-ranking officers, as outlined above, demonstrate that the ABC had formed the opinion that there was a shortage of leadership within the organization. It felt under pressure to demonstrate leadership internally and externally in order to promote the ABC more effectively among city stakeholders, throughout the region and across local and national government sectors. This is a view that was shared by the UK government concerning leadership in the public sector more generally and is very heavily promoted in its own publications (Cabinet Office, 2000b).

From this point of conjunction, questions concerning the understanding of leadership and the kind of leadership to be developed provoked answers that are less sure and definite. If leadership is an organizational component, what kind of leadership is being referred to? Reference to the government's own publication does not help, as the document provides a rather comprehensive literature review that makes clear the inadequacies in understanding referred to in this book and confirmed by numerous contributors from within the field (Bryman, 1996; House and Aditya, 1997; Jackson and Parry, 2008; Rost, 1993; Yukl, 2002).

Western (2008) asserts that functional models of leadership have become the dominant normative models of leadership theory, and this is replicated within the ABC. During interviews with prominent members of the ABC management team, statements were collected regarding leadership and what it meant to the ABC population. As quoted above, "it should be about setting clear objectives and helping people deliver the objectives but not managing the process ...

leadership is setting the broad objective and helping people to get there". This statement, combined with the "visionary" perspective of the ABC strategic literature (ABC, 2008), leads to the conclusion that the attainment of "One Council" represents a corporate vision, requiring, therefore, leadership as outlined in neo-charismatic leadership theories (Beyer, 1999; House and Aditya, 1997), typified by Full Range Leadership Theory (Bass, 1999; Bass and Avolio, 1994a) and the public sector transformational leadership Model (Alimo-Metcalfe and Alban-Metcalfe, 2004). While the ICC did not specifically outline its model of leadership or the causal and practical links between leadership, culture and performance, much of the supporting presentations provided by the directors of the ABC during the "From Good to Great" seminar were visionary in content: "we must build brilliance; release the magic and switch on to the potential". Such statements allow for the reasonable conclusion that this attempt to raise the motivation of the follower population alludes very strongly to a neo-charismatic, normative model of leadership.

Alternative opinions regarding leadership were canvassed, and while other models were loosely touched upon, it is the contention here that the neo-charismatic model was highly dominant, at least at the outset of the fieldwork. From this observed conclusion, attention needs to be given to the reasons behind the dominance of the model. The authors consider that this is due to four contributing factors.

The first factor concerns the nature of local government and the reforms imposed upon it by central government. As outlined in Chapter 2, it is the contention of this study that normative models of leadership are at their core a product of a functionalist paradigm (Rost, 1993; Western, 2008). The New Public Management defined earlier as being essentially managerialism and economic rationalism is underpinned by the same research traditions as normative models of leadership (Parker and Guthrie, 1993). The promotion of these models in conjunction with a progressive move toward greater managerialism not only supports the models, it also sustains managerialism (Bryman, 1996).

The second contributing factor is the complexity of the task to be undertaken by the ABC, involving complex societal issues that have no immediate or easily understood resolution. Effective leadership is seen as making a major contribution toward solving these "wicked problems" (Grint, 2005b). Problems of this type tend to be ambiguous, both in the root cause and nature of the problem and, therefore, also in the suitability of a workable solution. At times of great uncertainty, normative models theorize that a leader will emerge in order to supply solutions to "wicked problems" (Bass, 1985). Informed by the theoretical models, the emerging leader has charismatic status and is likely to be perceived, therefore, as being "heroic" by followers. It is also inferred that as the leader raises the performance of the followers, the influence of transformational leadership will be shared throughout the organization (Burns, 1978). It is the contention here that the concept of emergence and sharing heroism is strongly appealing, an attraction made more potent by the ambiguous nature of the work environment.

The third contributing factor relates to an expectation of what effective leadership should look like. Rost (1993), among others, has provided a persuasive argument which states that normative forms of leadership have gained inflated levels of acceptance. The models produced from a functional perspective have a tendency to reduce the complexity of the phenomenon under scrutiny and, therefore, become more readily assimilated by a wider practising population. This represents a commodification of leadership supported, in turn, by those with a vested interest in the financial value of leadership (Mintzberg, 2004).

This phenomenon is further aggravated by reproducing and reinforcing "leader categories" and, therefore, leads to an institutionalization of normative leadership theories (Alvesson and Deetz, 2006b). If leadership, be it heroic or otherwise, receives enough attention, it gains importance in social situations. In the case of the ABC, deficiencies of public sector service provision are well reported (Toynbee, 2009), and effective leadership is seen to be the solution. Media and business stakeholders within the city have made very public depositions for more leadership from the city as an important factor in competing with cities perceived as being more successful locally. The leaders of the comparator cities are judged to be more charismatic and therefore "leaderful" than those of the ABC. Simply put, expectations of leadership as voiced by these agencies force the ABC into aspiring to adopt normative models.

The final contributing factor is possibly the most significant and the most clearly evident. Central government as a purchaser of "leadership" promotes normative neo-charismatic theories of leadership as they are most immediate and theoretically replicable. It is asserted that this, along with the factors outlined above, closes off the possibility of any alternative to a prescriptive and widely held view of leadership.

As normative leadership understanding is evident within the ABC, the view of following does not hold the same currency. If there are leaders there must be followers (Kellerman, 2008). If this is the case then they would appear to be absent from the ABC, as shown by repeating the remarks quoted above:

> I may lead my team, but I don't follow.

> I don't follow leaders; I have to find the tactic to get what I think is right ... I'm not following leaders anymore.

> I wouldn't consider myself a follower ... that doesn't mean I'm a natural leader either ... I would accept that I'm a supporter, if I'm on board then I am a great supporter.

The appreciation and awareness of normative leadership models held significant currency among leaders at the ABC. This was not reflected among followers, where the concept of following suffered almost universal rejection. This questions the viability of leadership practice and the possibility of a wider acceptance of the model, if one constituent part of the leader–follower relationship declines to accepts its leadership responsibilities. Burns (1978), among other neo-charismatic scholars, maintains that the process of leadership is a joint process, shared through all levels of the organization. For normative models of leadership to be endorsed and utilized within the organization, followers must acquiesce to the potency of such models and practices. The fact that this acquiescence is not evident within the ABC is a compelling indication that overt evidence of such leadership practice is rare.

As followers disassociate themselves from following, they demonstrate that they are not a compliant population. Leaders and followers have expressed a view concerning leadership enforced by expectation and tradition. In practice, however, followers appear to have rejected the notion of following, and have thereby rejected their involvement in the leader–follower relationship as expressed in normative terms. If what is occurring between leaders and followers within the ABC is a complex form of leadership, this study confirms the view of Alvesson and Sveningsson (2003b) that the construct in its functional normative guise is open to serious question.

One further interpretation of the empirical material presented in the previous section needs to be addressed. Statements collected suggest that leaders, when expressing their views on leadership, are also acting in accordance with expectation, and that they may regard such expected views merely as hopeful rhetoric; this is illustrated by the remarks already quoted above:

> So we bring in consultants to tell us what leadership is … I don't need to be sold this stuff.

> It's a fad, isn't it … part of it says that it's a fad, what we need round here is a bit of common sense, get on with things and stop navel-gazing.… Increasingly I see things and I think it's just bollocks … people are hiding behind jargon, concepts, potted theory.

> We're all about leadership now, it's the new buzzword, it's not changed what I do on a day-to-day basis; I've been re-badged.

The rhetorical nature of the commitments expressed about leadership, and "From Good to Great" in particular, is of interest and promotes a complex view of the leader–follower relationship. In earlier localized interventions, the ICC had gained considerable support from managers within the ABC. Commitment to the initiative was almost universally expressed at the "From Good to Great" seminar. Over time, nevertheless, overt support for the seminar and for the primacy of leadership development withered, and statements such as those presented above and throughout this study became more and more commonplace. It is asserted here that the use of the consulting company has an ambiguous effect on the members of the ABC. Zanzi and O'Neill (2001), in a study concerning the positive and negative aspect of politics at work, concluded that the use of expert outside help could be perceived in two ways. The expression of positive or negative opinion regarding the use of consultants is unlikely to be explicitly for or against; in all probability people will feel both positive and negative toward the consultants, dependent on the situation and other contributing factors the individual is exposed to at the time of expressing their opinion. Over time, as expectations are not met, the likelihood is that opinion will become more negative and that people will start to react accordingly by providing less support or deliberately impeding progress.

Interpretations of the data suggest that leadership is held in esteem and that the position of leader is seen as desirable. The position of follower has no such appeal. It is the contention here that the fixing of identities as leader and follower, as within a normative framework, is difficult and potentially dangerous. On the one hand, actors have been seduced by the romanticism of leadership as defined by the organization's rhetoric, and on the other they are reluctant to be seen as followers, choosing instead to adopt a pejorative view of the function, a perception made worse by the confusion related to the practice of leadership and the ambivalence shown to the ICC and their interventions.

A post-structuralist view of following suggests that followers may possess many identities (Collinson, 2006), and the possibility that one of these may be "leader" must be given credence. While leader-centric viewpoints devalue the role of follower, all leaders have to play that role more often than they may be aware. This is evident within the ABC, as designated formal leaders, such as the strategic directors, also significantly follow an elected membership as well as superordinate officers and peers. Furthermore, a public sector ethos underpinning a notion of consensus (Pratchett and Wingfield, 1996) demands that those leaders – elected or organizationally constituted – follow. The role any agent plays is highly complex, ambiguous and therefore open to interpretation.

In conclusion, it has been suggested here that the models of leadership voiced by individuals within the ABC do not bear up under scrutiny, but that they are understandable given the high levels of societal pressure to conform to expected leadership behaviours. The influence relationship between leaders and followers is not, however, actually constituted along normative lines. The organization possesses high degrees of ambiguity in structure and in task definition. This ambiguity pervades the organization by its very nature and thus impacts upon the fixing of the roles of leader and follower. It is asserted here that these roles are highly fluid and that individuals in the act of leading do so from a rehearsed platform of following, a platform that has been enforced through practice, consensus, accountability and structural pressures. When the identification of who are leaders and who are followers becomes more fluid, as within the ABC, it is concluded that a principal dynamic of the leader–follower relationship is ambiguity.

6 The limitations to leadership and the dynamic of the environment

> We're always going on about bureaucracy, the policies and procedures are getting in the way. Are they helpful or hindering? We know why they are there, because of public money and accountability.
>
> Chief Officer Maun, City Development

The audit and regulatory framework

This next illustration is particularly focused on the ABC's regulatory framework. The illustration is concerned with a preliminary meeting set up to establish the scope of assessment of a future Corporate Assessment (CA) and Joint Area Review (JAR) of the effectiveness of the ABC's corporate centre and Children's Services Directorate.

Interpretation of this illustration suggests that the bureaucratic apparatus, both internal and external, is so powerful a dynamic, it can be seen as being the leader in a relationship with the ABC. It is asserted in this study that leadership cannot be appreciated devoid of the context within which it is located, and the contextual environment is identified as a significant dynamic of the leader–follower relationship.

Background

Within the ABC, and the public sector generally, there is a strong tradition of accountability as part of a public sector ethos. The reforms of central Labour government, culminating in the commissioning and publication of the *Modernising Government* policy (Cabinet Office, 1999), specifically attempted to increase the performance of the public sector. In doing so it adopted a functionally managerialist perspective, imposing a series of wide-ranging performance measures for government administrators, both central and local. Furthermore, the government's spending watchdog, the National Audit Office, while not directly responsible for the auditing of local government finances, became responsible for auditing the Department for Communities and Local Government and other ministerial departments that have delegated service provision to Local Authorities. This reinforced the concept of public financial accountability and the imperative of searching for "best value" within the public sector and the local government community.

In responding to the requirements of public accountability which were made more acute by legislative changes such as the Freedom of Information Act (Cabinet Office, 2000b), the ABC employs a rigorous internal programme of balances, checks and scrutiny. This comprises Scrutiny Committees, chaired by elected members, which oversee the activities of the council. Not surprisingly, in order to serve the demands of such committees the ABC has developed an extensive bureaucracy, comprising external audits related to financial accountability, assessments of performance against stated objectives, and assurances related to public accountability.

The assessments discussed here were conducted by government agencies – the Audit Commission and OFSTED (the Office for Standards in Education, Children's Services and Skills). In Chapter 3 the regulatory and auditing framework as experienced by the ABC was outlined; the complex reporting framework agreed by the ABC is presented in Figure 6.1. The discussion below refers back to this framework and provides detail regarding the auditing framework imposed on the authority.

Central government regularly audits the effectiveness of local authority service delivery and inspects the corporate effectiveness of the internal processes, procedures, legislative compliance and financial management systems. During the fieldwork undertaken for this study, the ABC was assessed as part of the Audit Commission's Corporate Assessment (CA) for corporate effectiveness and OFSTED's Joint Area Review (JAR) for service delivery in Children's Services. The

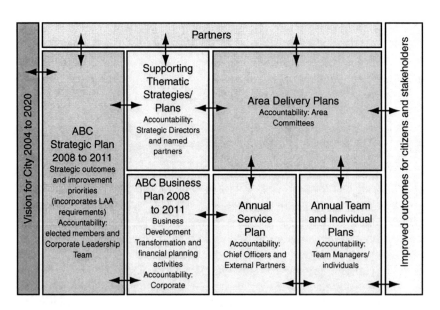

Figure 6.1 The ABC planning framework (ABC, 2008 p. 8).

CA is primarily related to issues of financial management, compliance and effectives of policy and process. Both the CA and the JAR assessors are independent government auditors whose assessments could have significant impacts upon the authority being examined. A failing authority may have special measures taken against it, which could include the insertion of Whitehall administrators appointed to manage the affairs of the authority. In practice this never happens, but the senior management team and politicians may be called to stand before a Public Accounts Committee hearing or to account for shortfalls before Parliament.

From conversations with many of the members of the corporate leadership team (CLT) and with members of the corporate centre, it became apparent that the objective of attaining a four-star appraisal as part of the CA process was at the forefront of the ABC's ambitions. This had become a particular issue for two reasons. First, in the previous years, the Comprehensive Performance Assessment, an external assessment by government auditors on the effectiveness of overall council service provision, had delivered a four-star assessment. In order for the ABC to maintain this status, the CA needed to match the government's Comprehensive Performance Assessment. Second, from a national perspective, the four-star award gained considerable prestige for the city, the region, the organization and in particular the members of the senior leadership. It was something of a surprise, therefore, that the attainment of the four-star award did not rate with such significance with the elected membership, who approached the assessment as a process likely to provide them with opportunities to identify shortfalls in performance.

Leader voices

A factor that was commented upon frequently from both leader and follower perspectives was the bureaucracy of the organization. It is maintained that central government and the strictures related to "public accountability", as the examples given above demonstrate, contribute significantly to the seemingly all-encompassing situation within the ABC. In addition, some of the comments made by senior-ranking officers have suggested other possible antecedents for the make-up of the administrative life of the council.

> This is a very conservative council, cautious, risk averse. It's not ... if I had a pound for every time someone said to me we do it this way because four years ago it went badly and we now have this process in place, it seems like overkill ... I've got numerous examples.
>
> (Chief Officer Leen, City Development)

> The council historically had a culture where members called officers to account overspending and the rest ... bullying officers and that mentality still underpins that process ... some of the processes that are in place are a reaction to the gross overspending, so that when you're at scrutiny board the members have disappeared.
>
> (Chief Officer Leen, City Development)

This last statement is particularly telling, as it refers to the belief that while elected members are formally responsible for adherence to budgets and, in particular, those budgets associated with capital projects, overspends are answered for by officers in isolation from their elected counterparts. This supports the view that while the "bullying" of overspending officers may be less than overt, it is still the officers that formally assume responsibility for issues related to financial accountability.

It would appear that the perceived rigorous nature of scrutiny and checking underpinned by a seemingly pervasive bureaucracy produces an internal dichotomy. On the one hand the bureaucratic framework is understood and appreciated as vital:

> There are frameworks on how you should best do things such as options appraisals. There's nothing worse than a bad report.... There's an acceptance among most of the officer corps that we want good quality reports.
>
> (Chief Officer Poulter, City Development)

Nevertheless, on the other hand, it is acknowledged that in practice the policies and procedure of doing business within the ABC can be appreciated as being less than helpful.

> We're always going on about bureaucracy; the policies and procedures are getting in the way. Are they helpful or hindering? We know why they are there, because of public money and accountability.
>
> (Chief Officer Maun, City Development)

This, in turn, leads to an element of frustration,

> Privileged and yet exasperation with the politics and trying to make sure that the processes don't become the most important thing, that actually what we achieve is that the processes help ... as a big bureaucratic organization we are really good at processes, we can do them to death!
>
> (Director Trent, City Development)

Follower voices

Many of the statements taken from a leader perspective allude to an element of frustration caused by the constraints that the bureaucratic framework imposes upon the workplace. However, the frustrations expressed are concerned primarily with the restrictions of senior managers and their relationships with elected members and the framework itself. Additional statements, however, from the same population of managers show that frustrations may also be derived from less senior managers' interpretation of the bureaucratic framework.

> Here I get a five-page report to spend 7,900 pounds, one, two, three, four, five, six, seven ... eight [counting] pages ... that has come to me to make a

decision, that is an amazing waste of time. How much has that cost – probably upwards of 1,000 to make a decision to spend 7,900 quid – utter nonsense ... and that's the downside and that replicates all over and this goes on to an executive member and it is an utter nonsense of decision making, the process is slow and over-bureaucratic.

(Chief Officer Erewash, City Development)

– He had to sign for a 200-quid shed.
– It was a 500-pound shed actually – two-and-a-half pages for a 500-pound shed!

(Chief Officer Erewash, City Development)

Additional statements from those in the middle of the management hierarchy show that frustrations become compounded:

But the systems we have to work in are absolutely Byzantine.... How do you get over those?

(Head of Service, Children's Services)

The example of delegated sign-off being restricted to the point that a £500 purchase is not possible without authorization suggests that the managers who have substantial budget authority feel restricted in committing those budgets; either due to formal or informal reasons, most likely a combination of both. The senior management body seemingly feels more equipped to negotiate the bureaucratic framework as it exists.

Rules, regulations, policies, procedures, practices and a whole host of people doing things on daily basis ... in a sense the ability of the successful people to get up and run the place is those that can find their way around the policies, procedures and practices. If you understand them, you can find your way through them rather than round them; round them implies that you're avoiding them. How do you use those policies to best advantage ... and knowing when you can break them and when you can't?

(Chief Officer Idle, City Development)

... and then I said who is the report to and I was told that I had to write it to myself, I said I'm not going to do it, it's a complete nonsense ... it doesn't get me in to trouble because of the role I'm in.

(Assistant chief executive, Chief Executive's Unit)

However, the final statement concerning the bureaucratic framework is probably most telling:

Procedures can be changed but not over any form of longevity.

(Assistant chief executive, Chief Executive's Unit)

The illustration

The committee room for the preliminary meeting regarding the Corporate Assessment and the Joint Area Review was a large room with space for more than 50 delegates situated around large wooden benches, organized as a room-sized rectangle with a void in the middle. The wood-panelled and old-fashioned room was set out with a meeting PA system of personal microphones and speakers. The members of the meeting spread out around the room, even though the total number attending was only 15. Each member insisted on utilizing the room PA, although it was not necessary. This added a surreal quality to the meeting, as instructions for using the PA were continually reiterated, and failed attempts to use the system occurred frequently, leading to extensive repetition, extending the meeting and producing a rather bizarre and comic scenario.

At the end of the room, where the chair of a council committee meeting would sit, were positioned the chief executive and the deputy chief executive. To their right, but at the far end of the wooden rectangle, sat the assessors. It was immediately apparent how difficult it was to conduct an effective meeting, and signs of frustration started to creep into the mannerisms of some of the attendees. At no point did anyone suggestion a reordering of the room to make the meeting more conducive to progress. It seemed that people preferred to soldier on rather than make an impolite or unwarranted suggestion. The chief executive had placed himself in the position of formal authority at the top of the table, but appeared to recognize that he wasn't officiating at the meeting and looked uncomfortable. The assessors, on the other hand, felt it their position to defer to the chair and the chief executive and did not overplay the hand dealt to them by the fact that they were the assessors empowered by legislation, the Audit Commission and OFSTED. The result was that the meeting was stilted, drawn out, repetitive, formal and deferential.

The meeting was opened by the chief executive, who first explained that the meeting was due to be chaired by Councillors Wharfe and Nidd (the joint leaders of the ABC), but they had sent their apologies as they had been detained by some emergency business and were in a "crisis meeting". The use of the word "crisis" was very casual, giving the impression that the organization itself was under no particular threat and that the crisis could be seen as a code to assert that this was political or personal.[1] Nobody gave much attention to the announcement that the two leaders were engaged in a crisis meeting. Next, the chief executive gave a five-minute opening statement about the importance and value of the assessment and the ABC's aspirations for the assessment. As was typical of the CE, the statement was full of light humour and was self-deprecating: "Events are all under control ... they are under control.... Yes? ... I wish!" After which he formally handed over to the assessment teams.

There were two distinct groups of assessors, one from the Audit Commission (John) and one from OFSTED (Wendy). John began by introducing himself as the "lead" and introduced the remainder of the team and the deputy leader. The areas of assessment closely followed central government guidance and priorities.

While the core of the presentation was easily followed, it was heavily laden with very specific jargon and acronyms, making the detail of the presentation unintelligible to anyone from outside of this particular work sector. The tone of the presentation and therefore, one assumed, of the audit to follow was one of transparency and of providing assistance. Language and phrases such as "areas of strength and areas for focus", "deal with successes, strengths, challenges and priorities ... areas we would like to see more focus" were comforting and deliberately conciliatory. Finally, John outlined a timetable for the assessment before handing over to Wendy. The second presentation followed the presentation from John almost identically, being sector-specific but even more laden with jargon and acronyms. The JAR assessment would focus on the five shared priority areas and on "four areas of high delivery across the authority." The sense of duplication and repetition was palpable; both groups of assessors mentioned issues of "diversity as a cross-cutting initiative", leaving one feeling as though the auditors were checking the assessors and, consequently, wondering where the cycle of continuous checking would end. Obvious displays of anxiety from the officers present were noted: fidgeting, shuffling of papers; almost as if the assessors were referring to areas in which those officers present were aware of specific "areas for focus".

The only real contribution made by the officers present was related to issues of timetabling for the assessment related to the Youth Offending Service. It was declared by all that a robust discussion had taken place, at the end of which the officers had been granted some concessions in the itinerary. Despite this, nobody looked any more comfortable than before the concessions were made. At this stage the group had been joined by Councillor Nidd, who was given a summing up from the CE regarding assurances of cooperation interspersed with the usual element of humour: "I'd like to tell you we're raring to go ... But!" He made what were intended to be closing remarks that lent heavily on rhetoric and management cliché – "period of change", "move fast enough", "adopt flexible postures ... to maximize opportunities" and a frequently-heard ABC phrase applied to external consultants and/or partners, "critical friends". Notwithstanding Councillor Nidd's concluding remarks, the chief executive felt obliged, effectively, to conclude before breaking up the meeting so that the assessors could continue separate meetings with their respective constituent groups.

The assessment team led by Wendy stayed in the large committee room, while John's team left with the responsible officers of the corporate centre, leaving behind the officers with responsibility for children's services behind. As the changeover commenced, more officers joined the meeting, making the numbers present similar to before. Wendy moved from the bottom right-hand corner of the room to the top table and took the place vacated by the chief executive. Again, introductions were made and the meeting took a very similar path to the earlier one. The researcher made three other observations. First, the meeting dealt with more level of detail, as the assessors' brief is to assess the service; with more detail came more jargon and a bewildering collection of acronyms. APA process, LAC, LDD, CAMS, LLN, YOS[2] are examples of the acronyms noted. Later it was learnt that many of the acronyms refer to areas of service related to potentially difficult clients. LDD for instance is Learning Difficulties and Disability; the acronym has a strange way of depersonalizing the individuals being discussed.

The second observation concerned the fact that the CA process and JAR assessment were to run concurrently and, in addition, along with the consulting group, KPMG was contracted to audit the CA, JAR and CAP assessments. Furthermore, the Youth Offending Service was also to be scrutinized by a different team of regulators and then again under the JAR assessment. In this apparent duplication, one particular assessor, Mike, would conduct both assessments; this was referred to as "synergy".

The third observation relates to the assurances given by the assessing team that the assessment would be conducted in a fair, supportive and transparent way. When the assessor was reading out a list of areas to be covered, the officers asked him to slow down. He replied, "I'll give you this", referring to the list he was reading from. "The purpose of the JAR is … not to add to the bureaucracy … collaborative and open … to be very straightforward with you". The impression was that the assessor team were there as enablers and that the whole process was to be as painless as possible; the consensual nature of the discussions and agreements related to timetable and further communication gave the impression that officers had some control over the process.

The environment

In the previous chapter, evidence was presented and interpretations made to conclude that the roles of leader and follower are ambiguous concepts and that this ambiguity comprises a principal dynamic of the leader–follower relationship. In this section, the arguments of the previous chapter and the evidence provided in the previous section is built upon to explore issues related to the construct of leadership itself and who or what provides the predominant leading influence.

It was concluded that the environment within which the actors are obliged to operate is highly pervasive and, as a consequence, members of the organization had become skilled manipulators of self and information. The interpretations made in this section are discussed, and the conclusion reached that context and environment constrict leadership and, therefore, comprise important dynamics in the leader–follower relationship.

It has been suggested that leadership is an essentially contested concept and can be expressed as four possibilities (Grint, 2005b). The first concerns "who" are leaders, the second "what" constitutes a leader, the third "where", and the final possibility, "how" are things done that make leaders. This section differentiates itself from Grint's position in that the author defines the "what" as being a consequence of results, but maintains the leader position as held by a human acting in an influence relationship with other individuals. The authors suggest that dynamics outside of the human leader–follower relationship heavily influence the timbre of the relationship and that the "what" of leadership may not comprise human agency. This in turn influences how other parts of the leadership phenomenon are interpreted.

Leadership expressed as a dynamic influence process is usually seen as a social influence process between leaders and followers who are conscious human elements of the overall leader–follower relationship. From a leader-centric, normative position, leaders influence followers. From a follower-centric position, followers are neither homogeneous nor compliant, but may moderate, substitute and construct the leader–follower relationship (Jackson and Parry, 2008). An alternative interpretation from a more openly critical viewpoint suggests that individuals in an organizational setting respond to the organizational context, in all its definitional possibilities, in order to play out a relationship moderated by the parameters of the environmental context within which the actors find themselves located.

From a normative perspective, the models derived from its functionalist orthodoxy see leadership as a product of leader agency. From a neo-charismatic platform, leaders influence followers' consciousness by an appeal to a higher ideal or vision, thus transforming followers and the organization (Bass, 1985; Burns, 1978; Parry and Bryman, 2006). Bryman (1996) has stated that this view of leadership is too closely fixed to an overtly rational perspective of organizational behaviour and that earlier theoretical antecedents to the neo-charismatic school of leadership have been excluded prematurely. For example, the contingency models of Fiedler (Fiedler, 1967) and the Ohio School of Leadership were ultimately rejected by New Leadership theorists for lacking explanatory power and for being too complex to apply to organizational life. It is the contention here that this study corroborates the complexity of organizational life and that leadership is contingent on the organizational environment; the outstanding point of difference is extent.

It was remarked upon in the previous section that the ABC operates within a legally constrained regulatory framework impacted upon by successive legislation and government reforms, as exemplified by the New Public Management (NPM; see Chapter 3.) The clarification or prescription of task is assumed to enhance performance, but is also associated with a commensurate requirement for monitoring performance against stated objectives (Lee *et al.*, 2009). Subsequently, the traditions of local authorities have come under significant pressures as consensual public sector ethos has become exposed to managerialist tendencies drawn from the private sector (Greenaway, 1995). The ABC has developed an extensive bureaucracy and system of internal scrutiny because of reform, legislation and the requirements of public accountability, a bureaucracy that has the capacity at times to exasperate the members of the ABC, whether they be leaders or followers: "But the systems we have to work in are absolutely Byzantine.... How do you get over those?" The system is acknowledged as being highly resistant to change and reform: "Procedures can be changed but not over any form of longevity".

The central government and its associated apparatus could be seen as playing the role of "leader" in a relationship with the "following" ABC. Its engagement with the ABC, however, must be seen in exclusively transactional terms, as budgetary control remains central government's primary tactic (Lee *et al.*, 2009). While transactional tactics are noted as being important within the leader–follower relationship (Bass, 1999; Bass and Avolio, 1994b), questions must be raised as to the efficacy of relying on a solitary tactic. In the absence of any discernible evidence of transformational behaviours, then it should be concluded that in this context transactionalism does not comprise leadership at all, but represents a controlling management – evidence of a conflation of concepts that is a common occurrence in attempts to theorize leadership practice (Rost, 1993).

In studies on public sector leadership, the impact of central government on the leadership of the public body has been recorded. Studies by Blackler (2006) and Van Wart (2003) demonstrate that bureaucratic discretion for leaders in public sector organizations is diminished, leading to instances where chief executives of public bodies can be seen to be mere conduits for centralized policy. It is maintained here that this diminishment of senior managers of public bodies constricts the leadership capacity of organizations and individuals alike. This is of no surprise considered in the light of Weberian analysis that control underpinned by a bureaucratic apparatus gives rise to specific modes of social domination (Morgan, 1997).

The evidence collected here shows that the ABC had to maintain and be part of a highly sophisticated system of investigation regarding its compliance with objectives, processes and the spending of public money. The system has become so pervasive that the organization demonstrates high levels of frustration regarding the framework within which it operates but with which it generally complies. Within this arrangement, central government, with its transactional treatises, comprises the principal managing and leadership role, leaving little scope for managers or elected members to express their own sense of ideas beyond further compliance to a notion of public service being systematically eroded by an ever-encroaching managerialist paradigm.

Despite the rigidity of the bureaucratic apparatus, the possibility of changing the system is rarely seriously entertained. This suggests that in some way the organization has become complicit in its own levels of scrutiny. Evidence collected indicates that while central government imposes a rigid framework of prescriptive tasks, procedural requirements and examination, the ABC has embarked upon a process of bureaucratic embellishment as a product of its own history. Collinson (1999) has suggested that the consensual growth of routinized surveillance and the associated audit culture produces followers who have become skilled exploiters of self and manipulation. In a later study, Collinson (2006) demonstrates that such systems comprising auditing, Human Resource initiatives and technology advances impact on the identity of followers and produce complex forms of anxiety. The relationship between anxieties and manipulation has not been shown, but this study concludes that this possibility exhibits, as some members of the ABC have demonstrated, clear skill in manipulating systems and processes to attain goals, and others exhibit anxiety through a slavish adherence to policy and procedure. It is highly improbable that an individual member of the ABC would be entrenched in such binary opposites as complying and manipulating.

It has been demonstrated that a failure in the public sector can be career-ending; an example is the case of Sharon Shoesmith, Director of Children's Services of Haringey Council, who was summarily dismissed by the Children's Minister after a failing within her own department. Examples of this kind reinforce the organizational status quo and the systems of investigation, which the ABC are not only complicit in but have also served to embellish. The organization is forced to accept the leadership position of central government and, subsequently, adopts a follower posture with the commensurate maelstrom of anxieties, identities and manipulations. It is for these two reasons that the leadership capacity of the organization is thus constrained. In considering the dynamic of the leader–follower relationship within the organization, an obvious conclusion to make is that leaders and followers are influenced by the leadership of the central government and thus are required to meet the expectation of that relationship. The principal dynamic here, therefore, is the environment within which leaders and followers are located. As a fundamental consequence, whatever occurs within the leader–follower relationship is not leadership, at least as it is theorized in normative terms, as the associated bureaucratic apparatus renders this virtually impossible.

7 The negotiation of leadership and the dynamic of resource acquisition

> ... and we'd have the discussion and say "yeah" and nothing would happen, and then six months later we'd have the same discussion.
>
> Assistant chief executive, Chief Executive's Unit

The corporate leadership team

This illustration is focused on part of an observed meeting of the corporate leadership team (CLT). The meeting concerned plans for a strategy on equality, diversity and community cohesion. The illustration deals with issues related to management style and governance on the one hand and, more specifically, with the management of potentially difficult situations.

The interpretations made in the subsequent section deal with concerns related to leadership as good management. The interpretations suggest, however, that there are additional considerations to be made by leaders in managing potential situations of conflict. The section concludes by establishing leadership, as practiced, as an almost exclusively transactional relationship within which leaders use access to resources as their primary contingent reward. It is asserted that the acquisition and utilization of resources is a primary dynamic in leader–follower relations.

Background

The CLT meeting is the principal executive meeting of the officers of the ABC. It is comprised of the most senior officers of the council including the chief executive and the four strategic directors from the principal service functions (City Development, Children's Services, Housing and Neighbourhoods, and Adult Social Services). Included also are senior officers of the associated arm's-length organizations (Education, Health) and additional officers from the chief executive's Department, including Deputy and assistant chief executives, Council Legal Services and officers from the central services department (Finance and HR). Its total membership is 11 when all are present. In practice, the formal membership rarely meets in its entirety, as others drawn from within their own departments may frequently represent one of the members. Elected members are not represented on this committee.

In recent months, the committee had chosen to rename itself, changing its title from Corporate Management Team to Corporate Leadership Team. The change in name was seen as an integral part of an organizational restructuring under-taken during the previous 12 months. The rationale behind the restructuring was the belief that the organization had become too focused on operational detail and therefore was deficient in its concerns for the wider strategic issues affecting the ABC. Central to the restructuring was an associated shift in emphasis and job role for the newly created directorates. Directors were now required to be more strategically focused, and the new Labour policy of following a "third way" between markets and hierarchies, referred to as "strategic commissioning", would be the principal modus operandi, alongside delegating operational responsibility to the relevant chief officer. It was felt that the new director appointments should be engaged in a strategic leadership role. Previously the directorates had been made up of a number of service-specific departments administered by a responsible director. These had now been absorbed into the new directorate structure, and traditional service functions such as Leisure and Sport had ceased to exist.

The restructuring was provoked by the implementation of legislation from central government, requiring local authorities to create a service department that dealt specifically with the wide range of activities and services related to young people – Children's Services. Consequently, some of the old service departments were now incorporated into the new Children's Service Directorate, leaving behind a reduced service function that no longer warranted director administration. In some cases, social services for example, the old department was split, with the functions that related to young people being moved to Children's Services and the remaining components either being incorporated into other departments or, as in the case of the ABC, forming their own administrative unit. The creation of the Children's Services department, as in the case of other authorities across the UK, led to widespread restructuring of the whole organization in order to fulfil the legislative requirement of a centrally created reform initiative.

As an internal demonstration of the commitment to the policy of strategic commissioning, and an elevation of leadership skills over administrative com-petence, the Corporate Management Team was renamed and became the Corpo-rate Leadership Team (CLT). Additionally, the authority had designed and implemented initiatives to spread leadership throughout the organization. The most recent had been described as

> Our leadership challenge, "From Good to Great".... This sets out the behav-iours and culture we are aspiring to create and covers both council and partner representatives recognizing the need to respond to the challenge of leadership across the city.
>
> (ABC, 2008 p. 11)

It was envisaged that the newly constituted CLT would demonstrate its own col-lective leadership skills and send out a significant signal throughout the rest of the authority concerning the change in emphasis in the style of management of the ABC.

> I was taking a number of presentations that basically said, "Do you realize that this is how we are viewed? Do you realize that the view within the city is that the city council lacks effective leadership?" ... We have an opportunity to effectively address this and we should take the opportunity to address it. It was hard work actually because for eight months we went forward two steps to go backward three steps. We had to change the mindset of those individuals on the CLT who were in a very different place and couldn't quite grasp the concept of what we were trying to take forward.
>
> (Assistant chief executive, Chief Executive's Unit)

In leading up to the re-configuration of the ABC its members had engaged in "away-day" awareness and team-building activities at which issues related to the production of the ABC strategic vision were discussed and high-level strategy finalized. As the quote above demonstrates, the most senior officers were committed to the changes designed for the ABC and were, outwardly at least, engaged and supportive.

Leader voices

The process of change within the ABC had clearly been provoked by the requirements of central government. Initiatives related to strategic commissioning and the development of Children's Services came as a response to a perceived lack of national focus, as evidenced by the Victoria Climbié affair. While pertinent, this must be appreciated as another in a long line of government-endorsed reform initiatives aimed at the public sector. Contrary to the pervasive view that the public sector does not embrace change, as shown by leader articles in the UK's national newspapers (Toynbee, 2009), the ABC more generally perceived change, reinforced by central government reform and intervention, as a constant imperative.

> One of the key agendas has been about change. In Children's Services it is the biggest and the deepest ... it's a cross cutting theme that may not be explicit but it *is* implicit ... but here it's largely driven by the Children's Act ... it's due to government agendas that have come in and start to challenge areas of work for people that have been internally focused to their service.
>
> (Chief Officer Penk, Children's Services)

> All about change – change initiatives.
>
> (Chief Officer Soar, City Development)

> The speed at which we have to be more flexible and to change quickly ... because of all the different types of proposals from government or changes

in government or initiatives they want to use to change local government, whether it's efficiency savings, introducing legislation which affects us like transport plan or whether it's giving us new responsibilities that will affect us.
(Chief Officer Welland, Housing and Neighbourhoods)

The ABC acknowledged that the motivations and provocations for change were principally external, but there would also, at least on the surface, appear to have been an acceptance of the need and potential value for more change, motivated by the desire to deliver enhanced levels of service throughout the city. As with many organizations that embark upon an explicit and deliberate programme of change, the journey within the ABC has not always been straightforward. This would appear to be equally applicable to the CLT which, despite its position as the most senior executive committee of the authority, has also experienced problems related to the change journey, despite being, ostensibly at least, committed to demonstrating change within the organization.

It got to the stage that the same things were coming up, we'd have a discussion and it would be, "Right, what's wrong with the organization?" and we'd be good at saying we don't have enough time, we spend too much time on detailed operation, that a lot of politicians don't take difficult decisions, that we don't spend a lot of time determining what our priorities for the city ought to be … and we'd have the discussion and say "yeah" and nothing would happen, and then six months later we'd have the same discussion.
(Assistant chief executive, Chief Executive's Unit)

While this should not be seen as unusual, as the dynamics and difficulties of organizational change is well-documented (Greenwood and Hinings, 2006), it might be that problems related to change were heightened due to a number of unanswered questions related to the process and outcomes of the journey.

The introduction of a Children's Services department has had wide-ranging impact upon the ABC, not only structurally but also in terms of the method of working. Aspects related to the conduct of work within the organization are covered in later sections of this chapter. At this stage, however, it is pertinent to deal with aspects of change related to structure, where the remodelling and redefining of the scope of the CLT is the initiation point.

The appointment of the director team was relatively current, having been finalized within the previous six months. Following the appointment of directors, further structural reviews were ongoing, leading to the appointment and reassignment of more chief officers. The scope of the organizational review and the potential implications of the structural changes became clear to the researcher only at a chance meeting with a senior officer in the Chief Executive Unit, who mentioned the "Council change programme … pretty much everybody will be re-interviewed for their jobs …" (Director, Finance and Central Services). This was later confirmed in a meeting with the Director of Strategic Human Resource Development. Similarly, it was also confirmed that the process of change that the organization was undertaking was due to become more formalized and wider ranging within a very short time. "We have got proposals now to better join those things up and so I am going to chair what has been called the Business Transformation Board" (Assistant chief executive, Chief Executive's Unit).

Follower voices

The illustration here is of the meeting regarding a strategy for equality, diversity and community cohesion strategy. In the interest of following a leadership story represented by this particular illustration, and the desire to give credence to multiple voices, the researcher decided to explore an agenda item related to "Diversity and Equality" by giving those that had been responsible for the presentation of the item at the meeting an opportunity to supply their interpretation of the events. In this situation, it is reasonable to perceive the officers who delivered the presentation of the paper to the CLT as followers to the CLT leaders. During the course of interviews, the following insights were captured.[1]

In the first instance, it became clear that the officer's job role was shrouded in ambiguity. Despite legal requirements and central government policies in support of equality and diversity, the internal audiences for a presentation in this area were not always as receptive as perhaps expected.

> Yes, so you tailor what you provide them with stuff that's relevant, that they can buy into it much easier … if I went along to the members, because the law requires us to do it, at least half of the council will switch off, maybe another quarter will be like, you are not telling us what to do, and then the other quarter may well be asleep. Who knows? Because it is not an issue for them, they don't deal with it. There are certain politicians I would not go to talk about sexual orientation but what I do is I talk about age. It is just finding that balance and linking the commonalities of one agenda with another agenda and knowing what they are signed up to.

The final part of this statement suggests that the task in hand requires significant levels of judgement on the part of the officer in order to maintain a train of progress, and that continued persuasive effort is required in order to deliver on targets established by central government. The CLT's capacity to accelerate the legitimacy of the equality and diversity agenda is compromised, as both officers had a rather ambivalent attitude toward the CLT, typified by the following comment.

> [My line manager] tells me afterwards that CLT respects people like me and you can challenge them. But actually I am not going to sit at CLT and challenge them, make enemies of the people I need to support me to do my job.

While it may be explicitly stated that CLT requires officers to contribute, present and maintain a position, the reality of doing so, at least in the eyes of the subordinate manager, is fraught with potential risk. Each paper that is brought to the CLT must be signed off by the sponsoring director of the directorate from which the document originated.

> Generally I know what happens when I go to CLT.… He [line manager] doesn't even say anything … [He] actually asked me afterwards, "was that OK, did I support you enough?" and that is the first time he has ever asked me that.

This gives rise to the potential that the sponsoring director may not feel compelled to support the paper and to challenge opposition to the initiative. This suggests that other factors are at play in the discussions of the agenda item under scrutiny.

> What I witnessed was political jockeying, a power struggle going on around the table … between the [Director of Housing and Neighbourhoods] and the [assistant chief executive]; historically, there has been some tension between [them].

The interviews turned attention to whether the officers felt that any progress had been made, as to an outsider, "progress" appeared to have been limited; nevertheless the officers were able to point to positives:

> I came out, and the word I used was "disappointed" because I suppose I didn't get the decision that I wanted, but I was happy we had a discussion on it … [we] came away and had a coffee and debrief and the outcome of it was, yes it was frustrating, but at least we had a positive discussion on it. We are starting to raise the profile more.

Additionally it was considered whether the remarks made by the chief executive had coloured the debate, and it became apparent that they had:

> I think as soon as [chief executive] set that scene ("I worry about this. Is it right? Is it the right direction for us to go?") I just knew which way the conversation was going. So that set the scene, didn't it, for what went rapidly downhill [laughing]?

Moreover, in the view of at least one of the officers, this was to be expected,

> I have been to CLT once where they have come to a decision. You know there was no decision made. There was sort of a decision.

Furthermore, when discussing the paper that was to be redrafted and brought to the CLT at a later date, as stipulated in the minutes of the meeting (see below), it became apparent that despite the debate and the minutes, ambiguity was still contained within the specified task. The officers expressed little confidence that the path or actions related to their initiative would be agreed regardless of completing the directed task, as the following dialogue illustrates:

> OFFICER: On the day it could go through, you're right, or it could be that same old protracted discussion. You know I can't predict it. I really can't predict it.
> RESEARCHER: Would you feel more confident about the outcome?
> OFFICER: No.
> RESEARCHER: Honestly?
> OFFICER: Yes, honestly!

The interview widened to accommodate the interviewees' experiences of reporting to the CLT:

> I don't think I should be going to CLT about changes on grammar or the way paragraphs are written. "Did you not notice that that paragraph doesn't make sense?" Fine. But actually, that's not what you are here to tell me, you are here to tell me that you think that is right and appropriate for the way you think the organization is going. Not actually that that paragraph doesn't make sense, can you re-write it.

And in summation of their experiences at the CLT meeting attended, one officer countered,

> There is about £2.5m of salary in that room – was that £2.5m worth of leadership?

The illustration

Reproduced below are the notes that relate to the agenda item extracted from the meeting minutes circulated to the members of the CLT.

Equality, Diversity and Cohesion – a way forward

Officer A outlined the purpose of the report, which was to return to CLT offering proposals for a single Equality, Diversity and Community Cohesion strategy. It was felt that these two areas are distinct but linked and the legal obligations and additional drivers such as the Equalities Review, single Equality Bill, single Commission for Equality and Human Rights, and the proposals from the Commission on Integration and Cohesion were outlined. It was noted that indicators on cohesion will be built into the LAA and will form a key focus for the corporate assessment. In view of the above, it was proposed that a single Equality, Diversity and Community Cohesion strategy is adopted by the council.

There was a discussion about the proposal and concerns were expressed that the challenges were different for each area and that a single strategy may prevent a strong focus remaining on key aspects of community cohesion. The "value-added" nature of a single strategy was also questioned.

It was felt that there needed to be a clearer articulation of the cohesion challenges and actions to address them, both within the new City Strategic Plan and LAA objectives, and at a local level. It was felt a single strategic approach may be useful although it would be possible to adopt different implementation approaches in different service areas, where necessary.

It was agreed that there should be further consideration of the proposal to adopt a single strategy but that both strategies should be reviewed and linked together. Included in the review should be the proposals from Director Housing and Neighbourhoods and assistant chief executive regarding respective leadership roles and responsibilities.

(CLT Meeting Minutes, 24 July 2007)

The CLT meeting took part in a room at the very top of the Civic Centre, with staggering views of the changing landscape of the city centre. A joke was made regarding the number of tower cranes that were in view and that the city had more cranes involved in active development than a perceived more successful "competitor" city. Numbers of cranes and the associated developments were all easily recalled and remarked upon as an indication of the wealth and success of the city, though this image of success didn't really tally with the environment that the meeting was to take place in. There should be little doubt that grandiose displays of success equated with the allocation of council funds and would not sit well with the ABC. During the researcher's time within the ABC, principles of public accountability, prudent use of public money and the search for "value for money" options were habitual topics of conversation. Nevertheless, the room was so ordinary, it could have been anywhere, and was completely out of kilter with the success, wealth and affluence of the city itself. There were no outward displays of identity, corporate colours, icons of the organizations, nothing of its people and even less of its plans and aspirations. It was noted that some of the Venetian blinds were not working; one had come loose from its mount. In one corner a computer appeared to have been disembowelled, as its guts spilled out over the floor in front of it like miles and miles of electronic spaghetti. The room was dominated by a very large clock, which after three hours of meeting and discussion seemed to tick more slowly.

Prior to the meeting, papers had been circulated, attached to the corresponding agenda items, built up into a large pack also containing the minutes from the previous meeting. The meetings were held weekly, and the amount of work that had gone into this meeting was clearly evident. Even more obvious, however, was the effort required on behalf of the participants to keep abreast of the issues at hand and particularly to be cognizant of the detail that the issues inevitably contained. It was observed that the previous meeting had produced a comparatively short set of minutes, of only five pages. The papers submitted were all noticeably similar to each other in format. The front page provided a brief summary as to why the papers had been brought with additional supporting material. The front page however contained no conclusion, but only the outline of options available for consideration. The papers were all signed by the author and by the sponsoring member of the CLT, without which a paper could not be brought forward for consideration. The agenda comprised eight specific items, and comments had been made so as to avoid any doubt that the proceedings of the meeting were likely to be "a chore".

It was noted in this meeting and other meetings attended how deferent the committee body was to the formal chair of the meeting. This was more than a gentle compliance to the position of the chair as the most senior officer present. As the meeting unfolded, the role of the chair and their position as senior officer present was critical to the progress of the meeting and the formalities that underpinned it; as a counterpoint to this, however, was the informal nature of the meeting itself. After only a couple of minutes, the chief executive, possibly as a gesture representative of the task at hand, removed his tie and opened his collar; other members took off their jackets and placed them over their chairs. Other members of the meeting continued to have a light lunch, collected coffee and water, or left the room as they saw fit. There was however a formal cordiality to which each member subscribed; frequent checking of phones would occur, but no one left to take a call, and only very occasionally did members reply to texts.

One of the items on the agenda required a paper to be presented by the Diversity and Equality team regarding the merging of issues of equality, diversity and community cohesion into a singular strategy for the city. A long and rather detailed presentation was given, during which time the sponsoring director appeared distant, engaged in the papers in front of him and occasionally doodling on a scrap piece of paper, but rarely acknowledging either the speakers or the points made. The presentation, although well accomplished, was difficult to comprehend fully. The language and jargon utilized, coupled with the nature of the issues involved, meant that the overall impression of the presentation was one of crushing complexity. This impression was not, however, limited to this particular item but was applicable to many of the items on the meeting agenda. All the items followed a rather formulaic path of introduction, presentation, questioning, debate and conclusion, all packed into a very particular form of language that appeared to be appropriate for the audience only. It resonated heavily with jargon and acronyms, references to legislature and other organizations, and was primarily concerned with issues that may be described as "wicked problems" (Grint, 2005a) – intractable issues that have no easily considered or operational solution.

Following the presentation the meeting fell quiet and turned to the chief executive, who, having introduced each item, would also initiate the debate. In practice what this meant was that the chief executive set the parameters within which the debate could operate. Not all of his opening statements were recorded, but his initial statement for the Diversity and Equality item was "I worry about this. Is it right? Is it the right direction for us to go?" thus effectively closing off any open debate about the real concerns of the paper and the issues involved. Despite this, however, the "debate" continued for the next hour and a quarter. The three main proponents were the chief executive, the sponsor of the paper, and the director of Housing and Neighbourhoods, with some nominal contribution from one or two others present. It appeared that, although the principal proponents were treading very carefully, the chief executive was acting as referee to a very public, yet politically motivated, verbal boxing match between the other two officers. The closing decision regarding this issue was that another paper dealing with the issues would be brought back to the CLT after further consideration by the officers of the Equality and Diversity Team.

The two officers who had presented the paper appeared a little deflated as they left, and the two senior officers around whom the debate had been conducted looked nonplussed. The remaining members of the group looked relieved; a palpable sense of tension had been dissipated with the closing of this particular debate.

Acquisition and utilization of resources

In the previous chapter, evidence was interpreted to suggest that the central government, due to the rigour of its auditing framework, had effectively occupied the leader position in a leader–follower relationship with the ABC. It was concluded that the ABC had contributed to the pervasive nature of this environment, which in turn had constricted the leadership capacity of the organization itself.

In the present illustration, the researchers conclude that the transactional and constricted nature of leadership impacts upon the interactions of agents within the ABC. The control and making available of resources are principal tactics in maintaining the position of leader in the organization. Resources may be financial resources, material resource – staff, office space, technology – or symbolic resources such as title, access, privilege, status. The availability of resources becomes the focus of negotiating leadership and, therefore, comprises a significant dynamic of the leader–follower relationship.

The illustration in this chapter demonstrates the transactional qualities of the chief executive in instigating and chairing the debate related to diversity and equality within the city and the ABC. This could be seen as evidence of a conflation between leadership and effective management (Rost, 1993), although those that presented the agenda item did not interpret the actions of the wider group as being leadership: "There is about £2.5m of salary in that room – was that £2.5m worth of leadership?"

During the fieldwork the researcher attended numerous meetings and not only recorded that they were similar in format and operation but also that members of the meeting group deferred to the chair of the meeting, who was usually the most senior officer present. In meetings when both officers and elected members were present, the officers in the meeting still deferred to the most senior officer in the room, regardless of whether he/she was attending or chairing. Within the officer population of the ABC there is a very clear appreciation of position and status derived from location in the organization structure. A rigorous formal structure, as evidenced by title and grades, which relate directly to banding of pay, requires commensurate levels of formalized process and procedure in order to make operation possible. The operation of the bureaucracy coalesces with the organization structure via the instrument of delegated levels of authority, which cascade through the organization chart to the incumbent post holder.

It may be possible to assert that the reliance of government and the chief executive upon a conflation of good management and transactional leadership, ostensibly to get things done, is an example of practice that is replicated throughout the organization. In other chapters the dominance of technical knowledge over other forms of skill (see Chapter 8) is noted, and while the possession of excellent technical awareness should not be taken as a weakness, a lack of general management and appreciation may impact detrimentally on the relationship between leader and followers (Dansereau, 1995).

Furthermore, it is those with a perceived good technical grasp of an area of service that get noticed and promoted, which is the ultimate contingent reward as part of a leadership transaction. It is the conclusion of this study that an overtly transactional or technical professional approach impinges upon the leader–follower relationship. Leaders attain a level of authority as a consequence of their position in the structure, augmented by a perceived technical competence in an area of service provision; a combination of personal and position power (Bass, 1960). These constructs theoretically interact over many different levels, making it very difficult to distinguish between the two (Yukl, 2002). There is evidence, however, that both power bases are utilized within the ABC, and it is the contention of this study that a product of the two is significant in attaining access to resources.

The issue of power within leadership studies is yet another hotly contested area. Within the literature review provided in Chapter 2, the word "power" is more prevalent than any other conceptual variable of leadership. To many, the absence of power is the true test of leadership, in that leadership can only be expressed when influence is exerted from a non-coercive platform (Rost, 1993). Setting aside the definitional debates ongoing within leadership studies, Rost's position seems to be one of the very few conceptual definitions where leadership is differentiated away from management (recognizing of course that a definition of management itself presents some difficulty). Regardless of the elegance of Rost's definition, there remains a problem attributing any influence to non-coercive factors when there is a strong evidence of hierarchy combined with commensurate levels of positional and personal power. Again, it must be concluded that whatever is going on between leaders and followers, within the ABC, it is not leadership as understood in a normative guise.

The preceding paragraphs have been concerned with the observation of status and position through which the individual may be called a leader. The activities and behaviours of the leaders are not leadership as is understood in normative terms, due to the absence of any transformational appeal to followers. Despite this, however, it should not be assumed that the activities and behaviours of the ABC's leaders comprise bad leadership. In the illustration accompanying this chapter the chief executive can be accused of establishing the parameters of the debate. This is only one interpretation of the illustration. A second alternative interpretation is that the chief executive deliberately planned and set out to establish the parameters of a conversation knowing full well that the ensuing debates could be detrimental to one of two members of the CLT. The chief executive skilfully manipulated the conversation to conclude that the two proponents sitting at the table should collaborate to produce a further document that was more of a compromise between the two individuals. While the officers who had presented the paper felt disappointed with the outcome, their initiative had not been dismissed and they had indicated they were pleased with the level of debate that had occurred during the meeting.

While it is the contention of this study that issues of power are a contributor to the style of leadership and management employed in the maintenance of status within the hierarchy, questions are raised as to how this use of power impacts upon followers. In an earlier chapter, it was noted that followers had rejected the notion of following but had an appreciation of the value of leadership. Furthermore it was also noted that fixing the role of leaders and followers is fraught with ambiguity, principally because the roles are interchangeable, and that most of the time, individuals acted from a platform of following as opposed to leading. The designated leaders of the organization are capable of maintaining their position within the structure when they adopt the posture of leaders; however, because of the changeable nature of their position, they are equally adept at maintaining their position within the structure when operating as followers. Adherence to process and protocol; reporting all possible alternative courses of action; collaboration; dissemination of "relevant" information; and timing are all tactics that are utilized in order to maintain position. It is not suggested here that leaders/followers will engage in position maintenance exclusively and to the detriment of other causes. The public sector ethos requires that other operational or legislative issues will take precedence, and position maintenance is not, therefore, the only objective, merely an important one.

Furthermore it is suggested here that this study's evidence permits the conclusion that subordinate officers operating in a following mode are able to engage in similar tactics to those outlined above, not only to maintain their position within the authority but also to grow their position. This requires moving up and through the organization structure. Followers require leaders because they hold the access to resources. Leaders and followers engage in a meaningful transactional relationship concerning progression and maintenance through the availability of resources. In the absence of any transactional negotiation concerning resource availability and allocation, followers will seek allegiances with leaders who have and are prepared to make resources available. Followers, of course, are also a resource and are subsequently valuable to leaders, but more so is their ability to acquire additional resources. The debates within the CLT can be interpreted as a public display of bargaining and negotiation regarding the acquisition of resources. Issues of equality and diversity have heightened value within central government circles and, as a consequence, attract significant levels of resources from numerous sources. The chief executive is ensuring that the ownership of resources is shared out, possibly to ensure that no one acquires too many resources and tilts the position of power and authority, and that the benefits of resources are felt across a wider platform. It should also be noted that resources might be defined to include political currency held by the individual. To lose out during public bargaining would be very detrimental to the political currency of the individual – a factor that the chief executive would appreciate. The principal dynamic in the leader–follower relationship here, therefore, is resources, and most notably the availability, utilization and acquisition of resources.

8 The balance within leadership and the dynamic of symbiosis

> Every six months they've been told they're doing fine, so the organization has developed a theory, and it's always had it – at least since I've been here – that you deal with people who are not performing with restructuring.
>
> (Chief Officer Poulter, City Development)

Accountable and responsible

The previous three chapters have dealt with empirical materials and made interpretations, primarily from a leader perspective, to make conclusions concerning the dynamics between leaders and followers. The ensuing three chapters continue this approach but shift the emphasis to demonstrate the role of followers in the relationship.

This illustration is not a unified observation but is a composite of bits of observations assembled to make an important illustration. It concerns an organization initiative designed to uncover the accountabilities and responsibilities of the chief officer job role. The followers in the illustration perceive the motives behind the initiative differently; subsequently, it is deemed to lack transactional benefit and to be potentially detrimental to chief officers. The illustration outlines the followers' response(s) to the initiative.

This chapter establishes the importance of followers in the leader–follower relationship. Interpretations related to this illustration conclude that the relationship is reciprocal and establishes a complex dynamic, termed here as symbiosis, as an important dynamic of the leader–follower relationship.

Background

ABC had sought to clarify and explore matters related to management responsibility and accountability within the chief officer population, and had contracted a nationally known consulting firm that specialized in human resource issues, here called Human Resource Consultancy (HRC), to assist in this work. The consultancy had drawn up a matrix (referred to internally as RACI – Responsibility, Accountability, Communication, Information) pertaining to each directorate. The matrix laid out in tabular form the task or job description in the left-hand column on a sheet of A3 paper and listed each chief officer across the top. The intention was that chief officers should indicate on the table whether they were accountable or responsible for a particular job role or task; making the process more complex, there were degrees of accountability and responsibility dependent upon one's individual or collective contribution. Furthermore, the definitions of "accountability" and "responsibility" were general descriptions, giving rise to interpretive flexibility and allowing the various managerial teams the opportunity to embellish or redefine the concepts to fit their own particular environments. Some matrices ran over more than one sheet of paper depending upon the particular directorate team.

What became very apparent with this particular illustration was that, despite the researcher's attempts to locate responsibility for the development of this initiative, the rationale behind the RACI matrix remained elusive. During the course of the "From Good to Great" event, the two most senior officers of the Human Resources Department introduced the consultant from HRC to the researcher with the explanation that the consulting firm were doing some work for the ABC. It was only at a later date that it became apparent that the RACI matrix was the work for which the HRC had been commissioned. During interviews with the HR officers, RACI was very rarely mentioned; the outcome of the work was never made transparent and, consequently, its intent was never fully appreciated during the research.

The RACI matrix was one of a number of substantive people-related initiatives that were taking place within the organization during the time that the empirical material for this study was collected. As well as the RACI initiative there were also the "From Good to Great" initiative and a culture audit based on the "cultural web" model of Johnson and Scholes (1999) designed to complement the "One Council" strategy; both of which are conjoined and justified as developing continuous organizational improvement. The chief executive explained some of the rationale for initiatives: "If it isn't delivering ... demonstrable improvement to the punter, the fact that people are happier being here isn't sufficient" (Chief Executive, ABC).

Leader voices

The apparent relationship between the HRC and the senior officers of the HR department witnessed at the "From Good to Great" event at least demonstrates an association, even though the association became less and less apparent as the fieldwork progressed. From a chronological perspective, the HR–HRC relationship was witnessed at the outset of the fieldwork conducted as part of this study. Over time, there were fewer and fewer references to RACI. Furthermore, in management team meetings when RACI was referred to, it was clear that managers associated RACI with the consulting firm and not with the HR department. It appeared that HR specifically took action to distance themselves from the RACI project. While this is a possibility, it will remain an issue of conjecture, but other "distancing" actions by HR were observed elsewhere, primarily in writing a paper for the CLT that presented the involvement of the ICC (the international consulting company that was employed to implement the ABC's model for leadership, cultural and performance development) and "From Good to Great" in particularly poor light.

The organization formally placed significant emphasis on appraisal, and formal performance appraisals were undertaken throughout the ABC on an annual basis. The appraisal pack sent to the appraisee is formidable, growing in volume at every step in the hierarchy until directors and chief officers receive an appraisal pack which is the size of a lever arch file, comprising in excess of 150 A4 pages. The contents and the pages started with guidance on conducting appraisals for both appraisor and appraisee. This was followed by an "elements of performance" assessment and then the "accountability port-folio", which comprised a series of corporate reports, including "sustainable communities" and "transport", "resident survey", "equality, diversity, cohesion and integration", "HR governance report", "RACI", "ethnic minority group", "women's group", "governance indicators" and, finally, a job description.

The importance of the annual appraisal was often stated, and yet the observable utility of the appraisal appears to suggest that statements of value concerning appraisal were more rhetorical than actual. The appraisal document originated in the HR department; when asked about the format of the appraisal, the officer who compiled the report said he did so because they had been instructed to do so. Senior officers of the department corroborated this view. "The deputy chief executive wanted everything included so we just bunched everything together" (Head of Strategic Human Resources, Central Services).

This statement could be considered indicative of the way the organization perceives its own appraisal system. Certainly, the following statements appear to support this perception. In conversation with one of the directors (whose anonymity has been protected) about appraisals in a very busy office, in which cascades of paper were pushed up against a far wall, the director drew my attention to appraisal documents by stating,

> There's last year's, you see. Oh! And the year before's.

Later during the conversation, the director highlighted a continued frustration with appraisals and, more specifically, the way in which they were implemented through their department. Again, this appears to be an organizational frustration, as the Human Resources department made a similar point.

> So you're going to discipline someone … did you address this, have you mentioned it in the appraisals, and you find nothing has happened. Then actually what they have done is not give themselves the tools to deal with the issue.
>
> (Head of Strategic Human Resources, Central Services)

Generally, the directors voiced a level of dissatisfaction with appraisals and the apparent lack of honesty in making assessments about an individual's capacity to do their job. Furthermore, this appears to be reflected in the way the directors' own appraisals are conducted.

> So we went through the process bit and then that was it ... no talk about what I've done in the job.

> We are really focused on the processes technical and administrative, we manage budgets brilliantly ... where we fall down is this caring more about this [the appraisal document] as opposed to them.
>
> (Director Trent, City Development)

Appraisal interviews, therefore, seemingly focus on those elements related to compliance, as opposed to the job role and tasks associated with the job role. Subsequently, it would appear that senior managers, to some extent at least, have questioned their suitability and validity.

Follower voices

While the most senior of officers appear to be aware of a shortfall in the administration of appraisals from an appraisor perspective, the question remains as to how appraisals are perceived from an appraisee (follower) perspective, recognizing that the vast number of people contained in the population makes any consensus of opinion difficult. One interview with an officer in the Chief Executive's Unit touched upon work levels, and comments were made regarding appraisals, which confirms the view that formal support for the appraisal process may be relegated in the light of other more pressing work priorities.

> The appraisals are always put back, postponed; I probably have an appraisal every 18 months rather than annually.
>
> (Senior Officer, Chief Executive's Unit)

Furthermore, meetings between the manager and subordinate were seemingly given less consideration than other duties undertaken during the course of a typical day within the ABC:

> I had to insist actually at my last appraisal, "it's not fair, you cancelled my one-to-one, and I don't get to see you".

And,

> When we have scheduled one-to-ones I don't waste his time; a scheduled one-hour meeting might last 10 minutes!
>
> (Senior Officer, Chief Executive's Unit)

More generally, the views expressed concerning meetings with managers contained much paradox. From an official point of view, the meeting between manager and subordinate is critical in the management of performance, although in practice the formal methodology lacked veracity, particularly at the most senior levels of the hierarchy. From a follower perspective, meetings with managers were formulaic, in which the time of the manager was protected, and were more generally seen as opportunities to promote oneself by suggesting that there were no problems to be concerned about. There was no freely manifest openness regarding difficult or ambiguous areas of a job role, specifically when relating to the jobholder's technical competence, as it could be construed as weakness. The relationship between manager and subordinate was deliberately conducted and maintained from a healthy, but respectful, distance.

During the course of the observations it was noticeable how little engagement of a personal, social or humanistic nature occurred. Small attempts at breaking routine, introductions of levity, snippets of conversation concerning the football results, made up the sum total of evidence that the population under observation were in some sense a group together, engaging collectively and sharing – working toward a common outcome.

The ABC, as alluded to in the next comment below, is an organization that is driven to technical delivery of services to a public, but there should be little doubt of the commitment and sense of vocation of the vast majority of people working within the ABC.

> General management is not valued, technical skills are valued and people play up to that.
>
> (Head of Strategic Human Resources, Central Services)

> There are lots of people that are really enthusiastic about what they do, and they're often at the lower levels ... they really care about what they are doing.
>
> (Director Trent, City Development)

> You would think they would be completely distanced from the council, they have got very particular jobs, particularly community care; most of them work part time, perhaps only six hours a week, but the pride they take in their work is fantastic.... It has nothing to do with the centre, I think it's more to do with the ethos of those services.
>
> (Senior Officer, Chief Executive Unit)

It could be argued, however, that the commitment given to the public – in some cases, a very demanding public – has supplanted any need for a social perspective internally. In some cases, the fact that people are dealing with another human being, possibly one at risk, may be lost in the conduct of delivering services.

We're still keeping the 55 per cent reduction target but you now have to deliver it in three years. So what we're saying to government is that, "We hold our hands up. You can rap our knuckles, you can rap the organization's knuckles", and, "Teenage conception is an important issue because of the impact it has – and we accept we haven't done anything about it, and we accept the admonishment we failed in that, but let's be realistic about what we are going to do going forward." And there is no way we are going to achieve 55 per cent in three years, we will be lucky if we achieve 25 per cent, so can we please agree a target that makes us focus on it as an issue. And we don't end up in three years not hitting target and the whole LAA [Local Area Agreement] is considered as failing ... are we winning the argument? We weren't at the beginning of the week.

(Assistant chief executive, Chief Executive's Unit)

There is a slight tension between the clients of the service and the intention of the service. In the case above, the issue relates to the reduction in the number of teenage pregnancies within the city; however, the teenagers for whom the service exists, and the reduction of pregnancies, appear to exist outside of the very client base itself. In other words, the objective appears to be established for all the right reasons but seems to lack humanity; a factor acknowledged at senior levels within the ABC.

You see that very much in communications, look at a lot of our communication to residents, they're very technical in nature because they are written by very technical people, actually if you understand the subject matter then they're fantastic.

(Assistant chief executive, Chief Executive's Unit)

The natural sphere of engagement for the members of the ABC appears to be technically oriented and rarely encroaches on the social and humanistic elements of work and organization. Internally, as externally, the technical aspects of the job are pre-eminent and the sense of the "human" gets lost in the sense of the "resources". However, this should not be too surprising, as the ABC has promoted staff based on technical competence and not on any sense of general management capacity.

In the past we have promoted people on their technical skills and not whether they have leadership skills. So what we have is a number of managers who are technically brilliant at what they do, but not managing because they are still doing the old job.

(Head of Strategic Human Resources, Central Services)

This could be interpreted as a frailty within the leadership and work relationships more generally. In order that this assertion should at least be corroborated, questions were asked from a rather tongue-in-cheek stance during interview: the interviewee was *provoked* into considering if the ABC was "technically competent, but socially inept". The response was surprising:

> I think that sums up the challenges we have.
>
> (Director Trent, City Development)

> I think that's probably, yeah, I think that's probably quite good.
>
> (Assistant chief executive, Chief Executive's Unit)

Leaders appear to be hesitant to make entreaties through a direct appeal to either the intellect or to the emotions, a hesitancy which is also reciprocated by followers – a dyadic reluctance by the leader and follower to engage on anything outside of the technical or procedural. Questions remain, therefore, as to whether this self-confessed frailty contributes in any way to the following observation:

> There is a general dissatisfaction working within the centre of ABC [Civic Hall] ... yet sickness levels are down at less than two days per person, they turn up every day, they're really good at what they do, but they don't really care about the organization.... You have to make a decision that some of those people are not going to change. If they're coming to work and they're really good at their job, it doesn't matter how many away days, how many workshops, how many nice things we say, how many newsletters we send out, how many award ceremonies, how many times you give them a metaphorical and physical hug ... they're still going to go, "they don't care", because we don't pay them enough.
>
> (Head of Service Admin, Corporate Services)

Performance appraisal within the ABC is clearly a more complex procedure than the purely formal process as outlined in formal documents, which stipulates the official expectations of the organizations. The following statement, provided by a long-serving chief officer, provides an insight into alternative ways in which the ABC manages the performance of its members.

> Every six months they've been told they're doing fine, so the organization has developed a theory, and it's always had it – at least since I've been here – that you deal with people who are not performing with restructuring; or you devalue their job to such an extent that they get embarrassed and they walk. And that's what RACI is about. The game is all about how many Rs and As can you get in your column.

> There will be some sort of reasonable adjustment made, which will filter through into job descriptions and, ultimately, into levels of remuneration – or is there a case for a chief officer at all.

> They won't kick good people out; somehow you'll survive.
>
> (Chief Officer Poulter, City Development)

The illustration

The project was initiated at a team meeting at which members of the team were invited to take a copy of the matrix and fill it in, whereupon the HRC team would collate it. The deadlines for completion had overrun several times and so the matrix was to be brought back to a team meeting for further discussion and clarity. It was understood that the discussion concerning the matrix had already been extensive and, in some cases, had become quite heated. The exposure to other team members' work and interpretation had initiated a continual iterative process of utilizing information gained to reclassify one's own work responsibilities and accountabilities in line with their peers.

During the ensuing discussion, the following points were noted. Members of a team ensured that they were not underrepresented on the matrix. A lack of As (Accountabilities) relative to peers might suggest that one had minimum levels of accountability, thus paving the way for questions concerning the current job role and future validity. Furthermore, if members felt that their job role had been poorly represented by the HRC team, they took it upon themselves to add aspects of their job role to the left-hand column. In time, the job task column came to represent even the minutiae of the various job roles, as members assigned As and Rs to the matrix for the most minor of tasks. Many had arbitrarily based their own accountability and responsibility structure on the idea that if a team member had claimed to be accountable or responsible for a particular task, then they must be also. The validity of the matrix was made even more questionable by the fact that each team of people undertaking the exercise approached it in a unique manner, making cross-comparison difficult.

It had been maintained that the matrix had been used in other organizations, although this was never substantiated. It was clear that the HRC's consultants were taken aback by the response to their work. The level of questioning regarding the complexity of job role and task, further exacerbated by the tactical machinations of those taking part, soon rendered the matrix inoperable and irrelevant. The project was rejected universally eight months after its initiation, due to management recalcitrance and lack of relevance. At no point did any director feel compelled to sit with each of their reports and have a meaningful discussion concerning the responsibilities and accountabilities of each job role. The impression was that with 14 direct reports, the commitment to the project by each director was outweighed by the absence of likely benefits to be derived from the process. Furthermore, directors were not able to adequately suggest which criteria chief officers should adopt in order to be more prescriptive in their approach to completing the matrix. What was to happen to the matrix and the subsequent developmental work on completion was never broached, as support quickly dissipated from the project. Again, the impression was that officers were relieved and self-congratulatory in contributing to and witnessing its final demise.

Symbiosis

The position of leader and follower is ambiguous, and to suggest that certain dynamics pertain to leaders and not followers, or vice versa, is erroneous. The dynamics uncovered in this study are dynamics of the relationship and not specifically the constituent parts. The dynamics impact on both leaders and followers, possibly in different ways and to different extents, but they are highly unlikely to be totally absent in the relationship.

The previous section outlined an initiative apparently driven by Human Resources, referred to internally as RACI. This illustration demonstrates how individuals can read different meaning and intention into initiatives. The chief officers' reaction to RACI firmly establishes the independent agency of followers, but, furthermore, uncovers the importance that both leaders and followers have to each other. The principal dynamic of the leader–follower relationship uncovered during the interpretive process is one of symbiosis.

In the introductory paragraphs to this illustration, it was suggested that the ABC wished to resolve or explore issues related to the responsibility and accountability of the chief officer population. It should be stated here that this, as a rationale for the project, is inferred by the researcher; at no time was the reason for undertaking such a piece of work made explicit. Furthermore, it is reasonable to suggest that neither the Human Resources department nor the consulting company who devised the project could have envisaged the protracted and complex nature in which the project was approached. This may be due to the following four reasons.

First, the consulting company approached the matter from a purely functional perspective and failed to capture the nuance, complexity and ambiguity of the roles chief officers undertake within the ABC. From a formal perspective, job role descriptions are extensive documents designed to capture the requirements of the job based on a role responsibility and personal specification. From a different perspective the job descriptions are, to an extent, historical documents that fail to capture the pressures that chief officers have to deal with on a day-to-day basis; pressures that may reinforce, deflect and/or conflict with the formal job requirements. From an overtly rational functional basis, the project of tabulating the accountabilities and responsibilities of chief officers was, at best, only going to represent a percentage of what chief officers do while working.

Second, the ABC was undergoing extensive structural reorganization as a response to central government's requirement for a Children's Directorate. Following this, the ABC restructured its existing directorates to create a new structure with strategically focused directors. The second tier of management, chief officers, was also undergoing structural reorganization and new reporting lines. This included the creation of new chief officer roles, and chief officers had been appointed from outside the organization accordingly. Under the new structural arrangements, the new chief officers had been provided with a delegated authority commensurate with the old director position. However, directors had not completely delegated their authorities, but were operating under a "concurrent delegation"; this delegated authority to chief officers, but directors still retained the right to "step in" should it be required. Some chief officers, typically those in post for a longer period, had not received these new privileges and were operating a hybrid system of managing day-to-day services without the formal acknowledgement of delegated authority.

Evidence was collected and has been presented here to show that chief officers were not only aware of the double nature of the chief officer role, but that some resentment and anxiety had been created by the structural reform. It is reasonable to conclude that chief officers approached the RACI project with a degree of caution, as they were very aware that the matrix did not represent their role, and the variance in role meant that there was a huge disparity between accountabilities and responsibilities. Newly configured chief officer positions were able to represent the delegated authorities previously held by directors. To some extent, therefore, they were being asked to take part in an initiative whose outcome was obvious from the start.

The third reason contributing to the outcome of the RACI initiative was the interpretation made by the chief officers of the reasoning behind the project. Although the desired outcomes of the project were not made obvious to the researcher, it is reasonable to assume that some benefit to the organization would have been derived from seeing the project through to a satisfactory conclusion. It would appear that the chief officer population, however, had arrived at the view that while the stated benefit might be attained there were other non-explicit reasons for the introduction of the initiative. The collective experiences of the chief officer group and their associated understanding of the history of the workings of the ABC led them to interpret the initiative as an attempt to inform the restructuring of the chief officer population. From this perspective, the chief officers felt that in cooperating they might hasten their own demise, and so they made little or no attempt to progress the project, but made successful attempts either to mould the project in terms beneficial to themselves or to see it finished without conclusion.

Finally, the RACI project was legitimized with a high degree of formal approval from the HR function and the respective directors of the departments. In other words, the formal leaders of the directorates had stated the intention that the project would be undertaken. Nevertheless, somewhere along the journey the project had become derailed, principally because of the deliberate actions of followers. This however cannot be taken as evidence of weak leadership in any terms. Normative leadership theory stops short of asserting an unquestioned obedience; also there are a number of leader elements that are absent in this instance. There is no appeal to any higher sense of transforming the organization; there is however a transactional request which was ultimately declined as the rewards were either seen as not valuable enough, or not in the interests of followers. While such appeals are important in neo-charismatic leadership models, contrary to this, the Full Range Leadership Theory model predicts that leaders may engage in "laissez-faire" behaviours (Bass, 1999; Bass and Avolio, 1994b). In this example, leaders made few forcible entreaties toward completion of the project, and it is safe to conclude that leaders took a laissez-faire approach. The reasons for this, however, are less obvious and will be commented upon later in the section.

Followers are usually appreciated as a homogeneous and compliant group (Kellerman, 2008), and normative forms of leadership see leadership as a zero-sum game where leader agency can only be achieved at the expense of follower agency (Reicher *et al.*, 2005). However, in this instance followers are acting under their own volition and contrary to the designs of leaders. This strongly indicates that following, as opposed to being a follower, is an essential component of the leader–follower relationship and establishes the agency of followers. This finding runs contrary to much of the theorizing concerning followers, principally because the relationship with followers is only conceptualized from a basis of leaders influencing followers (Bass, 1985; Hogg, 2001). Even theories that attempt to focus on the activities of followers stop short of indicating that followers can act with independence from leaders. Studies conducted by Collinson are an exception to this, as he has demonstrated that followers' identities are complex and differentiated and that they change in line with their social environment; followers are capable of responding differently to leadership (Collinson, 1999, 2006).

A different response to that predicted under normative leadership models is often categorized as workplace resistance. However, studies have concluded that an individual's response to leaders need neither be compliance nor resistance but can be what is referred to as "observance" – a combination of the two giving rise to both positioning and reflexivity (Iedema *et al.*, 2006). It is maintained in this study that the complex and ambiguous nature of being a leader or follower contributes to observance, allowing followers free range to both comply and resist leaders. More than that, however, in cases where the net potential outcome of an action is perceived to be less than favourable toward the individual or group, followers will engage in behaviours that appear compliant but are wholly resistant. In response, leaders may adopt laissez-faire behaviours if the initiative is not in the best interest of either followers or leaders.

During the course of the RACI project from inception to conclusion, there were opportunities for the leaders in this situation to stage interventions to promote more satisfactory progress of the project. During the fieldwork for this study, seemingly ineffectual actions of leaders were observed. This view is clearly a functional reaction to what looks like poor management. Underpinning such laissez-faire attitudes, however, must be more complex motivations than at first assumed. The ambiguity of the leader role in the ABC contributes significantly to the apparent lack of forcible actions by a leadership population. All the leaders within the ABC are required to spend considerable time acting from a follower platform. The group that leads the ABC senior managers can be seen as comprising a variety of constituents ranging from central government to notions of public sector ethos; from elected members to institutionalized bureaucracy; and from external stakeholder expectations to formalized superordinate managers. The point of stating this is to demonstrate that the position of leader within the ABC is not too far divorced from being a follower. In engaging with followers there are still significant dynamics that impact upon leadership behaviours and the relationship with followers. Leaders are able to empathize with followers due to the proximity of their own position and their understanding that they require followers in order to maintain their position within the organization. Leaders understood the rhetoric behind the RACI initiative, were not convinced of its value, and had experience of the history of the workings of the ABC which gave them shared insights as to the rationale of the project. Hence it became more favourable to adopt a laissez-faire position as opposed to taking a functionally managerial position and inflaming the tensions and resentments of the follower group, provided that the follower group played its part in the subterfuge.

In this illustration, evidence has been provided concerning the autonomy of follower actions. In an environment such as the ABC, followers, in response to the ambiguity of position, role and task, are capable of reacting to leaders in different and surprising ways. Subsequently, leaders, who are not too far divorced from the position of follower themselves, are able to develop equally skilful and manipulative positions in order to maintain their own position in the group and the wider organization. Leaders wait to see how the actions of the group play out before deciding upon their own interventions. The principal dynamic involved in the leader–follower relationship in this illustration can therefore be appreciated as being a complex dynamic of symbiosis. Leaders and followers need each other and, due to complex multiple identities and observances, they can at times be the same thing.

9 The negotiation of leadership and the dynamic of politics

I've just decided that I'm stuffed anyway so what the heck.... There are a lot of bullish people in the ABC and he who shouts loudest does get to do what he wants. He did get to move his section and form PPPU [Public Private Partnership Unit] because he made life too difficult for managers in other areas and I know that for a fact.

Chief Officer Soar, ADS (Architect and Design Service)

A management meeting

The illustration in this section is concerned with a Directors' Team meeting that was observed during the fieldwork. The illustration highlights that formal activities do not always give credence to the perceptions of a group. From a functional perspective, the group debates the future of a particular business activity. Further unveiling of the illustration shows that the functional aspects of the illustration could have occluded the political nature of the backdrop to the illustration.

Interpretations of the material presented here demonstrate the political nature of life within the ABC and concludes that political activity is an important dynamic of the leader–follower relationship.

Background

Directors utilize team meetings as an important tool for conducting business within their departments. The working week is heavily time-pressured and, consequently, time is at a premium. Each director has a large number of direct reports, making regular individual meetings impractical. Consequently, in their place, most directors will hold a weekly team meeting with all the chief officers present, supplemented with additional relevant attendees from the Corporate Centre dealing with items related to diversity, strategy, HR, budget, compliance, legal issues and so forth. The meetings would take a full morning or afternoon. It was felt preferable to hold the meetings in the morning, as lunchtime brought an effective hiatus to proceedings and, subsequently, delegates could engage in further activity in the afternoon. Meetings held later in the day had a tendency to drift into the early evening.

Leader voices

Localized management actions, underpinned by personal alliance, need to be considered alongside a major operational shift because of the introduction of strategically focused directors. As the directors are compelled to operate from a platform of "strategic commissioning", legitimized by the Labour government's stance of following a third way between free market and consensus, implications are being felt throughout the organization and, specifically, by chief officers primarily because of "concurrent delegation":

> I'm quite critical and fairly openly; one of the critical points was to give directors more critical capacity but I'm not sure that's happened.
>
> (Chief Officer Maun, City Development)

In order for chief officers to assume day-to-day responsibilities, concurrent delegation which provided the same delegative powers as directors was required. Concurrent delegation had only been partly implemented, giving rise to a situation where, within a population of chief officers, some would have concurrent delegation and others would not – the arbiter of which appeared to be the date of appointment. New chief officers received concurrent delegation on appointment, while long-serving chief officers did not, which led to a degree of dissatisfaction among the general population.

> From the chief officer perspective, who as a population had welcomed the additional authority associated with the structural change, a degree of confusion existed regarding it in practice; where were the effective limits of their authority, would a "step-In" be implemented? ... Everything had changed, but nothing had changed. Not surprisingly chief officers were starting to show levels of cynicism over the restructuring and even levels of resentment concerning the working reality of their situation.

> The buck stops with the chief officer. And we would not have the situation where strategic directors would be interfering on a day-to-day basis. But, and there is always a "but", the big "BUT" is that a director can intervene, there is a process of intervention, there is a veto over the activities of a chief officer. So if something gets out of hand, out of control, if a chief officer has not exercised good judgement, it's becoming a major political issue then the director can step in – step-in rights, you might call it, which is a concern to all of us.

> I don't really see the difference; nobody said in so many words what the benefits would be ... the focus was very much what the strategic directors wanted. From below, it didn't look any more different then, the blame stopped with me, and I got a lot more emails (laughs). So the workload has increased, it's obvious there is only a certain amount of capacity between

the director and the chief officer, and if the director says, "well I'm gonna vision now", the work doesn't go away. So as a natural consequence, some stuff comes down, – and of course we're all sitting here saying, "well I'd like to vision as well", because the level I'm operating at, I feel like I should be doing more than just delivery.

(Chief Officer Poulter, City Development)

Unsurprisingly, issues such as concurrent delegation, the right of "step in" the ongoing structural review of the ABC, the definition of the role of chief officer and director, and the recruitment of new chief officers with enhanced levels of responsibility compared to residual members of the team, had caused a degree of concern and anxiety:

Uncertainty, real uncertainty, have I still got a job in this new structure ... I think there is real uncertainty particularly among chief officers, and it's difficult to not transfer this down the line.

(Chief Officer Leen, City Development)

Follower voices

Following on from comments made by the director, the Head of the ADS (Architect and Design Service) volunteered an opinion regarding the lack of success of the organization. Rather surprisingly, the points raised were entirely absent in the formal debate concerning the future of the organization. What was discovered is an example of resistance to a corporate decision that appears to be tolerated. The Head of the ADS explained the predicament.

At the review it was agreed that all the design function of the council would be done in design services (ADS). But lots of people have not kept their promises ... she has got another person ... occasionally recruiting from within the council so-called client officers to commission us to do the work, but they build up their own teams ... they're revenue funded.... In Landscape Architects the staff were transferred into this service and they re-grew their own people in Parks and Countryside. So instead of the work being done here, the work is still being done back in Parks and Countryside.

(Chief Officer Soar, ADS)

In essence what had occurred here is that a decision was made, following a review conducted by the assistant chief executive, that all ABC architect and design services would be commissioned by the ADS. This effectively never happened, as those people in the department who were transferred to the ADS were reallocated back into departments by recruitment drives designed to rebuild their own design function. The rationale for this was that as internal departmental services were paid for from revenue budgets, the design service cost, which could range from anything from 6 to 15 per cent of the total build cost, was covered by the departmental revenue budget allowing the full amount of capital available to be spent on the project. In practice, this move increased the total development fund, as design costs were covered elsewhere.

Furthermore, internal departmental design services were commissioning a schedule of work that would not have been possible from within design services. The ADS specified works that were driven primarily for purpose and fit, while departmental services were driven exclusively by cost. Not surprisingly, the ADS developed a reputation for being expensive.

Additionally, as the departments re-established their own internal design services, they recruited from the ADS. The work force of the ADS was effectively, therefore, being denuded and cannibalized by colleagues from different service functions. The remaining staff in the ADS were collectively regarded as less desirable work colleagues than others.

Finally, a member of the ADS was seconded to the deputy chief executive's department (at his own insistence) to establish what became known as the Public Private Partnership Unit (PPPU), effectively to oversee and commission capital developments gained as a result of the government's private finance initiative (PFI), the strategy of using private sector money to finance public sector capital works. Subsequently, work that was originally designated as the responsibility of the ADS was now hived off into the new unit that, on paper at least, appeared to generate millions of pounds of additional revenue for the deputy chief executive's department.

> I've just decided that I'm stuffed anyway so what the heck.... There are a lot of bullish people in the ABC and he who shouts loudest does get to do what he wants. He did get to move his section and form PPPU because he made life too difficult for managers in other areas and I know that for a fact.
>
> (Chief Officer Soar, ADS)

The head of the ADS requested and took early retirement less than six months after the interview took place.

The illustration

The format for the meeting is very similar to that of the Corporate Leadership Team meeting reported in Chapter 7. In many cases, senior management team meetings are held in the same room as the CLT meeting. A formal agenda is prepared and papers drawn up in support of the various agenda items, the papers being circulated in advance of the meeting. The agenda was surprisingly large with over a dozen items; the supporting pack of documentation was equally intensive. Questions were raised about the amount of time that an attendee would need in order to fully understand and be conversant with all the relevant papers. The impression was that individuals relied upon scanning the documentation prior to the meeting, hoping that they would either follow the discussion or use their own experience and intuition in order to contribute.

The atmosphere and conduct of the meeting were very similar to many other meetings that were chaired by a senior member of the CLT. ABC meetings are deferential and formal, but not adversely so. Plenty of humour abounds, and the group work is jocular and pacey; nevertheless, the group is always respectful toward the chair. At certain times and at the initiation of an agenda item the group collectively seeks guidance from the chair, particularly during challenging or difficult agenda items when it is noticeable that certain members of the group would rather be elsewhere.

One such item related to a discussion concerning an agenda item about the central Architect and Design Service (ADS). It quickly became apparent why someone from the Corporate Services team was present. Before this item, the meeting had been very upbeat, focused on organization and departmental successes. Despite this, the impression was all very earnest, somewhat self-congratulatory but also modest. The mood changed with the introduction of agenda item 4. One was left to wonder if the previous 25 minutes had been mainly concerned with positioning.

It was learnt that item 4 had previously been raised by the CLT and that, consequently, a best-value report had been conducted. The findings of the report had been circulated before the meeting with the other papers and they were to be presented by a person from outside of the department. The Head of the ADS was at the table. The report was presented as being the speaker's work, leaving questions concerning the involvement of the Head of the ADS. The ADS is a partnership organization between the internal design services function and a private sector architectural and design company. The ADS is meant to be responsible for the delivery of capital building projects within the ABC; the scope of such works can vary from hospital refurbishment and art gallery redesign, to the design, build and commissioning of an Olympic swimming pool.[1] The associated paper outlined the discussion and issues concerning the ADS, which fundamentally were related to the current forecast of the ADS making a deficit of £0.5 million.

Following the presentation was the debate concerning the ADS. The tone of the debate was deferential and respectful. Contributions from the attendees, however, were virtually uniform. It was clear that the group was informed and had an opinion. Each delegate's opinion appeared to carry equal validity; eventually, members started to defer to those with more technical experience and position, and consequently maintained their overtones of respect to the chair. One is reminded of romance tales concerning the court of King Arthur and his knights collected at the round table.

The debate had continued for some 20 minutes when the chair (director) first made an attempt to close the conversation. The last few minutes of the debate had become repetitive, with members starting to revisit previous contributions. Iteratively the meeting descended into increasing levels of complexity, intricacy and personal experience, which added little to the apparent fact that the ADS loses money because internal departments choose not to use the function but, locally and unilaterally, decide to use external bodies for design and building services outside of the ADS and the ABC in general. As to agreeing a course of action on the future of the ADS, the group seemed no closer to agreement than 20 minutes earlier. The director concluded by stating that the work needed to be addressed and that a paper should be brought back for discussion regarding options, at which point it could be submitted to the CLT in six weeks.

It was only after some considerable debate that the head of the ADS decided to contribute. His initial comments in the discussion were fully understanding and supportive of the process. He stated openly that the ADS was an issue and it must be decided what to do with the partnership. His comments were carefully structured and very guarded, in keeping with the general tone of the debate to that point. Criticisms of the ADS were made around the table, which he acknowledged. Collectively, however, the comments were a continued critical assault and were not very helpful. The Head of the ADS became increasingly withdrawn and frustrated, and started to look hurt and annoyed.

Despite the director suggesting some action to allow the group to move on, the finance manager and another member of the committee reinitiated the debate. There seemed to be a reluctance to conclude. The field notes state it was like "the last voice wins", and the feeling was reminiscent of a wildlife programme where the pack sense the weakness of one of their own and turn upon the unfortunate, ultimately driving it from the pack. The director attempted to close this debate again but failed – more conversation and, again, further attempts to end the discussion. The debate lasted some 75 minutes, at which point the director managed to close this agenda item and call for a break. There had been no agreed action taken.

During the break the ADS chief officer was heard to say, "I feel a bit pissed off." Further sporadic but increasingly heated spats interspersed the coffee break. As an aside, the director attempted to explain what had been witnessed. Fundamentally, the director drew attention to the complexity of personal alliances and relationships throughout the ABC, which enabled the possibility of localized management decisions, many of which might be contrary to the formalized expectations of the organization centrally.

Politics

In the preceding chapters, a complex picture of organizational life at the ABC has been presented. This has included the outlining of significant dynamics that impact upon the leader–follower relationship. The interaction of the dynamics strongly affects the leader–follower relationship and, subsequently, the organization. The interpretations made in this section focus on how leaders and followers deal with the complexities and ambiguities already uncovered in earlier chapters to conclude that widespread use of political activity comprises an important dynamic of the leader–follower relationship.

Leaders have become skilled in progressing activities within the ABC in a style that is particular to them. Officers that had been recruited from outside the ABC had remarked upon how they had found the methods of working different to their previous organization. Within the ABC, leaders had developed a consensual style that attempts to create a positive and supporting environment. Allowing and encouraging debate and contribution, ensuring that peers and subordinate officers are not exposed to detrimental pressures, either from elected members or other officers, and demonstrating strong personal ethics in accordance with the notions of the public sector ethos: all are factors that contribute to the overall successful operation of the organization.

Underneath the surface of the awards and successes of the organization lies a maelstrom of dynamics; shaping, reinforcing and reinventing relationships between leaders and followers at all levels. Some of these have been identified, and so attention must be given to the processes of how the dynamics coalesce, converge and progress.

There is an increasingly large literature that supports the presence of politics in organizations. Mintzberg's analysis shows that organizations can be appreciated, either wholly or in part, as a political arena (Mintzberg, 1985). The activities of elected members between themselves – the resignation of Councillor Wharfe, the early retirement of the ADS chief officer, the observed struggle and subsequent mediation by the chief executive at CLT, the actions of chief officers toward RACI, rhetorical statements concerning the value of leadership – all appear to be politically motivated actions and behaviours. Observation of specific events within the ABC leads to the conclusion that political activity resonates throughout the organization.

The observation and conclusions made here could lead to the classification of the ABC as a totally political arena, due to the intense and pervasive nature of the political activity to be found within it. However, classification is not too important here for two reasons. The first is that other classifications described by Mintzberg could fit equally well; second, a critically motivated observer may be able to discern political motivations in all of the actions within the organization. However, the weight of evidence, complimented by much of the literature, allows for the characterization of the ABC as a political arena where the levels of political activity and behaviour are high. Furthermore, the literature supports the notion that politics and political behaviour can have profound effects on organizations and, therefore, by association, the leaders and followers of the organization. Despite this, however, there is very little consideration given to politics in leadership studies, an observation considered surprising by some leadership scholars (House and Aditya, 1997).

Motivated in part by the comments of House and Aditya and the conspicuous absence of politics in leadership studies, Ammeter and colleagues, in an extensive study, begin to address this deficiency and model a political theory of leadership (Ammeter *et al.*, 2002). This breakthrough study provoked a special edition of the *Leadership Quarterly* entitled *Political Perspectives in Leadership* (volume 15, issue 4, 2004), generating additional contributions to the subject.

Ammeter and colleagues are very specific in their view of politics as a contributor to organizational leadership. They define politics in organizations as a neutral activity but also state that politics in organizational leadership can be seen as the "constructive management of shared meaning" (Ammeter *et al.*, 2002 p. 751). It is the contention here that this definition and application is too narrow. The authors express the view that leadership studies have been rationally constrained and have traditionally considered a limited set of variables while ignoring other potentially relevant aspects. Furthermore, they argue that leadership theory is deficient in areas related to leadership style, particularly when directed to superiors and peers, and that there is a need for theory to be placed in context. During the course of the study, the authors focus on leadership traits and, therefore, continue the status quo in leadership studies. The reason for conducting their research from this platform appears clear. First, the authors adopt a definition of leadership as giving "purpose, meaning, and guidance to collectivities by articulating a collective vision that appeals to ideological values, motives and self-perceptions of followers" (Ammeter *et al.*, 2002 p. 753). This definition is a clear reference to the neo-charismatic view of leadership and is, therefore, inculcated in a variety of definitional shortcomings already noted. Specifically working from such a definition, the authors are placing political activity within a framework that contributes to their own definition of leadership. It is the conclusion of the present study that political behaviour as a dynamic of the leader–follower relationship need not contribute favourably at all. Political acts may have repercussions not designed by individuals and they may become part of the context within which the leaders and followers are acting.

There is an implied assumption within leadership studies and, in particular, normative appreciations that leadership is a beneficial commodity to be sought, developed and nurtured within organizations. If leadership is taken as an influence process then there is the distinct possibility that the influences may be detrimental, negative, evil, pointless, self-serving and so forth. Issues of bad leadership have been largely ignored within leadership studies, with the exception of some contributors, notably Kellerman (2004), Kets de Vries (2003) and Conger and Kanungo (1998). Ammeter *et al.* do not touch upon issues related to the negative possibilities inherent in an influence relationship, and by ignoring the possibilities of negative aspects of leadership, a complete understanding of leadership will always remain distant. It is not possible on the one hand to have a leader but on the other to have a "power wielder"; the definitions do not bear up to scrutiny.

The present study shows that political activity may not always be beneficial to the collective. Certainly, in the example of the chief officer of the ADS, the political activities created millions in revenue for one part of an organization to the detriment of another. However, the principal casualties remain the ADS itself and its chief officer who, despite years of good and accomplished service, felt overburdened by the political environment to the extent that he left the ABC and took early retirement. Morgan reminds us of the possibility of political activity underpinned by large-scale bureaucracy giving rise to a particular form of normalized control that can dominate entire organizations (Morgan, 1997). This study demonstrates that narrowing the area of research to meet only the positive aspects of leadership does a disservice to all.

It is important to recognize the issues around why individuals feel the need to engage in political activity. The study by Ammeter and colleagues does not cover this as an antecedent of their theory, preferring to rely upon the limitations of definition to state that leaders engage in political activity as a functional requirement of benefiting the collective. The authors recognize that political behaviour may be undertaken for other purposes but choose not to recognize those activities as they do not fit the definition of leadership. Political behaviour is, therefore, taken to be a neutral activity, neither good nor bad, but an essential part of organizational functioning. The present authors agree that political activity is an essential part of organizational life but hold that the division of political behaviour as either included in leadership or excluded from leadership, based on the outcome of the behaviour, is erroneous. Political activity by leaders has repercussions across the organization, the outcomes of which are undetermined. Behaviours can result in outcomes that are both favourable to the organization and detrimental to the individual, or any other permutation imaginable.

The political theory of leadership, as outlined in the study by Ammeter and colleagues, is in essence an exclusively leader-centric theory. Political activity is undertaken by leaders in order to narrow ambiguity and promote understanding where uncertainty exists. Followers, as in many other studies, are theorized to be the recipients of political behaviour and act as a homogeneous and compliant whole. In the study by Ammeter and colleagues, it is stated that leaders need to adopt political behaviours that match the situational assessments of their follower counterparts, which is a simpler process if followers act as a compliant and homogeneous grouping. When followers have independent agency, and are capable of a moderating identity and being manipulative, the issues of adopting appropriate political behaviour become exponentially more complicated. Ammeter *et al.*'s study does not incorporate follower engagement in political behaviour into its findings. It is the conclusion here that followers have a level of agency beyond that usually theorized in leadership studies, and that they are as skilled and as manipulative as their leader counterparts. As leaders engage in political activity, so do followers.

This finding has implications for leadership studies. Normative models following a functional paradigm have asserted the predominance of the leader to the detriment of the follower. Few writers in the mainstream have focused attention on the contribution of followers, appreciating them only as moderators or constructors of leadership. It has been maintained that followers do not engage in followership (Rost, 1993). As the follower is one of the constituents in the leader–follower relationship, the act of following is part of the relationship. When followers act in a way that is seemingly not in accordance with leader designs it is often referred to as resistance, but as the actions of followers have an impact on leaders, it is safe to conclude that followers do engage in followership, as they are acting from a position of informed agency in order to achieve something.

Evidence has been presented in the preceding section and elsewhere that political behaviour was both intensive and pervasive within the ABC; some consideration should be given now to make interpretations as to why the incidence of political behaviour was so high. First, it is evident that levels of political activity were high within the ABC, to the extent that everyone had the capacity to engage should they wish. Pfeffer (1981) has argued that there is a match between political skill and the individual's preference for political organizations. In other words, the political nature of the ABC draws people with ability at political engagement toward it. Once inside the organization the individual is met by a set of unique constraints imposed by, and upon, the organization; this requires political ability to make sense of and circumvent some of the more restrictive arrangements and the impositions of elected members. In a sense, political activity is the modus operandi by which business is conducted within the ABC as officers model their behaviour on other perceptibly more successful officers. Second, political skill is required to protect position and resource allocation within the structure. Ferris and colleagues assert that political skill is a prerequisite for survival in organizations (Ferris *et al.*, 2007); consequently, those in positions of seniority are likely to be those with political ability. And finally, it is the contention here that application of political behaviours and skill will enhance individual career prospects. This proposition is given more attention in the next chapter.

In defence of the findings and theory development reported in the study by Ammeter and colleagues, the present study supports many of the arguments contained within it. As Ammeter's study relies heavily on leadership trait analysis conducted within a functional research paradigm, its conclusions are orchestrated to match the theoretical underpinnings of their normative counterparts and are, therefore, not as far-reaching as they perhaps could have been. Nevertheless, the authors have initiated debate and research into an important dynamic of the leader–follower relationship. In agreement with the aforementioned study, this study concludes that politics is an important dynamic in the leader–follower relationship.

10 The agency of followers and the dynamic of game playing

I think how I got on was I realized, I learned you had to play the game. A lot of what we do is playing that game, isn't it?

Chief Officer Greet, Corporate Services

Meeting the leader

This illustration is actually comprised of two events that occurred sequentially. Both concern meetings between a director and the elected leaders of the ABC.

Interpretations of the meetings show how an individual in a formal follower position is able to resist leaders. As it was demonstrated in an earlier chapter how leaders establish their leadership, this chapter is concerned with how followers establish the strength of their own followership. The interpretations deal with aspects of power within the authority and conclude that strong followers and leaders continually negotiate their relationship in accordance with rules of a "game". It is the game, therefore, that comprises a dynamic of the leader–follower relationship.

Background

As the hierarchical changes in structure was relatively new to the ABC at the time this research was undertaken, the changes in emphasis were still effectively being embedded within the organization. Some officers, as will be shown, felt that enough of the system had been experienced in order to make comment and to identify areas in which the elegance of the ABC structure was becoming slightly unravelled. The illustration demonstrates the complexity of the task to be accomplished and gives further insights into the dynamics of the leader–follower relationship.

The shift in senior manager emphasis presented a particular challenge for the organization, as it constituted a fundamental change in the way the organization was to be administered and managed. The continued progression of the ABC was perceived to be dependent upon the application of skills and competencies by the four principal directors in balancing the operational responsibility for a very complex service function while developing a higher strategic focus. Additionally this transition required the delegation and reallocation of responsibilities between the directors and their various reporting chief officers. As the directors assumed a more strategic view, so the chief officer was required to assume operational responsibility for the delivery of their particular service function.

The directors, however, maintained a fall-back position of being able to "step in" should the need arise and to reassume personal control and responsibility for those areas for which they are formally accountable. This process was referred to internally as "concurrent delegation". The organization considered this organizational design to represent the optimum chance for progress against many of the obstacles to be overcome. Aligned with this structure was a contingent belief that a strategic perspective and the competence of the directors to deliver effectively on their responsibilities required an upgrading and an emphasis on individual and organizational leadership skills.

A further significant change in the structure of the ABC had materialized as elected members had realized more executive authority within the council (see Figure 10.1 for a diagram of the ABC management structure). An Executive Committee had been established comprising elected members, some of whom

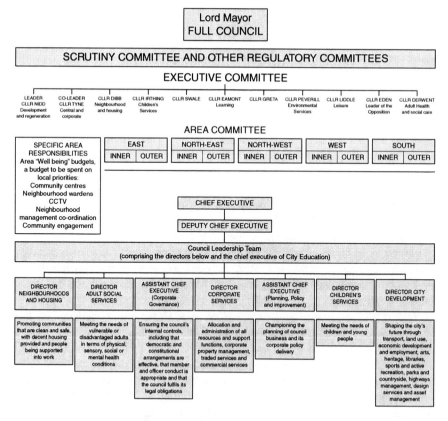

Figure 10.1 Management structure of the ABC.

had been granted additional responsibilities by the full council that comprised portfolios for central and corporate council functions. An additional and significant change was that members had been provided with offices within the civic centre of the council. This had resulted in a fundamental shift in perspective and operation. Before these changes, elected members were required to visit the offices of the specific officer with responsibility for the service under question. Now council officers were required to attend the member in their own office to discuss the issue at hand.

> Perish the thought that councillors would be based on the premises.... It's a massive change in the psychology of the relationship between officers and members. The change came when [name removed] was leader of the council and he got himself ensconced in an old office in the annexe.... He had three comfy seats outside his office and he used to summon the directors to come and see him and have them waiting on the comfy seats for up to half an hour. Now that sends a massive signal as to who is in charge."
>
> (Chief Officer Poulter, City Development)

Furthermore, the role of councillor had provided a small stipend. This grew to a substantial salary for those members with executive responsibilities. The consequence of this is that the councillors were a body of employed elected officials, many of whom required no other additional employment or income. Elected members were much more visible than they had been previously, and this had contributed to a rise in the overall volume of work that officers were required to do in order to support the elected membership, not all of it considered to be valuable.

> Massive change in the culture of the organization creates a lot more work and pressure, and it's nuisance value really.
>
> (Chief Officer Poulter, City Development)

Due to the nature of the hung council and the alliance between two minority parties in forming the ruling administration, directors were required to meet, on a frequent basis, both leaders of the ruling coalition parties. At any one time, one party would be the formal leader while the second was a kind of under-leader. So while Councillor Nidd is the formal leader, Councillor Tyne maintains his position on the executive but acts in a supporting capacity as the formal leader chairs the Executive Committee. The roles of the two alternate every six months, with the co-leader becoming the formal leader and chair of the Executive Committee. The executive responsibilities of both councillors remain the same during their time in office. Councillor Tyne had been in post for a short while following the leadership election, as a consequence of Councillor Wharfe's resignation. Councillor Tyne was not the favourite to win the election, being perceived as being a slightly grey and innocuous candidate. The favourite, a well-known, committed and astute politician, failed in the election; this was attributed to overconfidence and a lack of canvassing.

Leader voices

As a consequence of these circumstances, the impact of the elected membership on the organization and, in particular, the perceived impact on the careers of officers has grown significantly. One officer saw as significant an early posting to the corporate centre that has close links with the elected members:

> I've had quite a lot of [political] exposure – as you do if you're at the corporate centre.
>
> (Chief Officer Poulter, City Development)

Part of the job role, in this case, was that junior officers would be present in a room when members of committees were conducting reviews with more senior officers.

> What was particularly interesting is that we would be in the room for the full session and the directors at the time would come in and out for various items.... And what was particularly interesting was what was said to them while they were in the room and what was said about them after they had gone out.
>
> (Chief Officer Poulter, City Development)

By all accounts, the members at the time were apparently quite candid in their opinions of directors who had been consulted over particular issues. Younger, more junior members must have been affected by such a performance and would have in all likelihood been equally candid outside of the meeting with what they had witnessed.

Although five directorates are acknowledged, the Chief Executive's Unit does comprise a notional sixth department. Although this department is comparatively very small in terms of personnel, a considerable amount of influence is held by the department, which is unsurprising considering that the most senior roles of chief executive, deputy chief executive and assistant chief executive are located in it. The formal reporting lines of the other five strategic directors also end within the Chief Executive's Unit. The role of assistant chief executive appears anomalous within the overall structure of the organization, as it has no direct service responsibility but maintains accountability for internal functions such as communications or legal services.

Many of the initiatives relating to organizational strategy, effectiveness and efficiency are oriented around the office of the assistant chief executive. One of its primary initiatives is the development of a "One Council" ethos. This headline development, from an outside perspective at least, encapsulates many of the other initiatives that are ongoing within the ABC. Forming part of the council's change programme, branded "Smarter Working: Better Results", established in 2006, the notion of "One Council" as taken from the corporate strategic plan (ABC, 2008 p. 11) outlines the importance of the ABC being perceived as, and acting as, a "coherent whole", ultimately leading to cultural change and establishing a more professional corporate organization.

An interesting and alternative view of the authority and influence of the leading population of the ABC came from an unscheduled and informal meeting with the ex-leader of the council. Set in a restaurant in the city, the meeting took place a couple of weeks after the councillor had announced his resignation as leader. During the course of this meeting (due to the ad hoc nature of this meeting notes were only taken after the event and the conversation went unrecorded), a number of insights were volunteered. The ex-leader had felt that his time in office had ultimately proved very frustrating. It was his opinion that the officer corps had become very skilled in dictating the pace of business within the organization. Initiatives that the ruling administration had wanted to implement were, in the opinion of the ex-leader, filibustered and ultimately never saw the light of day. He mentioned that he felt significantly underpowered in his capacity to steer the organization in a direction and that, consequently, he focused on areas that he could affect as opposed to those that he needed to affect. Similarly his motivations for becoming a councillor had been to make the lives of his constituents better; this he found difficult as he became very frustrated by the machinations of the organization and, in particular, the officers whom he regarded as being responsible.

Follower voices

It is evident that the members' influence on the ABC had been quite substantial and not all of this influence should be seen as detrimental when considered from the follower perspective. As reported above, it is clear that officers can specifically benefit in terms of career enhancement from a close association with the elected members. Similar benefits may also occur should the respective officer enjoy a close association with the corporate centre. It is in this arena that blurring occurs as to which grouping may have most impact on the career path of officers. An association with the corporate centre means that geographically the officer is directly associated with the senior, most powerful officers of the authority but, also, through the course of day-to-day interaction, comes into close association with elected officials.

The following statements support the notion that careers may be enhanced by close corporate or political association. One such example concerns the appointment of an individual who had risen to the attentions of the corporate centre as a talented and committed officer.

> He's very talented and he's recognized as such – corporately. So part of it is saying, well here's an opportunity to give him a leg up. He'll be consolidated at that level some time in the future; it's almost a signal to the rest of the world, I suppose, that here's a fast-lane character and don't be surprised when he gets the next chief officer job – which is the way the organization has always worked.
>
> (Chief Officer Maun, City Development)

The individual had been seconded to another role in a different department for three months initially. Under agreements with the union, this is the maximum amount of time a secondment can be allowed without the job role becoming subject to agreed procedures of open opportunity and competitive recruitment.

> He was only supposed to go for three months, and we all knew that was nonsense – it was done to pacify the unions, because they said if he's going to be employed in that role for more than three months it should be advertised. He's been there three months now and there's no sign of him coming back.
>
> (Chief Officer Maun, City Development)

A second example as reported above relates to the apparent fast-track development of the assistant chief executive who had either enjoyed or deliberately cultivated strong associations with the corporate centre and subsequently with the elected membership.

> Yes, he punches way above his weight in this organization, which some of us struggle to understand why, not because he hasn't got ability, but it's difficult to comprehend why, somebody who, before he went to the corporate centre was way below chief officer level and in a very short period of time has risen to assistant chief executive level and is punching above strategic directors. In actual fact, and I struggle to work it out ... sometimes you have a theory, but I don't have a theory in this case.
>
> (Chief Officer Idle, City Development)

The second issue, drawn out of statements made from a leader perspective, is one of frustration. Members and the leader of the council, in particular, reported frustration at not being able to conduct the business of the council primarily due to the obstacles provided by the officer corps. Officers of the council, on the other hand, were aware of this position and shared the frustration,

> We're all trying to operate within a framework, but within that framework be as positive as we can. We take the agenda of the current administration and we say, "Well, within this framework can we help them deliver that agenda." But from a member's perspective that can seem quite rigid.
>
> (Chief Officer Leen, City Development)

The almost inevitable result was that frustrations boiled over into more confrontational behaviour:

> Councillor Liddle has lambasted me on any number of occasions.... "You're here to do what I tell you!" and I say, "No, I'm here to do what the executive board decides to do within the law of the land". And some

members get frustrated with that, even the leader from time to time ... particularly when we appear to be black-hatting.[1]

> (Chief Officer Leen, City Development)

These two statements combined not only demonstrate the awareness of members' frustrations but is also an admission that, occasionally, the officer corps is specifically responsible. At times, members have been able to create a situation where officers have aligned themselves with the members' cause, despite possibly being in opposition to the officer corps.

> For councillors the ideal is that somebody breaks ranks from the officer corps and says I can write that report as you want it.... They weren't highly regarded in the past, but now people feel sorry for them.
>
> (Chief Officer Leen, City Development)

This statement appears to present the relationship between members and officers as an oppositional relationship. It is, however, one of the central contentions of this study that work-based social relations are rarely so straightforward, and that relationships may be both oppositional and symbiotic. Officers are well aware, as demonstrated above, that opportunities for political exposure can be very beneficial to their career prospects. The association involved, however, is not one of pandering to the aspirations of elected members, as this as a course of action may prove detrimental to the individual.

While both elected members and the corporate centre may provide opportunities for career enhancement, the association with the corporate centre, as with the elected membership, also has the potential to limit career prospects.

> There's a feeling now that you're invited to express a view, but it has to be the right view. There's definitely a feeling that you can't speak out – they're not actually listening to chief officers.
>
> (Chief Officer Leen, City Development)

Additionally,

> When I meet my boss I get the impression that she doesn't want me to change. There's an element for all of us about "playing the game." There's almost an element of fear among some of the strategic directors about speaking out because of being seen to be "on message".
>
> (Chief Officer Leen, City Development)

This concept of "playing a game" was mentioned on more than one occasion:

> There's an element for all of us of playing the game, we're all on board with "From Good to Great" officially, but ...
>
> (Chief Officer Poulter, City Development)

and,

> I think how I got on was I realized, I learned, you had to play the game. A
> lot of what we do is playing that game, isn't it?
>
> (Chief Officer Greet, Corporate Services)

The illustration

A meeting with Councillor Nidd

The committee room was fairly typical of the ABC, nondescript and lacking per-
sonalization or identifiable associative features of the authority. Within the room,
Councillor Nidd was positioned at a large wooden round table at the far end of
the room; the director was invited to sit directly opposite, leaving a good three
metres of space between the two. The atmosphere was informal and friendly but
still deferential. Councillor Nidd required reference to himself to be made using
his formal title of "Leader" while in formal office, but as Councillor Nidd when
performing the co-leader role. He was never referred to by his first name, in
marked contrast to Councillor Wharfe, who had tried to promote a level of
informality in his dealings with the senior officers of the authority.

With the usual deferential overtones, ensuring that "place" was maintained,
the meeting was initiated in an affable environment. However, the opening statement of the leader set the tone: "got me on a bad day," he stated, which was followed by an account of the leader's perception of inefficiencies in the director's
fellow officers. The leader came over as being very comfortable in his surround-
ings and also quite arrogant. The director did not particularly acknowledge the
leader's criticisms and did not seek to defend or put in context any other officer's
actions. It was clear, however, that the director and the leader had known each
other for a considerable time and were comfortable in each other's company. No
agenda had been set for the meeting and so the director was left simply to
respond to whatever point the leader wished to discuss next. Usually each topic
was provocatively introduced with an associated action. "What we want to do is
to issue a press statement"; "This won't wait"; "We're more of a "can do"
council ... get it knocked down!"; "Right ... what's next is ..."

The meeting lasted approximately half an hour, during which there were two
substantive points. The first related to the acquisition of more temporary car
parking in the city, which was, first, contrary to the ABC travel strategy and,
second, difficult to achieve due to the planning requirements of the authority. It
was revealed that more parking spaces would raise more revenues for the city.
The second point related to a statue of a prominent individual in the city's
history and the maintenance of the statue, which merged into a further point
regarding the amount of public art in the city generally. Both points raised were
demanding but, despite the practically impossible nature of the two requests, the
director accepted both points with a minimum of concern. Moreover, the director
was happy to appease the leader with a series of acquiescent statements about

"looking at it". This was confirmed later in the day when, during a meeting, the director received a message to call Councillor Nidd and that it was urgent. It was some 40 minutes later that the director returned the call and after the call simply said, "It wasn't urgent, it never is … he already knows this. Happens all the time." The director explained that one of their team had been asked to brief the leader directly on the issue discussed over the phone. The director knew that this briefing had taken place and that the leader had been satisfied with the content. Nevertheless, at a later date, he had sought either to undermine or ignore the advice given, going directly to the director to tread over ground already walked upon.

A meeting with Councillor Tyne

As with Councillor Nidd, the meeting took place at the party offices within the Civic Hall. The meeting room was entirely similar but had a rectangular table and a workstation and desk in the corner. The formal cosiness of the conversation meeting with Councillor Nidd was not replicated here, the director being more guarded and slightly more anxious. The conversation took on a similar line to the meeting with Councillor Nidd earlier in the day.

Councillor Tyne introduced himself, principally for the benefit of the researcher. He was keen to maintain a posture, similar to Councillor Nidd, of being action oriented: "Bring me the hard choices!", "Yeah, do it!" he said, and maintained that he was not in a popularity contest and was prepared to make the hard decisions required, although it was not clear what hard decisions he was referring to. Much of this appeared to be posturing, and Councillor Tyne, like Councillor Nidd, appeared to be slightly out of step with the modus operandi of the council and not fully cognizant of the processes that were put in place to stop officers and members alike from acting in an arbitrary manner outside of the committee structure.

Much of the conversation, as in the meeting with the leader, dealt with operational issues; matters which the organizational structure had empowered chief officers to resolve. There was no prepared agenda, and the director did not know in advance what the issues were to be tabled for discussion. The first point dealt with the ABC's display in a National Flower show, which had been criticized by the local media due to its cost. "Do you believe we had a good story?" the councillor asked. The director answered politically, but was very transparent, making Councillor Tyne aware of a difficulty, risking exposure to criticism. Councillor Tyne appeared to become defensive and, consequently, moved on to a discussion related to income levels from the city's sports centres. The director admitted to a deficit of approximately £1 million but defended it as part of the ABC's commitment to service delivery and wider social agendas related to provision of sport and health. Councillor Tyne suggested that the council should "Close it." The director maintained that the department would bring some options, although it was not clear who should receive and deal with the options, as leisure provision within the city was managed at executive level by Councillor Liddle, a member of an opposition party but part of the ruling coalition. Following a further topic relating to an issue of viability, a topic that had clearly been covered before and on which the director suggested that one of their chief officers should arrange to talk through it, Councillor Tyne concluded the formal part of the meeting by asking, "Is there anything you want to say to me?"

The meeting lasted for less than 20 minutes, but as the director made to leave, Councillor Tyne initiated a further discussion regarding government funds of £14 million in support of cycling. It emerged later that Councillor Tyne was a keen cyclist. He suggested that the city needed a champion to support bids for development capital. "Make sure he wears a helmet", he added. A final issue was raised; it was almost as if the joint leader had dealt with the business of the council from his perspective as leader and was now engaging in more local issues associated with his role as ward councillor. This final issue related to the rights of use of a common within the city boundaries and a building that had been leased to a local group at a favourable rate. The councillor reported that this rate was too high and that the council should seek to help the tenants additionally. He implied a level of expectation and it emerged that the common in question fell into Councillor Tyne's ward. Furthermore, the issue seemed to be incongruent with the previous discussion about reduction in income at sports centres, to which the favoured opinion appeared to be closing the centres; whereas in this context the councillor was seeking a reduction in the cost of a lease, which would lead to a reduction in ABC revenues.

"Playing the game"

The illustration given in the previous section shows how leaders and followers negotiate their relationship with each other. Exposure to leaders within the organization affords potential opportunities to followers. As earlier chapters have demonstrated the tactics leaders used in maintaining their authority, this section is primarily concerned with how followers are able to strengthen their own position by potentially obstructing leaders and establishing their own agency.

This section concludes that leaders and followers perceive their relationship among themselves, and with other parts of the organization, as playing roles in a game. The appreciation and practical application of the rules of the game are important in establishing the position of individual leaders and followers; it is the game, therefore, that comprises an important dynamic in the leader–follower relationship.

The illustration of the two meetings between directors and the leader(s) of the council demonstrates the capacity of followers to maintain their own positions while adhering to the formal requirements of the job role by acquiescing to a more senior colleague. The meeting is polite and deferential but the follower is able to divert any points discussed and, as a consequence, remains non-committal throughout the proceedings. To the observer, the meeting seemed to serve no practical value at all, but appeared to be imbued with political significance as both parties established their positions.

In these illustrations, the director acts from a follower platform but is able to establish the strength of their position as follower; there are other examples given where followers can be demonstrated to possess and protect their significance. For instance, the organization can be shown to hold a bureaucratic apparatus that permeates all levels of the organization. Officers can, at times, find it convenient to utilize the apparatus in an obstructive capacity and as a result to frustrate elected members. It is mentioned above that the outgoing leader of the council felt at times powerless in the face of officers establishing the strength of their own followership and, subsequently, filibustering the designs of the leaders. Officers in turn also recount examples of members' frustrations with officers and processes as being quite vociferous, and suggest that they may at times be deliberately "black hatting". Similarly, it is also possible to see other minor incidents throughout the organization as attempts by the officers to bolster the position of their followership and assert its strength.

It has been remarked how the technical competence of an individual is valued within the authority. This technical skill has additional value when it comes to asserting the strength of a follower's position. In complex issues, the officer with the technical knowledge pertaining to the issue will be able to maintain a position of strength against a less knowledgeable manager or elected member. Many of the issues faced by the ABC require considerable technical knowledge and expertise. This may range from practical engineering construction for capital projects to knowledge related to the statutory powers the ABC may on the one hand utilize and, on the other, restrict. This technical legislative knowledge can also apply to procedural issues. Officers within the Chief Executive's Unit are the experts related to the powers of the authority, its legislative framework and other statutory covenants that dictate the authority's powers of action. The ABC employs a large group of technical legal experts to advise officers and members alike on due process and to militate against the authority exploiting its legal powers illegally. In these examples, followers with a technical expertise are able to maintain the strength of their follower position by virtue of the knowledge they hold.

In some respects the ability of followers to assert the value of their own followership cannot be more clearly illustrated than when considering the example of career progression within the authority. Followers and, in particular, politically motivated and skilled followers recognize that a close association with the premier power bases of the authority can be particularly beneficial in terms of career enhancement. The power bases referred to here are first the elected members and, specifically, the Executive Board which comprises the political power base and the Chief Executive's Unit, which makes up the corporate power base. In the preceding section an example was given of an officer who was seconded to another department. The individual in question had come to the attention of the corporate centre and had been given the chance of a more senior role. This was an indication that this individual would become consolidated as a chief officer when the opportunity arose. Examples like this abound throughout the organization, where officers have risen to great prominence without having to face any form of recruitment process. Surprisingly this is reported to include the chief executive.

In the ABC, followers are given numerous opportunities to establish networks of connections with more senior officers throughout the organization. Skilled followers have the capacity to exploit these openings to build associations with the senior officers they come into contact with. In doing so, they establish their follower position with leaders; these are not limited by their formal superordinate managers. This process of establishing follower position enhances their influence throughout the organization, allowing them further chances to build more association, and so progress their careers within the ABC.

An example of a politically skilled individual rising through the ranks quickly is the assistant chief executive. The rise of this individual has taken many of his colleagues by surprise, but taken from the perspective of an individual establishing their follower position through politically motivated activity such as networking, building alliances and generating influence, the rapid progression through the hierarchy makes more sense. The individual has demonstrated courage or, at least, taken calculated risks in managing difficult projects; has become the name associated with the organization's change programme and business improvement initiatives; and is the external face of the organization, in that the individual is responsible for the marketing and communication function. Much of this has been facilitated by the individual's capacity to develop relationships with officers that are more senior and to cultivate influence through visible and careful self-promotion; the assistant chief executive enjoyed a very close alliance with the deputy chief executive. A relationship that is significant in establishing the strength of the followership position reciprocates by strengthening the status of the leader position of the superordinate manager.

This phenomenon is worth considering further from a wider leadership and political perspective. Mintzberg supports the Aristotelian view of politics and shows that political activity is undertaken when there is a diversity of interest (Mintzberg, 1985). A diversity of interest can be taken as individuals thinking and behaving differently. This difference is likely to arise during times of organizational stress and when the organization is responding to, or attempting to, change. Evidence has been given that the ABC is undergoing a great deal of change through the organizational restructuring brought about by the statutory formation of the Children's Services directorate, the Blairite imposition of strategic commissioning, continued focus and reform from central government, and the operational requirement of resolving a series of "wicked problems". From a normative perspective it is theorized that a heroic leader will emerge to inspire followers along a vision or course of action. Such heroic leaders possess the particular quality of charisma, hence the term "charismatic leader". Ferris and associates (2007) have expressed the view that political skill and charisma appear to be the same thing. This study agrees with this position in part; politically skilled individuals have the capacity to present themselves as effective leaders, charismatic or otherwise. This study would assert that there is closer liaison between leadership generally and political ability than just leadership of the charismatic variety. It is entirely feasible that a diversity of interest permeates every leader–follower relationship. This can be derived from the ambiguity of the role played and the different perspectives associated with being a leader or follower, and leads to the conclusion that political behaviour is not only inevitable in leader–follower relationships, but that it may comprise a substantial part of the whole relationship.

Studies have demonstrated that political activity can either be sanctioned or non-sanctioned (Zanzi and O'Neill, 2001). Sanctioned political behaviour matches the expectations of the organization, whereas non-sanctioned behaviour could lead to questions being raised concerning the suitability of that individual remaining within the organization. It has been asserted here that political skill is important in career progression within the ABC, as achieving a more senior leader position requires leaders to be convinced of a follower's credentials. Mintzberg maintains that the resolution of tensions within organizations may require political behaviour that could be defined as a game (Mintzberg, 1985). A number of statements are presented within the preceding section that support the notion of leaders and followers being engaged in a game.

It may be suggested that the "playing of a game" may not comprise a dynamic on its own, but is a product of the others. The previous dynamics comprise the playing field over which actors are engaged in playing a game. This point has been considered and it is represented by some of the empirical material presented. Yet it is maintained that playing a game represents a different dynamic. This is principally because notions of playing a game conjure up a sense of playing within a set of codified rules. One need only watch people playing games or sport to recognize that games incorporate high elements of gamesmanship outside the rules. For one to assume that those playing the game respect the rules smacks of a sense of Corinthian "fair play" and does not represent the whole picture.

Successful playing of a game involves being perceived to be operating within the rules, ensuring that one is not ejected from the game; this implies an element of risk. In playing the game both sanctioned and non-sanctioned behaviour may be utilized, as a leader may sanction behaviour of a non-sanctioned variety. Furthermore, political activity of a legitimate kind may be utilized to hide and/or legitimize non-sanctioned behaviours. It is the view of officers that being seen to be "on message" is part of the game. The behaviour itself is ostensibly legitimate but its intent is clearly not.

In conclusion, it is evident here that leaders and followers are engaged in a game comprising political activity, a game within which there are inevitably winners such as the assistant chief executive and, regrettably, losers such as the ADS's chief officer. A dynamic within leader–follower relationships is therefore the game, through which followers are able to develop their own follower position, are acknowledged by leaders, and thrive.

Part III

Discussion and conclusions

11 Discussion and conclusions

Leader–follower dynamics

In this chapter the dynamics outlined in previous chapters are viewed through a critical lens to make conclusions about how they influence each other, in order to uncover an influence relationship that is distinct from normative and functional conceptualizations. This section concludes by asserting that the leader–follower relationship as played out within the ABC is significantly focused on the use of political behaviour, to the extent that the influence relationship between leaders and followers, referred to as "leadership", is political. This finding leads to wider conclusions concerning the nature of leadership as a politically constituted phenomenon.

It is recognized that in attempting to outline the dynamic processes between leaders and followers, some of the complexity inherent within the relationship may be lost (Alvesson, 1996). The importance and significance of how the dynamics ebb and flow is dependent upon the actors involved, the experiences they bring to bear, and factors contained within the wider environment. Nevertheless, a broader discussion of the dynamics is necessary, and each dynamic needs to be considered in turn, specifically with reference to the themes of ambiguity, power and politics as developed within the Critical Theory literature.

In the first section we will consider together the dynamics of the "wider environment" and "organizational ambiguity", as they both have a common theme related to the existence of a generally ambiguous environment within which leaders and followers relate to each other. The second section covers the dynamics of "resource allocation and utilization" and "symbiosis", which are situated within a wider thematic framework of power relations within organizations. Finally, the third section discusses the interplay of politics from the perspective of "playing the game" and "political behaviour". We conclude by drawing together the various discussion points to state that this study has gone beyond the normative appreciation of leadership to provide an understanding of leadership in practice, a leadership that is centred on political behaviour.

Ambiguity and the leader–follower relationship

The interpretations of the illustrations provided in earlier chapters assert that the organization under study demonstrates high levels of ambiguity arising from a number of sources. These inherent levels of ambiguity have a powerful influence on the leader–follower relationship, which is in turn demonstrated to be also ambiguously constructed.

Alvesson and Sveningsson (2003b) maintain that issues related to ambiguity within leadership studies have rarely been considered and are therefore subject to neglect. The authors assert that a neglect of ambiguity has produced a level of theorizing in which leadership is seen as something stable, coherent, and fixed. In applying ambiguity to the organizational setting, the authors demonstrate a number of problems related to the conceptualizing of leadership as a real phenomenon, leading to the conclusion that the existence of leadership is dependent upon numerous assumptions and should not be taken for granted.

Ambiguity is taken to refer to persistent uncertainty that cannot be diminished with more information. It has the capacity to create disarray and compromise the purity of leadership as a phenomenon (Alvesson and Sveningsson, 2003b). In a study related to workers in a knowledge-intensive organization Alvesson draws attention to the possibilities of heightened ambiguity (Alvesson, 2001). It is the contention here that the local government setting has much in common with the organization in Alvesson and Sveningsson's study. Ambiguity in the public sector is further corroborated by additional studies, most notably Orr and Vince (2007), Pratchett and Wingfield (1996), and Lee *et al.* (2009).

In common with Alvesson and Sveningsson's study, similar observations concerning levels of ambiguity were made during the current study. In the first instance the very notion of "service" itself is ambiguous, as are the objectives related to the service and, finally, in the evaluation of the value of the service. What comprises a service as differentiated from an enterprise or "arms-length" organization has consequences beyond pure semantics. As an example, the provision of car parking within the city came under increased attention, as this service possesses the capacity to generate huge amounts of cash. As a service, however, it was implied that revenue generation is of secondary importance to the provision of adequate parking for the benefit of the local business economy.

As the notion of service is ambiguous, so is the service objective. This source of ambiguity is exacerbated by the fact that targets are established in the belief that they facilitate better performance (Boyne and Chen, 2007; Lee *et al.*, 2009; Noordegraaf and Abma, 2003) and are, therefore, almost exclusively established by external agencies, particularly the central government. Objectives for local authorities and other public bodies have a tendency to be focused on service provision for areas related to deep-seated societal issues, problems for which the solutions are not immediately available, rendering the problem "wicked", as opposed to "difficult" or "tame" problems where the solutions are more immediate (Grint, 2005b). While the destination is stated, the route to be taken is mostly through uncharted territory. Finally, ambiguity of service is additionally created by the evaluation of those services against the stated targets. Delivery of a target may be a quantified simplification of a problematic issue, the attainment of which either has no impact on the problem at hand or creates additional related problems.

In addition to the three sources of ambiguity related to service, other sources come from the way the organization is being forced to reform its methods of working and its structures. Many of the traditions and working practices of the public sector have been challenged by an extended period of functional reform inspired by the working practices of the private sector (du Gay, 2006). The rapid encroachment of managerialism, as recognized by the New Public Management (Rhodes, 1991), has had the impact of changing the way in which public bodies view themselves and operate. A requirement to operate in two worlds that are typified, on the one hand, by consensus and, on the other, by free markets has created crisis within public bodies (Boyne and Chen, 2007); tensions that contribute to additional ambiguities within the workplace (Pandey and Wright, 2006). This is further exacerbated by the state of flux of the organizational structure, the impositions of concurrent delegation, the operating styles of the directors, and the involvement of the international consulting company, among other factors.

It is our conclusion that the sources of ambiguity cited above are evidence of a highly ambiguous organization, and that these, combined with the ambiguity of leadership, impact on the very nature of leadership itself. It has been suggested that the solutions to "wicked problems" and the effective transformation of public sector services can be found in the initiation and development of effective leadership practices (Bryman, 1996; Performance and Innovation Unit, 2001). Like the New Public Management, the references for these normative leadership practices are those that have been drawn from the transformation of private sector enterprises. It is the contention of public stakeholder groups that these leadership characteristics would possess the same potency when applied to public sector organizations. Questions may be raised concerning the validity of the imposition of normative leadership models, as there are a number of interrelated factors that suggest that leadership as conceptualized by neo-positivistic research methods does not stand up when subjected to critical scrutiny (Alvesson and Sveningsson, 2003b).

As we have drawn comparisons between the public and private sector, it becomes abundantly clear that the paths of both show much in common. In addition to the equivalence in ambiguity as discussed above we have drawn attention to three other resemblances. First, late capitalist organizational change as experienced by the private sector is typified by flexibility, networks, speed, and frequent shifts of strategy and position (Boltansky and Chiapello, 2005). The requirement of more flexible approaches to organizational functioning has paradoxically coincided with a wider array of more detailed techniques aimed at the measurement and monitoring of performance against objective goals (Hassard *et al.*, 2009). This is replicated in the public sector, as reforms aimed at allowing managers to manage is superseded by others designed to ensure managerial productivity (Peters, 2010). A new organizational ideology for the private sector that is flatter, less secure and yet more demanding for managers (Hassard *et al.*, 2009) can be clearly observed within the public sphere (Cooke, 2006).

Second, as the path of reform can be variously interpreted and reconfigured, opinions coalesce concerning the overall pattern of reform, where the presiding influence over organizations passes from insiders, via a requirement to be more sensitive to external voices, to those on the outside. Within the public sector context, public bodies have been required to orientate their gaze toward market-based "third-way" reforms aimed at developing choice and internal markets. Additionally, external agencies have deliberately embarked upon a programme of guiding reform by applying private sector "best practice". Global bodies such as the OECD, the EU and the World Bank have been instrumental in spreading public sector reform through influencing of national governments, giving rise to New Public Management type reforms being observed in countries beyond the traditional reforming heartlands to encompass a truly global reach (Kettl, 2005).

Finally, a widely-held observation and additional similarity between the public and private spheres was initiated by the private sector supplying the exemplar model for the "effective manager" (Peters, 2010). Since the early 1980s, initiated by a raft of publications such as Peters and Waterman's (1982) *In Search of Excellence* and a succession of business biographies extolling individual leadership, the effective manager becomes the visionary leader. Both the public and private sectors have coalesced around the reported values of leadership as a resource essential to the resolution of the complexities and ambiguities to be found in the organizational environment.

It has been shown that officers within the ABC are aware of leadership models and particularly those from a neo-charismatic perspective. It has also been indicated that officers are compelled to adopt and demonstrate leader behaviours outlined by these models and, particularly, those developed by Bass and associates and incorporated by Full Range Leadership Theory (Avolio, 1991; Bass, 1998, 1999; Bass and Avolio, 1994a, 1994b). These compulsions are driven by the expectations of external stakeholder groups and the media, who portray leadership as a demonstration of charismatic and heroic traits, allegedly symptomatic of leaders from neighbouring cities. Internally, respondents have confirmed their understandings of leadership as containing a strong visionary element in accordance with normative conceptualizations. This view has a strong corporate backing, as shown by the "From Good to Great" seminar and the shift in job focus of the director group, whose role has been "elevated" to focus primarily on strategic direction and visioning.

This last point is significant and has been explored in studies by Alvesson and Sveningsson (2003a, 2003b). The authors conclude that while managers may entertain the possibility of performing leadership in a visionary guise, in practice, this remains elusive. Managers attempt to adhere to stated expectations with regard to leadership but fail to be either consistent in their approach or maintain their commitment for any substantial period of time, as the consequence of other pressures referred to as micro-management take over. Within the ABC, managers, and directors in particular, have been reconstituted to be strategic and visionary – to demonstrate leadership. In practice, however, this is elusive, as it is impossible to resist becoming engaged in aspects of day-to-day management for which directors retain accountability. Additional statements collected show that the aspirational claims to adopt leader postures decline and are replaced with cynicism about leadership, highlighting the initial statement as well-intentioned rhetoric.

Alvesson and Sveningsson maintain that the concept of leadership, at least as expressed in its normative guise, is underpinned by strong ideological overtones. Furthermore, upon such considerations, the observable phenomenon of "leaderism" is documented (O'Reilly and Reed, 2011). This leads to the consideration that leadership in practice is neither part of the norm nor typical (Alvesson and Spicer, 2011). The authors' study resonates heavily with those conducted by Calás and Smircich (1991) and Meindl *et al.* (1985), who focus on leadership as seduction and romance, and Gemmill and Oakley (1992) who see leadership as a potentially damaging, socially conspired myth.

The evidence from the ABC is in accord with the aforementioned studies and suggests that leadership in practice contradicts leadership as perceived. While there is a prevailing organizational view about what comprises leadership, the view is not robust enough to withstand either critical scrutiny or observation of practice. Evidence in favour of leadership is, however, almost exclusively expressed as leadership in the first person, with little consideration for other leaders beyond an organizational requirement for greater leadership capacity. Open questioning of leadership theory as a fad by officers is at its most striking when the comments are related to following and the universal rejection of the value of following. Scholars concur that leadership only exists where there are followers (Grint, 2005a; Kellerman, 2008), and an absence of mutually supportive followers would lead to the obvious conclusion that leadership in practice is absent.

An absence of leadership has been noted in other studies, which has led them to refer to "the good, the bad and the ugly" of leadership (Alvesson and Sveningsson, 2003a p. 968). The good represents the aspiration, the bad the practice and the ugly the ambiguity that exists in the clear discord between managers' conceptions of leadership (good) and its practice (bad).

Leadership-specific "ugly" ambiguity may be exacerbated by who or what plays the leader role. The "what" referred to in this case is central government, which has a profound effect on the organization and the leader–follower relationship as practised. A complex array of factors originating from central government's reforming agenda has resulted in an extensive bureaucratic apparatus designed to monitor and investigate public sector performance against stated objectives and ensure internal compliance with process. It has been shown that this reduces the possibilities for leadership, leaving only space for a derivative variant, referred to here as "constricted leadership", to be practised. This in part has been observed by others researching leadership within the public sector, where lack of leadership opportunity results in chief executives of public bodies acting purely as conduits to the politicized centre (Blackler, 2006).

This study has shown that the imposed bureaucratic apparatus of central government, comprised of commensurate levels of rules, regulation, process and procedures, is the leader in the relationship with the ABC. The authority of this leader–follower relationship cascades throughout the organization and, as the bureaucracy of central government is replicated, the ABC, because of its own historical anxieties, embellishes it. The result of this is that the leader–follower relationship between central government and the ABC informs leaders and followers within the organization, and relations are conducted in exclusively transactional terms, which contributes to the aforementioned constricted form of leadership being practised.

The authority of the central government's leader position is hugely potent and influential, as impositions on the ABC are virtually non-negotiable. Targets and processes are underpinned by the allocation of budget, which can be seen as government's primary transactional method of control (Lee *et al.*, 2009). While it may be possible to see the role of government and its impositions as all-encompassing, to assume that the ABC, as follower, acts in a purely compliant manner is incorrect. It is the follower's reaction within what would ostensibly appear to be an autocratic, overtly transactional relationship that indicates ambiguity in two guises. The first is revealed in the responses of followers and the second is in the relative mobility of the identity of leaders and followers. These, within a constricted leadership, further inform the ambiguous nature of the relationship between leaders and followers

It has been theorized, particularly by the school of New Leadership, that followers are a typically compliant population. Leadership is seen as an asymmetrical influence relationship where followers are a blank slate upon which the leader writes the script (Jackson and Parry, 2008). More critical studies such as those by Collinson (1994, 2003, 2005, 2006), conducted from a post-structural perspective, demonstrate that followers are not as compliant or homogeneous a grouping as normative theorists maintain. The studies show that followers, in response to anxieties created by organizational factors, are able to fulfil many different identities. Consequently, they become skilled at manipulating themselves and information, and have the capacity, therefore, to surprise leaders continually with their behaviours (Collinson, 2005).

It has been shown that the transactional relationship with the central government, underpinned by an extensive bureaucratic apparatus, establishes a particular form of social dominion (Morgan, 1997). It is the contention here that the relationship with central government (and other government-funded external agencies) has the capacity to create anxieties in response to performance against objectives and processes. Failure in either capacity may result in facing heavy penalties and/or, in the case of personal failure, may be terminal as far as career is concerned. It has already been shown that another source of ambiguity may be the problems associated with service evaluation, and this has an iterative impact on followers. Ambiguity in evaluation results in anxiety related to performance, which escalates the manipulation of self and information. Successful performance is, to a greater extent, the result of impression management (Alvesson and

Willmott, 2001), a skill that is essential for survival in an ambiguous public sector (Ferris *et al.*, 2007). This, as a process, has been shown to fit the evidence observed in relation to the leader–follower relationship between central government and the ABC, but is equally relevant to those relationships played out within the ABC itself, and gives rise to mobility of identity between leaders and followers.

The ABC has become skilled at fulfilling its follower obligations as far as central government is concerned. Its award of a four-star status is testimony to this. However, in attaining this award, the officers of the ABC "negotiated" their final award in a process that was reported to be quite aggressive at times. It is the contention here that, due to its relationship with central government and its rehearsed position of manipulating data from a follower perspective, officers of the authority are able to move from leader to follower status comfortably. One of the multiple identities available to followers is therefore "leader", thus diminishing the creditability of a theoretical relationship of polarized individuals. The nature of the bureaucratic apparatus, embellished by the authority itself, requires that even the most senior leaders are required to act as followers on a regular basis; subsequently, following is more of a natural state for members of the ABC, as opportunities to lead are rare and are associated with levels of risk due to the ambiguity of evaluation. Leaders/followers therefore can be appreciated as being in "calculable followers" or "informal leaders" states, that are in accordance to a hybrid of the two, with a slight element of bias dependent upon the situation the individual is faced with (Collinson, 2005). Our findings show that, while the identities of followers are variable, the identities of leaders are not fixed either but are heavily dependent upon individual, task and context. This clearly has the capacity to create additional levels of ambiguity.

The possibilities for leadership in such an ambiguous environment appear to go beyond the conceptualizing of normative leadership theory. Leadership, where it exists, is not stable and robust but is vague and contradictory. There is a dichotomy between leadership as a resolver of ambiguity and leadership as a creator of ambiguities.

Our findings corroborate the conclusions of Alvesson (1996) and Knights and Willmott (1992) concerning the importance of ambiguity in organization studies. This study puts ambiguity at the heart of the leader–follower relationship by concluding that the forces of ambiguity impinge upon the roles of leaders and followers alike. In support of Alvesson's study on leadership (Alvesson, 1996), this study provides empirical evidence which demonstrates that the normative guise of leadership is questionable.

Power and the leader–follower relationship

Normative representations of leadership are typically presented in binary terms. Leaders and followers appear at opposite ends of an influence relationship, where leaders are predominantly given voice and followers are rendered silent. Hence, mainstream leadership theories that prioritize leaders have assumed that leaders are powerful while followers are largely powerless. Similarly, such orthodox studies portray power and control as rational forms of organizational authority, while resistance is viewed as abnormal. Where power is considered it is generally conceived narrowly, either as positive, where leaders empower followers, or negatively as a form of coercion (Collinson, 2005). A lack of appreciation of the element of power within the leader–follower relationship has led to calls for the development of models that treat power and subjectivity as integral to the leader–follower relationship (Knights and Willmott, 1992). Through the incorporation of the dynamics of resource acquisition and utilization and symbiosis, we provide substantially more depth to the consideration of power within the leader–follower relationship.

Leadership is rarely viewed as a form of managerial behaviour toward subordinates, but more often as a relationship reflecting harmony and a convergence of interest, and involving, therefore, little or no power or coercion. Indeed, Rost (1993) defines leadership as an influence relationship conducted without coercion toward the attainment of mutually agreed aims. Coercive behaviour and the use of formal authority to establish rewards or punishments are predominantly appreciated as the activities of managers only. It is difficult, however, to imagine a relationship between leader and followers where an element of formal authority is not present. Full Range Leadership Theory, in common with many of the models of the New Leadership approach, does incorporate aspects of power within it in the form of transactional leadership (Avolio, 1991; Bass, 1998; Bass and Avolio, 1994a; Burns, 1978). This dimension of the model is heavily redolent of management relying upon such leader/manager behaviours as correction, negative feedback, reproof, sanctions or disciplinary action (Bass, 2000).

The findings of Alvesson and Sveningsson (2003a, 2003b), replicated also in this study, show that while managers may aspire to act as leaders they rarely achieve their ambition. In its place, managers rely on "bad" management which is closely associated with detail and operations. Given the problems of pursuing good management and leadership, the value of transactionalism appears to have been overlooked in models of leadership (Rickards and Clark, 2006). This creates a number of problems for leadership scholars and, specifically, those advocating neo-charismatic models of leadership, as they fail to account for the obvious management behaviours that are only possible where the leader holds and utilizes power over the superordinate position. The oversight regarding the prevalence and importance of transactional behaviour has led scholars to suggest that power and the asymmetries of the relationship should not be underestimated (Collinson, 2005).

In the previous section the nature of the relationship between the ABC and central government was expressed as one that is based on overt transactionalism, predominantly concerning budget (Lee *et al.*, 2009). Evidence has also been presented to show that the acquisition of and the utilization of additional resources is a core dynamic of the leader–follower relationship, of which budget is the principal resource. Budget as a resource is important, and the element of budget that remains discretionary is of paramount value. Discretionary budget allows for the further acquisition of additional resources beyond the non-discretionary element, as this is already earmarked for the continuance of operations. It should be noted that resources refer to not only financial resources but to other resources that are material – staff, office space, technology – and symbolic resources such as title, access, privilege, status. It has also been noted that the overt, transactionally ordered relationship between the ABC and central government acts as an exemplar method for others and, consequently, the relationship is replicated through the organization. Subsequently, leaders and followers base their transactional relationship on the acquisition of resources, as additional resources equate to increased levels of authority and power.

Generally, those in leader positions hold superior positions within the organization's structure, and this provides the basis within normative studies for assumptions concerning the asymmetrical power relationship between leaders and followers; leaders hold power, followers do not. From a critical perspective, however, these assumptions are less clear than the dualistic perspective alluded to above. Problems occur when power is conceptualized as a possession, as opposed to a social relation, in that the former perspective diverts focus from the interdependence of social relations (Knights and Willmott, 1992).

A small number of critical leadership studies are concerned with the importance of power. Smircich and Morgan (1982) demonstrate how leaders maintain control by "managing meaning" and define situations to meet their own designs. The authors conclude that leaders can create situations in which followers are rendered powerless and, therefore, surrender their own autonomy. Calás and Smircich (1991) contend that leaders "seduce" followers, while Gemmill and Oakley (1992) maintain that leaders produce learned helplessness. These studies show how power is an intrinsic part of the leader–follower relationship, but, by concentrating on the assumed powerful (leaders), they underestimate the potential of follower agency and fail to consider that meaning is co-constructed and that power relations are interdependent (Collinson, 2005); more will be said on this later.

It is the contention here that a leader's "possession" of power over resources cannot be sustained without the shared interpretations of less powerful others (followers). The meanings that sustain power relations have to be negotiated in the first place and need to be continually negotiated, as power cannot be stored, and does not exist independently of its exercise. The importance of this insight is that it highlights the importance of the practice and negotiation of leadership. To this end, power is integral to the dynamic social practice of leadership (Knights and Willmott, 1992).

Leader power and its correlation to control is a well-reported phenomenon, and this study confirms the requirement of and the engagement of leaders in managing power in order to maintain their own position within the organizational structure. In achieving this, leaders are able to exploit ambiguity held within the environment in order to increase their own access to additional resources, thereby developing power or protecting their own power sources. The establishment of the Public Private Partnership Unit (PPPU) business, which was designed to capture available funds through the government's Private Finance Initiative scheme, is an example of an individual doing exactly this to produce millions of pounds in revenue, but to the detriment of the internal Architecture and Design Service. This occurrence is the only example of its type contained within the empirical materials of this study, but other examples were discussed during the course of the fieldwork. It is evident that as the environment possesses many different sources of ambiguity, as outlined in the previous section, the opportunity for leaders to exploit ambiguity is extensive and has become institutionalized.

For leaders, a significant part of the power relationship with followers is the negotiation of position and identity. Leaders and followers reconstitute their identities as "leader" and "follower" on a continual basis, given the ambiguities inherent within the environment, the organization and the leader–follower relationship. As stated earlier, leaders require followers (Grint, 2005b; Kellerman, 2008). The absence of followers, given the ideological significance of the value of leadership, would therefore severely prejudice the continuance of the individual as a leader. This insight further illuminates the leader/control relationship. Leaders may strive for greater control, but there is no definitive regulatory process that gifts to leaders exclusivity of the power mechanisms that maintain control. The concept of utilizing power in order to gain control in an ambiguous environment means that control is never absolute. Similarly, the "powerless" feel no such compulsion to submit to leader designs. The concept of leaders requiring followers demands that following has a proportionate value in the sum of the relationship.

Mumby (2005) observes that, despite a growing literature, many studies prefer to dichotomize power and resistance as being a complete binary opposition that privileges either control or resistance. Such an approach asserts leader control to the detriment of follower agency. This study demonstrates categorically that followers do not follow blindly but are capable of their own designs and of establishing independent agency toward their own objectives.

The issue of followership has been one of contention within leadership studies. Many studies show followership to be the natural consequence of followers responding to the charismatic or transformational behaviours of leaders. Rost (1993) maintains that in the act of following, followers do not engage in any followership but are a complicit part of the leader–follower relationship. Followers can not engage in followership, therefore, but participate fully in the leadership relationship. Explicit, however, within Rost's definition of leadership is that leaders and followers agree mutual aims. This, although possible, is unlikely, given three factors: the ambiguity of the relationship; the transactional nature of leadership; and the agency of followers. Followership in this study refers to independent associated actions that followers are capable of, and may include resistance.

In order to achieve a level of independent agency, followers must be able to attain levels of power for their own uses, and this is clearly evident within the ABC. On a formal basis, followers are able to mobilize employment law protection which, due to the nature of the public sector and its associated levels of accountability and transparency, is relatively robust in comparison to that present in other types of organization. Accounts of grievances and "whistle-blowing" are not uncommon within the organization. These forms of resistance are made more possible by the protections that are afforded by high levels and traditions of unionization, as the union has a long history of resistance practice and is adept at representing the views of the "non-powerful". During the fieldwork, a number of "disputes" were current and in the process of being negotiated. On a less formal basis, followers have designed a range of tactics that have the capacity to impede the plans of leaders. The informal conversation with the outgoing leader of the authority during which he referred to the levels of frustrations he had experienced serves as an example of this. Followers possess power that may advance their own agency and that has in turn the capacity to diminish leader agency.

In addition to this, followers have obtained specific sources of power within the organization. Critical studies look to both material and symbolic forms of resistance. A list of categories of resistance that is comprehensive but not exhaustive has been compiled by Zoller and Fairhurst (2007) and includes such action as ambivalence, resignation, toleration, theft, non-cooperation, sabotage, confrontation, collective action, formal complaints, legal action, or violence, and all are applicable to the ABC.

With reference to the transactional negotiations ongoing within the leader–follower relationship, it is important that the reward of resources matches the expectations of the follower. Where there is a discrepancy in the perceived value of the resource reward, following may be withdrawn. Leaders for their part are aware of the fragility of their own status and will make overtures to followers in order to secure their support. This observance is not limited to the formal leader–follower dyad. Followers gain plenty of exposure and opportunity throughout the organization, in the forms of working parties, focus groups, cross-departmental working, multi-agency initiatives and equality approaches, to align themselves with leaders that are capable of matching the expectations of the follower.

In the case of the ABC, the two most prominent power bases within the authority are the elected members, specifically the executive committee and the corporate centre of the Chief Executive's Unit. The possibilities of aligning oneself with either one of these groups allow the individual the opportunity to acquire considerable resources, both material and symbolic. The result of satisfactory exposure to one of these groups may well mean accelerated promotion through the ranks, and it is the prospect of advancement that fulfils the criteria of the optimum contingent reward bestowed by leaders. It is important to note, however, that this reward is not limited to the gift of immediate superordinate manager or formal leader, and evidence has been provided of leaders undertaking actions, effectively, to transfer competent followers away from colleagues.

Followers have become adept at a whole host of activities that may be utilized to frustrate the designs of leaders, which in the context of the organization may be regarded as resistance. In the case of followers, being concerned with potential penalties and sanctions may result in more subversive or covert forms of dissent. Absenteeism was particularly noted, as was exploitation of flexible working practices. Increases in the awareness and competence of manipulating sophisticated forms of technology provide the opportunity for more covert but deeply subversive forms of dissent. By far the most common form of covert dissent witnessed, however, was the reliance upon procedure to slow, stifle, halt or reject leader plans and initiatives. This allows more junior officers to accommodate senior officers or elected officials while simultaneously concealing their own dissent and acquiring a degree of control. This is particularly relevant where certain officers or groups of officers have specific technical knowledge related to engineering, legislation or process.

The above, however, appears to demonstrate a lack of coherence in the behaviours of followers. On the one hand, they will align themselves to leader designs and, on the other, they are capable of resisting leader overtures in order to locate other leaders that have greater capacity to reward following behaviour. Post-structural analysis of follower relations demonstrates that followers are able to display multiple follower identities or social selves whose actions need to be understood as a consequence of the complex and ambiguous circumstances apparent at the time (Collinson, 2006), allowing followers to engage in behaviours that appear to be inconsistent, contrary and surprising to leaders (Collinson, 2005). As with issues related to power and control, it would be wrong to assume that only followers perform resistance. It has already been demonstrated that significant ambiguity is held in the positions of "leader" and "follower" and in the leader–follower relationship itself. Collinson's view of multiple selves can be extended to incorporate another "social-self", that of leader/follower or follower/leader dependent upon circumstance. This has been referred to earlier as a "calculable follower" or "informal leader" (Collinson, 2005) and occurs when the status of the actor is not clear. As an example, a director in a meeting with the leader of council acts as leader to the department and as follower to the position of the council. In deflecting the instructions of the leader, the director engages in a particular form of leadership recognized by Zoller and Fairhurst (2007) as "resistance leadership" or observance, by being both consenting and dissenting at the same time (Iedema *et al.*, 2006).

In showing that control does not reside exclusively with the leader group and that followers are able to travel a path of their own volition in pursuit of their own objectives, it is important to remember that leader-centric models of leadership have privileged the leader, and follower-centric models should not over-privilege the follower. As leadership has been shown to have romantic connotations (Meindl *et al.*, 1985), scholars should resist the temptation to romanticize the resistant follower. The relationship between the two is symbiotic; leaders and followers negotiate together for a variety of reasons.

The underlying consensus between leaders and followers should not be assumed to be the product of "effective leadership" bringing together a variety of disparate identities to form what has been referred to as a "committed polity" (Knights and Willmott, 1992 p. 766). It is more insightful to appreciate the consent between leaders and followers as precarious, achieved through the exercise of power. The development of shared meaning and joint processes is mediated by relations of power attained through differential access to material and symbolic resources.

Senior ranked officers in the public sector are subject to almost continual monitoring aimed at making them more accountable to various external stakeholders. In addition, the ABC has embellished the externally imposed bureaucratic apparatus so that new forms of control processes significantly affect individual identities. In response to such surveillances and the ambiguities of leader–follower identities particularly evident within public sector bodies, leaders and followers consent both to resisting control mechanisms and acquiring more sources of power. Rather than be appreciated as polarized extremes, as with control and resistance, dissent and consent may be shown to be ineluctably linked within the same ambiguous practices of leadership.

Politics and the leader–follower relationship

In this section we consider the very influential dynamic of politics and political behaviour on the leader–follower relationship by not only building on the findings of others but also illuminating some of the implications of extant studies. Within our analysis we differentiate the political dynamics using Zanzi and O'Neill's (2001) model of sanctioned/non-sanctioned behaviour, but unlike the aforementioned authors, we do not eliminate aspects of political behaviour from our interpretations on the basis of ideological convention.

There is an underlying assumption that the importance of political behaviour in organizational functioning has become more generally recognized in recent years (Ammeter *et al.*, 2002; Mintzberg, 1985; Pandey and Wright, 2006; Pfeffer, 1981; Zanzi and O'Neill, 2001), and so there would appear to be a general consensus concerning the presence of political behaviour in organizations. The rationale for an upturn in the importance of political behaviour appears to be connected to a concerted increase in the competitive nature of business. This observed tendency can be drawn from the interpretations of Pfeffer (1981) in which interdependence, heterogeneous goals and beliefs, and the scarcity and distribution of power, increase the use of politics in organizations (Zanzi and O'Neill, 2001). From a more practical perspective some authors conclude that political skill is a prerequisite for organizational survival (Ferris *et al.*, 2007).

Mintzberg puts forward the view that organizations can be appreciated as political arenas (Mintzberg, 1985), a view shared by a number of academics in the field (Ammeter *et al.*, 2002). In such political arenas, the amount of political activity in evidence is correlated to levels of conflict within the organization. In such cases, the more conflict there is, the more likely political behaviour will be undertaken. This is clearly a destructive process, as Mintzberg maintains: "The purpose of an organization is to produce goods and services, not to provide an arena in which people fight each other" (Mintzberg, 1985 p. 148). Despite this, however, the author concedes that politics within a political arena may deliver organizational benefits and should be judged by its long-term effects on the organization's ability to deliver the mission(s).

Mintzberg (1985) sees politics as representative of one of a number of influence systems within an organization. Among other potential systems is the system of authority that defines formal power allocated on an explicit and legally sanctioned basis. The system of ideology, although implicit, typically represents the norms and beliefs widely held in the organization, and the system of expertise represents power that is certified on an official basis and is sanctioned by a formal authority. A system of politics may be seen as reflecting power that is technically illegitimate. In other words, political behaviour is neither formally authorized nor widely accepted or officially sanctioned.

Mintzberg associates the source of politics directly with conflict in the organization. He defines a political arena as a function of conflict and has created subcategories of arena depending on the intensity and distribution of conflict within the organization. Conflict, as such, is not clearly defined, but the study associates political behaviour further with political games, and these give an indication as to how conflict is being conceptualized.

The outlined games are "played" out between individuals and groups of individuals against other individuals or groups of individuals. The descriptors of the games coalesce around a rationale of establishing power bases, which is the underlying reason for organizational conflict. In such cases political activity comprises supple overlapping activities but is guided by rules both implicit and explicit – the collection of rules, in effect, defines the game. The game is seen as a concrete mechanism in which workers regulate and structure their power relations. Games are, therefore, instruments toward organized action. Engaging in political games defines who the "competitors" are, removes weaker competitors from the field, and serves as a test to demonstrate the potential for leadership (Mintzberg, 1985).

Mintzberg's contention is that conflict is predominantly detrimental to organizational functioning – political behaviour is "typically divisive and conflictive, often pitting individuals or groups against formal authority, accepted ideology, and/or certified expertise, or else against each other". (Mintzberg, 1985 p. 134). Consequently, the eradication or containment of conflict allows the organization to function more efficiently.

This appears to be a simplification of the issues of conflict in organization. Morgan (1997) states that conflicts arise when interests collide, and establishes the basis of conflict as disparity of interest over power. Collinson (2005) draws upon Foucauldian analysis to state that the power/resistance relationship produces political activity as a response to a diversity of interest. Subsequently the attempt to eradicate conflict becomes a futile gesture, as attempts to control will inevitably produce resistance to any controlling actions.

Critical Theory commentators operate from an ideological-political spectrum, within which the existence and extent of political behaviour in organizations is to be expected (Alvesson and Sköldberg, 2005). Political activity can be seen as being inextricably linked to the maintenance and/or undermining of existing power structures; equally, it is the pervasiveness of micro-politics that leads to the politicization of everyday life (Layder, 1994). A definition of political activity that favours one end of a polarized continuum lacks creditability. Politics exists in organizations and within the prevailing power structures. Political activity has the capacity to be both a positive and negative influencer of organizational life. A critical view of politics in organizations would concur with the commentators above as to its occurrence, but would differ in terms of its interpretations, particularly within an influence relationship such as leadership.

The widespread appreciation of political behaviour stands alongside a similar appreciation of the value of organizational leadership. Given that social psychologists have extensively studied power and influence processes in organizations, and that most commentators on organizational studies admit that political behaviours are often a necessary part of organizational functioning and can have profound effects on those exercising them and the effectiveness of organizations, it is surprising therefore that there is little consideration of politics within leadership studies (House and Aditya, 1997 p. 455).

Some of the writers above make close reference to leadership in their assertions about politics. For example, Mintzberg refers to the games played as a training ground to identify potential leaders. Additionally, the author suggests that a test for "good" politics is the long-term effect the politics has on the organization's mission. Clearly, in making these statements the author is referring to a neo-charismatic type of normative leadership in which heroic leaders claim their position after winning at games in order to lead followers in pursuit of mission and visions.

An additional contribution drawn from the study by Mintzberg requires further evaluation from a critical point of view. In asserting that politics may be one of a number of systems of influence, neither formally authorized nor widely accepted or officially certified, Mintzberg directs attention toward the system of ideology held by the organization that represents the norms and values of the organization. It is a contention here that leadership, in its normative sense, comprises part of the system of ideologies of an organization that is formally authorized, widely accepted and officially certified and is, therefore, seen as the virtual opposite of politics as a system of influence.

Ammeter *et al.* (2002), in a study specifically detailing political activity in leadership, define political activity as central to the constructive management of shared meaning. This definition sees political activity as a neutral but inherently necessary activity of organizational functioning. However, the authors agree that political behaviour has the capacity to represent the dark side of management and prefer to focus on political activities that are deemed to be altruistic and, consequently, benefit the greater collective or organization. The authors therefore align political activity alongside the constructive management of shared meaning.

The management of meaning implies the creation of meaning where it does not exist and, consequently, is a vital mechanism for dealing with ambiguity within the organization, providing clarity in terms of the visions and associated plans of the leader. The authors state,

> Hence, many self-serving behaviours that are functional for an individual may be dysfunctional for the group and/or organization. Although such behaviours may serve to protect the individual's reputation and interests, such outcomes are often achieved at the expense of the organization's best interests. To us, such instances of self-serving behaviour do not constitute leadership.
>
> (Ammeter *et al.*, 2002 p. 767)

The attainment or maintenance of control is accomplished through continuing to hold disproportionate levels of power over the non-powerful. It is dangerous, and somewhat naïve, to assume that this is only achieved through legitimate or sanctioned behaviour. Control may be achieved through political behaviour that is not self-serving but, equally, it may be attained through behaviour that clearly is.

In the study by Smircich and Morgan (1982), the authors equate the management of meaning with a management strategy of maintaining control. From a critical perspective, the management of meaning privileges the views of managers/leaders – the powerful over the non-powerful – and thus reinforces the status quo of the organization's power structures through the legitimized vehicle of organizational leadership. Furthermore, it continues to assert the importance and value of leadership. The consequence of this form of iterative process of supplying meaning and asserting its own value eventually develops a state of learned helplessness as outlined by Gemmill and Oakley (1992).

Furthermore, they show that studies on political behaviour are predominantly focused on the top levels of the organizational hierarchy. First, this suggests that political skill is a prerequisite for organizational success, a view shared by other authors (Ferris *et al.*, 2007) and, second, this would appear to suggest that political activity is limited to leaders only. This view of political activity occurring at higher levels of the organization does not fit the observations and interpretations made here. Diversity of interest and imbalances in power require followers to engage in political activity.

To explain the observation made by Ammeter, a number of factors may be considered. First, the majority of leadership studies are conducted on the top teams of organizations. The observation of greater levels of politicking will be a consequence therefore of the general disregard for study on followers. Second, political activity conducted by members of the top levels of the organization is more likely to be legitimized, whereas any political behaviour by followers is more likely to be pejoratively categorized as dissent and resistance. Third, due to the intended target of the political activity and the possible risk of sanction, it is more probable that such activity as conducted by followers will be covert and, therefore, less obvious. Finally, since political will and political skill is linked to career advancement (Ferris *et al.*, 2007), those at the top of the organization structure are by association the most skilled proponents of political activity.

The political is rarely considered in critical theorizing of leadership, possibly because preferences are for an appreciation of deep power structures over relational perspectives (Zoller and Fairhurst, 2007). Where this has been attempted, however, the phenomenon is considered beyond the functional and is taken into the political realm associated with power and control effects. The privileging of leaders in asymmetrical relationships similarly takes no account of the agency of followers, who are capable of manipulating their own identities and information and are able, therefore, to engage in political activity and exploit ambiguity in pursuit of their own goals.

With reference to the empirical materials needed to explore the motivation of leaders and followers when engaged in political activity, it is possible to make explicit the use of politics as a method of gaining control and attaining power (resources). It has been shown that leaders of public sector organizations can be seen as a conduit for a political centre (Blackler, 2006). This in turn constricts the possibilities for leadership internally, as the bureaucratic apparatus of government significantly reduces any bureaucratic discretion (Van Wart, 2003). It has already been shown that budget can be used as a measure of control (Lee *et al.*, 2009) and, therefore, has value as the primary resource as a source of power. Leaders of public sector organizations (followers of the central authority) utilize their political skills, therefore, in attempts to gain more budget. Leaders will practice various forms of impression-management activity and enhance this with campaigns of coalition building, networking and lobbying. As has been asserted earlier, this example of behaviour is copied by politically motivated senior managers who compete for those resources available, material and symbolic. Through these actions, leaders maintain their positions within the organizational hierarchy.

As leaders use impression management and lobbying to gain resources, followers utilize political activity and the same tactics for similar reasons. Specific to their cause is the engagement in transactional negotiations to gain reward in the form of more resources or advancement. Followers will align themselves with leaders who are able to deliver the followers' expectations of reward. Where there is an imbalance between expectations and the reward offered, followers withdraw their support by utilizing forms of covert dissent, which may have the effect of damaging the impression built by leaders. Furthermore, in building alliances and coalitions with powerful leaders, followers are able to protect themselves from others and their attempts to liberate resources.

Leaders and followers negotiate their position within a framework of available resources which credits the individuals involved with associated levels of power in terms of resources held. Leaders need followers, first as a resource and second as the primary method for using and realizing the value of the resources held. Followers need leaders because of the opportunities they make available in resources and career advancement. Additionally leaders and followers engage in political activity to deal with the ambiguity involved in the relationship, the relative position held as "leader" or "follower", and in the evaluation of the services. Public sector ethos (PSE), defined elsewhere as a political institution, provides a supportive coping mechanism for resolving ambiguity under previously constitutive consensual methods of working (Pratchett and Wingfield, 1996). Contributors have highlighted that inconsistent, competing and irreconcilable demands contribute to an ambiguous working framework, which further complicates the constitution of policy objectives into meaningful action (Pollitt, 2000; Kirkpatrick *et al.* 2005). A more aggressive functional managerialism observed as part of the New Public Management has eroded the PSE, leaving in its place greater ambiguity as managers attempt to create consent through rhetorical recourse to visions and missions, and, as stated before, ambiguity provides opportunities for leaders and followers to fulfil their own objectives.

In acting on these motives and others, leaders and followers will use political activity that is both sanctioned and non-sanctioned in order to minimize disturbances to their own endeavours (Ackroyd, 1996). Non-sanctioned political activity is seen within this study as "playing the game". Mintzberg describes political games as being played with an explicit or implicit set of rules, which does not preclude the use of non-sanctioned political activity. Morgan defines gamesmanship as follows: "The organizational game player comes in many forms. Sometimes, he is reckless and ruthless, 'shooting from the hip', engaging in boardroom brawls, and never missing an opportunity to intimidate others" (Morgan, 1997 p. 190). This makes a very clear statement about the possibilities of non-sanctioned political behaviour being utilized. We note that either a follower or a leader in the pursuit of some objective may employ gamesmanship. Where undertaken by the follower, this is done because in all likelihood the behaviour will become legitimized and sanctioned by the leader(s) over time. As such, the rules of playing a game and gamesmanship are a product of the organization's own history. In order to illustrate this, the example provided in Chapter 10 is repeated here, but interpreted from a political perspective.

In this example, the officer establishes a new initiative and is motivated by the power resources it will attract. This is political behaviour that is non-sanctioned but is undertaken in the full knowledge of the deputy chief executive, who would be aware of the damage such action is likely to impart on the Architect and Design Service. The behaviour has become sanctioned and therefore legitimized by the leader. The follower has initially acted independently and has actively sought a leader in achieving his own aims. Leader and follower are acting as part of a designed plan, transactionally negotiated. They have been able to dovetail their aims into those stipulated by central government, and this gives the actions further legitimacy. The new enterprise will be located in the Chief Executive's Unit close to the corporate and political power bases of the ADS. The transactional basis of this and the contingent rewards for the officers are, therefore, transparent. The officer of the PPPU has exploited central government directives and the associated ambiguity inherent in the internal workings of the authority for his benefit and, ostensibly, the benefit of the organization. The officer of the PPPU took a risk and played the game; the ADS chief officer lost. To be resolved in this example are the reasons why the ADS chief officer lost out so badly. This will remain conjecture, but it is possible to surmise that once the issue was raised at CLT, the ADS became a drain on resources and, therefore, the power yielded by the director lessened. The chief officer lost his/her political ally and no other ally could be found; the chief officer was rendered powerless. Time dictated that, eventually, a face-saving solution could be found and that was to offer early retirement.

Politics and leadership

It is no real surprise that within a political arena, given its propensity to attract people with the will to act politically such as the organization under study, political activity is observable. It is, then again, not too much of a leap of imagination to suggest that extensive levels of politics within an organization will filter through its levels to impact upon its basic administrative, managerial and leadership functions.

We have shown how an interdependent relationship exists between ambiguity, power or control, and politics. We have also remarked that it is a surprise that there have been no substantive attempts to make provision for political activity in a theoretical interpretation of leadership, and where this has been attempted it is usually set within the parameters of existing normative understandings of the phenomenon. It is our conclusion that these theories provide a "politicized" theory of leadership and are deficient in stating the true contribution of politics to the leader–follower relationship. We explore this in the following section.

This section comprises two parts. The first deals with the deficiencies of politicized leadership models and the second draws the arguments together to make the substantive conclusion – that the characteristics of leadership as a phenomenon can be interpreted as a politically constructed influence relationship. This has significant impact on our understanding of the nature of leadership as we demonstrate that politics corresponds with leadership.

The treatment of politics in leadership studies

Exponents of the functionalist conceptualization of leadership have not made a serious attempt to incorporate an appreciation of politics into their theoretical models. More recently, studies have been developed to attempt this, yet they have not taken the full implications of politics into consideration. It is considered here that these models are deficient for the following reasons.

First, the limitation of incorporating sanctioned politics into the models of Ammeter and colleagues (2002) portrays only a part of possible political behaviour. The authors have deliberately neglected the inclusion of non-sanctioned political behaviour and gamesmanship, predominantly because the motives of usage do not subscribe to the definition of leadership as conceptualized by the authors. To draw on Alvesson and Svenningsson (2003b), the authors have highlighted the "good" but looked beyond the "bad" of leadership activity. In doing so, the ideology of leadership is maintained and perpetuated. Failing to consider a significant proportion of possible political behaviours fixes the motivations of actors and limits the veracity of the theoretical models subsequently derived. Leadership as an influence relationship takes place between leaders and followers. Therefore, whatever the form or make-up of the influence relationship, it comprises leadership, no matter how distasteful. In addition, by including a proportion of political behaviours and excluding the rest, the authors erroneously add substantially more ambiguity into an already ambiguous relationship. Part of the malaise of leadership studies, as reported in Chapter 2, is as a consequence of definitional shortcomings (Rost, 1993). Leadership studies, in promoting leadership as a powerful transformative force on the one hand, cannot turn a blind eye when faced with the acts of destructive leaders on the other by resorting to claims that one is the result of leaders while the other is the result of "power wielders". Moreover, leadership research serves to perpetuate the sanctity of leadership as a construct, which merely compounds the issue of what those who study leadership have to say about leadership in practice.

Second, those studies that attempt an investigation into politics and leadership appear reluctant to go beyond their own narrative to draw conclusions contained within their studies. Ferris *et al.* (2007) remark upon the similarities between charisma and political skill but insist on maintaining the integrity of the two constructs. Other studies, such as the frequently cited and influential study by Mintzberg (1985), state that political games are the proving ground and, consequently, a developmental programme for leaders. The study by Ammeter strips away the antecedents and the consequences of politics by asserting that "we hoped to depict that politics are simply a fact of life in organizations, and demonstrate how leaders need to work on and through others to accomplish personal and organizational goals" (Ammeter *et al.*, 2002 p. 788). A ready association between leadership and politics is apparent in the literature, and yet the implications of the association are never theorized and the construct's independence of the leadership phenomenon remains unchallenged.

Finally, the sanctity of leadership as a construct is maintained by the ideological foundation of the phenomenon. A determination to produce a leadership that is easily assimilable for a ready public is not representative of empirical evidence. A critical appreciation of leadership suggests that there are wider and deeper structures inherent within the leader–follower relationship that remain unexplored. The ambiguity of the leader–follower relationship in terms of constitution and practice has been negated by an apparently socially constructed need to believe in the value of leaders and what they practice. Establishing the ideological position of the value of leadership demands that possible alternatives are opposed without considering that the very act of opposing these alternatives is an act of control that reduces the genuine possibility of transformation (emancipation).

Appreciating politics as leadership

In evaluating possible alternatives not constrained by the ideology of leadership and the normative guises perpetuated by that ideology, we consider arguments that confirms a correspondence between leadership theory and politics to the extent that there is a direct correspondence between leadership and political behaviour. To make this correspondence, the Full Range Leadership Theory model (FRLT) (Avolio, 1991; Bass, 1998; Bass and Avolio, 1994a), as the apex of the neo-charismatic appreciation of leadership, is used to demonstrate how its constituent parts can be reinterpreted from a political perspective to display a clear correspondence between the two concepts.

The FRLT model as outlined by Bass (1999) comprises two parts, the first being the more frequently considered and apparently more potent component of transformational leadership (Burns, 1978), and the second, the comparatively neglected unit of transactional leadership. In reinterpreting the model, we consider each constituent part of the two components in turn. The larger component part of transformational leadership is made of four separate dimensions, the first of which is refereed to as "idealized influence or charisma". Ferris and colleagues (2007) have already noted the close association between politics and this component part of transformational leadership. If the ability to inspire people to action toward an articulated vision or set of mutually reinforcing and integrative goals is what is generally meant by charisma, then charisma and political skill would appear to be quite closely related. Bass and Avolio (1994b) consider the construct to be more akin to establishing oneself as possessing referent power and setting a behavioural example.

From a political perspective, this appears to correspond directly to impression management engaged, not least, as a response to possible ambiguities inherent in evaluating the success of work undertaken. Impression management requires leaders to build an aura, supported by followers of their capability, and success, either material or symbolic. From a practical perspective, leaders attempt to establish favourable impressions through reliance on rhetoric about visions and missions while inwardly aspiring to be leader-like, yet practicing micro-management and exploiting ambiguity (Alvesson and Sveningsson, 2003a).

The next component part to consider is referred to as "intellectual stimulation" and is appreciated by Bass and Avolio (1994b) as providing encouragement to break with the past and establish new ways of doing things. From a political perspective, this construct corresponds to generating appeal for superordinate initiatives such as promoting and aligning with a compelling vision, in all likelihood the vision of a leader, established through rhetoric and reinforced with transactional benefit (see below). In engineering this, ambiguity in the organization may be used by the leader to prevent unpopular but promising alternatives from being prematurely eliminated. Additionally, of course, the leader may also be able to use ambiguity to promote a favoured course of action over other potential alternatives.

The third component part is referred to as "inspirational motivation" and is perceived by Bass and Avolio (1994b) as potentially overlapping with idealized influence or charisma. The leader provides simplified and symbolic emotional appeals in support of the goals. Symbolic associations and displays of authority and power designed to promote confidence in the leader and the associated direction correspond closely with inspirational motivation. In the case of the ABC, the use of internal corporate promotions such as "From Good to Great" may be an example of the type of political activity referred to here, as may be the use of external agencies and, particularly, the use of well-known individuals or celebrities to engender support and commitment for forthcoming activities. More potent is the symbolism involved in rhetoric when engaging individuals in a compelling future related to an initiative, event or vision, particularly where counter-normative behaviour may be utilized or staged to demonstrate personal commitment and risk. Problems may arise in the building of consensus concerning the vision; inevitably, some groups or individual followers will be adversely impacted by the proposed changes and will resist accordingly to the associated controlling mechanisms and their own personal displacement. In such cases, the leader may utilize coalition-building skills and enhance personal status and impression through the negotiation of opposing discourses and by creating space for the novel exploitation of ambiguity.

In the final component part of Bass's (1999) FRLT model, leaders employ "individualized consideration", in which followers are treated individually with a concern to meet their needs and requirements. Tactics to achieve this, as recommended within the model, incorporate such activities as the delegation of assignments to enhance learning opportunities, the tailoring of individual feedback, and the use of coaching and mentoring. This component part of leadership corresponds well to the political interpersonal skill of making the individual appear important. There is a critical limiting factor to be considered when contemplating this dimension, principally the factor of time. An individual operating as leader cannot engage in such an activity with a large population. It therefore becomes expedient that leaders select subordinates toward whom they will bestow individual time and consideration. This is entirely congruent with our findings, and the assertion that leadership corresponds to politics and political behaviour. Evidence has been provided of individuals, both leaders and followers, aligning themselves with others with the intention of securing and maintaining more resources and power. In effect, this activity of alignment by the notional leader can be considered as coalition-building through effective networking among powerful constituents, the process of which renders impotent alternative discourses and paths of direction. The leader must engage in a form of selection among the most powerful/influential followers through which agreement can be arrived at, the associated process of aggregation delivering the chosen (leader's) vision as the most appropriate course of action to be followed. The leader, then, is required to individualize their approach and convince the followers of the course of action. In doing this, of course, the leader may find the application of transactional tactics to be more readily applicable and effective.

In this instance transformational behaviours were not commonly observed. The various component parts of transformational leadership coalesce into a conceptual singularity related to vision promotion, coalition building and impression management. Furthermore, other academics have noted that managers aspire to be visionary or leader-like but fail in their aspirations (Alvesson and Sveningsson, 2003a).

Aspirational leadership is replaced by a focus on day-to-day management activities, which has the capacity to promote more ambiguity; this may be utilized by the manager in promoting a particular vision.

The transactional components of the FRLT model may be, somewhat pejoratively, appreciated as less potent than its transformational counterparts; nevertheless they are considered valuable. Despite the implicit importance of this part of the FRLT model, however, the explicit conclusions must be that these component parts of neo-charismatic leadership behaviour are less important than those outlined above. Specific to this is the likely credence that transformational elements of the model subscribe more to the ideology of leadership as opposed to leadership in practice. Transactional components can be more aligned with "good management" behaviours and therefore seen as more in keeping with differing managerial discourses, without acknowledging the similarities and the close relationship that leadership has with managerial ideologies. Given the evidence presented here, our conclusion is that transactional elements have been underplayed. The possibility of this pattern of leadership behaviour being replicated elsewhere as a consequence of contextual and environmental factors that are evident in other organization types and sectors should not be underplayed in turn.

There are three components that are situated within the transactional half of the FRLT model, the first of which is referred to as "contingent reward". This part of the model rewards followers for attainment of performance targets. The key responsibility of the leader is to clarify the direction or participate in what the follower needs to do. Corresponding to this from a political perspective are the rewards given to followers for continued support; providing that the rewards meet expectations, the follower will engage in the objectives of the relationship. This is a principal mechanism for establishing control of and gaining consent from the follower group, and is particularly effective in impression management. The rewards referred to primarily involve access to additional resources, either material or symbolic, with the most effective contingent reward being related to advancement and/or the opportunities for advancement. Where there is a gap between expectation and reality, the follower will resist, most probably in a covert way, given the potential sanctions enforceable by the senior manager.

The second transactional element is known as "management by exception" and may involve either active or passive behaviours. These are tactics that directly involve the leader in resolving issues related to poor performance and failure to meet expectation. Management by exception is the clearest opportunity for the leader to engage in political behaviours that may be considered non-sanctioned. Management of performance can be tackled through the formal bureaucratic apparatus or, alternatively, through more conspicuously aggressive behaviours such as the use of intimidation and innuendo. The choice for the leader is dependent upon the effect of the failure in performance. Should this result in exposing an impression carefully nurtured and protected by the leader, it is more likely the leader will attempt to bring about the removal of the follower. In this way, the politically capable leader practices discretion based upon follower capabilities and their capacity to gain resources. The use of discretion is absent in the models of neo-charismatic theorizing and appears contradictory to the aforementioned transformational behaviours such as individualized consideration. While the use of discriminatory tactics may not comply with leadership theory, it is entirely congruent with a political theory of leadership.

The final part of the model, referred to as "laissez-faire", may be more accurately described as a sub-behaviour of management by omission or as a non-behaviour, as it is principally characteristic of the leader taking no action in the face of issues. The precise formulation of this sub-factor has not been fully conceptualized in leadership models (Rickards and Clark, 2006) and is not dealt with in any depth by normative conceptualizations of leadership. Despite the lack of consideration in theories of this kind, and the admission that leaders should take a more proactive stance (Bass, 2000), as with other less "glamorous" behaviours that do not accord to an ideological view of leadership, these behaviours should nevertheless not be sidelined. Failure to fully conceptualize these types of behaviours is more a testimony to the veracity of the models that incorporate them, as opposed to making meaningful statements about the importance of the behaviour. Within a political model of leadership, the appearance of passive or laissez-faire behaviour gains more significance when appreciated as a deliberate but politically motivated activity not dissimilar to the political art of filibuster. Furthermore, viewing leadership as a political construct gains additional merit due to its enhanced explanatory capacity.

Laissez-faire leadership therefore may be appreciated as pertaining to one or a combination of three probable scenarios. The first concerns the leader utilizing his/her position of power to take the time to consider the available courses of action. In doing so it would not be unreasonable to believe that leaders may decide to sit on their current position and observe how things unfold. A prescient leader may observe the path of an opportunity, only declaring an interest when the outcome was assured. Alignment with principal agents, coalition-building and networking are critical in obtaining material resources (information) and symbolic resources (goodwill, alliances) that illuminate the most suitable path to be taken. Furthermore, it is entirely within the compass of actions that a leader may seek to become a follower so as to obtain a position that would allow for the effective exploitation of the opportunity at a later date. What is pertinent here is that an individual can employ their own agency, within the remit of their own position of power, in order to obtain more resources to subsequently enhance their own position of leader among their own group of new and existing followers.

In the second scenario, the leader weighs up the benefits and disadvantages of forming a new alliance, or breaking or withdrawing from a previously negotiated alliance. The principal difference in this scenario is that the agent seeks to either exploit the ascendancy of another agent in the organization, or distance himself or herself from the decline of another. This is the exploitation of agency, as opposed to the exploitation of opportunity provided by the organizational environment as outlined in the previous scenario. It is entirely congruent that a leader may decide to employ the time resources at their disposal before deciding upon a course of action. The resolution of such a course of action and apparent consequences remain a matter of conjecture and should be more appreciated within the ebb and flow of human relations. A dramatic break with a sponsor or leader who maintains residues of power and resources may result in that sponsor or leader employing them directly or withdrawing support when it is needed. Mistakes in such arenas may prove to be detrimental and career-ending.

A third possible scenario concerns the array of possible actions to be undertaken when seeking to enhance positions of power and resources. As stated earlier, and drawing upon the analysis of Zanzi and O'Neil (2001), some leader actions may be perceived as sanctioned. However, other actions may be non-sanctioned but should not be ignored as part of a leadership influence relationship, as such omissions merely serve to maintain the ideology surrounding the leadership construct. We have stated earlier that this form of conceptualizing leads to a politicized form of leadership more in accordance with the sanctity of the leadership as opposed to any form of leadership empirically observed. Apparently passive behaviour may seem inconsequential with regard to the leadership actions on display but has a vital currency with regard to the thought processes leaders undergo in evaluating the benefits and risks involved in the considered action. Laissez-faire behaviour or the absence of activity may be better understood therefore as the space between sanctioned and non-sanctioned behaviour.

Additionally, as in the example given in Chapter 10, the activities of a manager may officially be regarded as non-sanctioned but may continue nonetheless as other more senior managers are complicit in the behaviour. In such cases the reward, in terms of resource and power allocation, is perceived to be significant enough to warrant the continuance and tacit support of the potentially questionable behaviour. Over time, and clearly dependent upon the outcome of such activities, the previously non-sanctioned activities are sanitized and presented as legitimate by more senior members of the organization. The period of ostensibly laissez-faire behaviour by senior members of the organization may on the surface be perceived as an absence of activity, but this should not be taken to mean that activity at deeper levels is not being undertaken. In such accounts, leaders may attempt to utilize the agency of followers in order to build their own access to resources and power and strengthen their individual leadership position.

An appreciation of the role of followers in such scenarios not only serves to highlight the importance of followers but also significantly undermines the diminished status reported within existing normative models of leadership. During periods of perceived laissez-faire activity, followers may be utilized as the primary consenting agent. Here the possible exploitation of a follower by the nominal leader to deliver enhanced resources should be acknowledged. However in such cases there are many risks to both parties. For them both to survive and acquire more resources requires that they act and support in tandem – symbiotically.

First, a follower could be coerced into undertaking non-sanctioned behaviour as the leader seeks to distance him/herself from that action, but this might provide too many risks for both parties. Without a negotiated position of mutual benefit, a coerced follower is more likely to engage in resistances in order to nullify the designs of the leader, and may ultimately withdraw their followership possibly to the detriment of the leader. Mutual benefit however does not suggest any degree of proportionality; in such scenarios it is probable that the power and resource ratio between the two is at least maintained but also could widen.

Second, in order to fully engage in discrete behaviour the follower might require that a more senior member of the organization acknowledge that the initiative is either ongoing or being considered. In doing this, the less powerful creates an accord with the more powerful, hoping to mitigate any possible risk associated with the proposed activity. Consequently, the follower must seek active agreement from a leader for the initiative in order to follow a path of action but also to secure any gains in resources. In such instances it is the follower that is the primary active agent and the direction of intent emanates from the follower toward the leader, making possible a change, or hybridization, of identity and/or role.

Finally, in making a proposal for a path of activity, a skilled follower will consider tacitly at least an array of important environmental factors before deciding on a particular leader to bring the initiative to. In doing this, the follower is predominantly concerned with ensuring that their proportion of the resources to be acquired is neither lost nor procured by others. In such scenarios, important political skills come into play, such as the selection of the leader and the judgment of their likely response, the presentation of an initiative in line with organizational and/or individual aims, the manipulation and presentation of information over time, and the alignment of other interested parties in support of the initiative. Such activities belie the supposed acquiescent nature of the follower and serves to illuminate the extent of follower agency and the commensurate political skills required in following. Thus followers can be seen to be not only "playing the game" but also contributing to its rule-book.

Conclusions

In presenting a more critical view of the leadership phenomenon we have not discounted the possibility of an extraordinary human candidate able to match up to the skills and characteristics, ostensibly at least, of the charismatic or heroic leader capable of large-scale organizational transformation; however, we suggest such an individual to be extremely rare. First, we question the interpretation of leader behaviours as being too functionally orientated and incapable of accommodating deeper organizational dynamics of ambiguity, power and political behaviour. Second, we disagree with such conceptualizations of leadership predominantly because the supposed classification of activities is so very infrequently observed. Moreover, while the claims of the neo-charismatic models may possess a degree of credibility acquired through a normative research platform, these claims must be countered therefore by evidence taken directly from the field.

Additionally, in wishing to engage in a critical study of the phenomenon under observation, we are readily open to other alternative interpretations of the data we have presented here. Accordingly, adherence to the truth criterion of positivistic research work was never an objective of this particular study. More pointedly it is our design and intention to widen the scope of contributive voices, and we would not wish to render impotent those voices that may be different but widely informative. We would openly ask other researchers to view their own work through a critical lens and consider its political implications and ramifications. The dynamics outlined here provide an iterative basis for exploration and further illustration, a process that may facilitate the uncovering of leadership as a phenomenon and provide a deeper understanding of the mechanisms beyond that achieved through a normative conceptualization of leadership.

We have identified and explored a variety of interlacing dynamics from a critical platform and shown how those dynamics are strongly related and influenced by aspects of ambiguity, power/control and politics. The organization in this case is highly ambiguous, exhibiting sources of ambiguity from factors related to concepts of service; definition of and practicalities of operation, aims and objectives; and the evaluation of effectiveness (Alvesson, 2001). We have deduced from this, given the approximation in environment and context, that the substantive conclusions of our work have an applicability beyond the original organization analysed.

We outline a literature that demonstrates that the scope of the "New Public Management" is no longer confined to its traditional heartlands. The drive for reform within the public sector(s) has a global reach, and the pace of reform has accelerated in the light of the macroeconomic environment and the austerity measures imposed upon public bodies. Furthermore, we have considered the antecedents of the public sector reforms to show that they can be seen as both a continuation and extension of contemporaneous developments within the private sector, considered to be the leitmotif for public sector reform (du Gay, 2006). This unidirectional process of exchange shows little sign of abating, despite the view that the private sector is undergoing similar challenges posed by a new spirit of capitalism (Boltansky and Chiapello, 2005): of a need for increased flexibility and efficiencies in order to cope with a dynamic, globalized and technologically enhanced environment constrained by unprecedented levels of privately held debt (Keen, 2011). This in term leads to greater workloads and the intensification of management roles throughout corporations (Hassard *et al.*, 2009). In organizations typified by project working, a high level of complexity, and knowledge intensity, high levels of ambiguity exist in objective, measurement and process (Alvesson and Sveninngson, 2003b), giving rise to an interpretive space within which ambiguity may be exploited strategically (Eisenberg, 1984). It is our contention that organizations that accord, to a greater or lesser extent, to this typology are not in the minority, but can be found in the public, private and charitable sectors, and are not restricted to any geographic locus of operation but can be found in the majority of the economically productive world.

By interpreting real-life leader and follower activities in an organizational context typical of the above outline, we have developed a series of substantive propositions applicable to an array of differing complex environments. Our conclusions drawn from the empirical materials have allowed for more radical propositions to be made about the leader–follower relationship, and this in turn allows, specifically, the discrediting of the normative view of leadership and of followers as a homogeneous and docile grouping.

In the first instance, followers are neither a compliant nor a docile grouping of individuals. They can be skilled manipulators of self and information and have the independence to search out their own objectives. Followers have an independent agency not considered in traditional conceptualizations of leadership. Second, the relationship between leaders and followers is almost entirely transactional. The transformational element of leadership influence is shown to be a very fragile construct, mired in rhetoric and very difficult to practice. The transformational proportion of leadership has been institutionally overplayed to the detriment of understanding related to the transactional components of the leader–follower relationship. The laissez-faire component of transactional leadership should not be appreciated as "an absence of activity" but more an array of political activities constituted by purpose. Third, the study of leadership as an influence process cannot be approached as something that is only defined in positive terms. This comprises only half of the leadership conundrum, as certain behaviours can result in something that is perhaps not intended but, ultimately, is demonstrated to be detrimental and damaging. Calling it something else to protect leadership is tantamount to conceptual eugenics. Fourth, leader and followers do not act in convenient dyads or controlled groups; they act in organizational settings that are ambiguous and prescriptive in equal measure. The historical context is crucial in appreciating the impact the wider environment may have on the behaviour of leaders and followers. Lastly, leader and follower relationships incorporate a substantial amount of politicking, political behaviour and gamesmanship. We conclude that leadership behaviours correspond directly to political activity as observed within the organizational context.

Within this specific case we have outlined a number of working practices, both historically entrenched and added recently as a response to the ongoing reform of central government, that contribute sources of ambiguity. Additionally, the leader–follower relationship is shown to be variable and transitory, providing additional sources of ambiguity (Alvesson and Sveningsson, 2003a), and in turn, counterintuitively contributing to those "wicked problems" instead of supplying resolution as designed. Ambiguity in this instance is derived from the gap between aspiration and practice and from the conflation of identities referred to here as "informal leaders" and "calculable followers" (Collinson, 2005). While these two identities are practiced, they are not the only identities that leaders and followers are able to adopt dependent upon time and context. Multiple identities create ambiguities and anxieties that allow for the manipulation of information by individuals enabling a variable presentation of their social-selves (Collinson, 1994, 2003, 2006). Thus followers are able to act in ways that are consistently surprising to leaders, and by association other followers. This is also observed in leaders, who are able to act in ways that cause alarm among followers. Both leaders and followers are able to, and have been observed to, discriminate either favourably or unfavourably through their actions towards others.

Aspects of power and control, when filtered through organizational ambiguity, promote a form of leadership relationship that is heavily dependent upon a transactional bias. Transactionalism was confirmed to be comprised of a governing emphasis upon the negotiation of rewards in turn for support and performance; leaders offer reward in turn for follower support. Followers require leaders, as they are the primary holders of resources; conversations concerned with resources comprised the central focus of the reward structure as outlined above. The acquisition and utilization of material and symbolic resources was of central importance to both leaders and followers, as this equates to the application of meaningful power and control throughout the organization (Collinson, 2005).

It has been traditional to view issues of power and the establishment of control as a tactic associated exclusively with the management population. Control is very closely related to issues of consent and is seen as a fundamental contribution to the efficient workings of the organization. However, as attaining consent is considered a legitimate practice of leaders, so displays of dissent are seen as illegitimate. Organizations can be seen as a network of interrelated power structures and relationships and, as power is present, so will resistance be in close attendance. The favouring of one constituent part of the leadership relationship over the other, however, underestimates the possibility of independent follower agency, and fails to take into account that meaning is co-constructed and that power relations are interdependent (Knights and Willmott, 1992). Leader and followers were shown to act jointly in the pursuit of additional resources and the acquisition of more power and control. In asserting their own agency, followers will withdraw their support for leaders where there is a discrepancy between the reward and the expectations of probable reward. As a consequence of the withdrawal, followers may engage in covert forms of dissent and will utilize opportunities to align with other leaders.

Acting as a bridge between ambiguity and the acquisition and maintenance of power is the skilled and deliberate employment of political behaviour by both leaders and followers, who are able to utilize the ambiguity inherent in the organizational system and the leadership relationship to develop better access to more resources. Political behaviour is utilized in equal measure by both leaders and followers, and this is seen as a naturally occurring product of diversity of interest as leaders and followers negotiate their relative position within a framework of available resources. Both populations are shown to be capable of politically exploiting levels of ambiguity within the environmental context in pursuit of independent goals. Despite apparent opposing views, political behaviour is shown to be a normal part of organizational functioning that includes both sanctioned and non-sanctioned political behaviour (Zanzi and O'Neill, 2001). Non-sanctioned political behaviour should be considered as more relevant to the production of gamesmanship (Mintzberg, 1985; Morgan, 1997). The rules of games are created as a product of historical precedent, as the actions of leaders may legitimize non-sanctioned behaviour over time. Nevertheless, there is an important and undervalued element of risk-taking in practicing non-sanctioned games.

Despite an increase in the appreciation of political behaviour as an organizational feature, there are very few attempts to relate politics to leadership (House and Aditya, 1997), regardless of both being, demonstrably and primarily, influence relationships. Moreover, a number of studies have alluded to a relationship between leadership and politics (Ammeter *et al.*, 2002; Ferris and Judge, 1991; House and Aditya, 1997; Mintzberg, 1985), without fully developing the conclusions at the risk of polluting the purity of leadership as a construct.

In opposition to these traditionally held views concerning leadership, the framework of dynamics outlined above necessitates that the nature of leadership, as theorized in its normative guise, be challenged. Our analysis shows that leadership is neither a static nor a robust phenomenon and it is asserted here that much of the conceptualization of leadership is derived from a system of ideology that asserts the value of leadership as benign organizational feature contributing to organizational performance. Such views contribute in turn to the notion of leadership as an asymmetrical influence relationship in which leader voices are shown to prevail, rendering followers as blank slates to be influenced by leaders. As such, the very concept of leadership contributes to the imbalances of the influence relationship, favouring as it does the opinion and perspectives of leaders, who are in turn able to use the status of leadership to assert their own levels of control. Lack of effective consideration of politics in leadership appears to be symptomatic of leadership as part of an ideology as, where politics is considered in studies, the political behaviour practiced is unquestionably posited in a favourable light. In such cases, the theoretical development comprises a "politicized" theory of leadership designed primarily to fit the expectations of the dominant ideological architecture.

We have set out a challenge to the ideological foundations of leadership and in doing so we have outlined a politically relevant interpretation of the dynamics of the leader–follower relationship that balances the power relations inherent in that relationship and provides a framework for enhanced explanatory enquiry of leader–follower relations in a wide variety of organizational settings. Many of the constructs contained within normative leadership models correspond directly to constructs of observable political behaviour, and so we conclude that there is a direct correspondence between leadership and political behaviour. In moving to a more widely developed model of political leadership, research needs to be conducted into a variety of leadership contexts, organizational environments and sectors and expanded to incorporate additional leadership models, including those less functionally oriented. We are not concerned with a political theory of leadership as a unidirectional model of leadership. It is neither leader-centric nor follower-centric but is concerned with a politically relevant interpretation of the dynamics of leader–follower behaviours that are linked in multiple ways. The hope is that this interpretation will stir additional scholarly enquiry aimed at a fuller appreciation of politics in leadership and a deeper, more contextualized appreciation of the leadership phenomenon itself.

Glossary

Audit Commission A notionally independent, government-funded body charged with auditing services across local government.

Concurrent delegation Delegative power granted to the authority's chief officers, commensurate to that of directors, as part of the restructuring of the authority.

Critical Theory A perspective for undertaking social research, drawn from and influenced by the Frankfurt School. Seen as a natural extension of a movement initiated in the Enlightenment, Critical Theory attempts to uncover asymmetrical power relations and political inadequacies. It therefore has a strong emancipatory intent.

Full Range Leadership Theory A neo-charismatic model that breaks leadership down into transformational and tracsactional components (see Figure 2.1).

Leadership An influence relationship between leaders and followers.

National Audit Office A national body established to audit the accounts of government bodies.

New Leadership school A collective name for the group of theories that grew up in the 1980s, portraying the leader as someone defining organizational reality through the articulation of a vision that reflects his or her conception of the mission of the organization and the values that underpin it.

New Public Management An epoch of public sector reform in which public sector bodies were reformed under direct influence from the experiences and practices of the private sector (James, 2004; Rhodes, 1991).

Normative leadership Leadership models that have been derived from a functionalist research paradigm. The most significant are the neo-charismatic models, which include the Full Range Leadership model (Avolio *et al.*, 2004; Bass, 1999; Bass and Avolio, 1994a) and the Public Sector Model of Transformational Leadership (Alimo-Metcalfe and Alban-Metcalfe, 2001; Alimo-Metcalfe and Alban-Metcalfe, 2004) (see Chapter 2 for a wider explanation).

One Council The vision of the ABC under which all services and processes would fall into a single corporate identity and requiring that service delivery should be equal across all service users.

Public sector ethos   The existing paradigm of administration as endorsed and practised by public sector employees. The PSE can be appreciated as a political institution in its own right, determining practice and highly resistant to change (Pratchett and Wingfield, 1996) (see Chapter 3 for a wider discussion).

Strategic commissioning   The strategy of developing relationships with external bodies in order to provide council services. This strategy was directly informed by New Labour's policy of following a "third way" between markets and traditional methods of public sector working.

Unitary authority   A local authority where the county council and district council bodies have been merged to form one administrative body responsible for all local government functions within a geographic area.

Notes

2 Leadership studies

1 It is acknowledged that psychodynamic theories have interpreted the role of leader and follower. However, due to the scope of this study, this literature will not be covered here; for a more comprehensive approach, the reader is directed to Gabriel, 1999, and Stech, 2004.

5 The challenge to leadership and the dynamic of ambiguity

1 The title of this seminar should not be confused with the book of the same name by Collins (2001). While it may be possible that there is an awareness of Collins's work, it was never referenced during the course of the "From Good to Great" seminar or at any other subsequent meetings and conversations concerning the seminar.

6 The limitations to leadership and the dynamic of the environment

1 Later in the week a telephone call with Councillor Wharfe revealed the nature of the meeting, in that he had felt compelled to tender his resignation as leader of the party, and with this was to stand down as leader of the council after the successful completion of a party leadership election. Later a more full account of the conversations and the reasons leading up to them were given, but for the sake of anonymity and to avoid betraying a confidence, little can be recounted here, save for the fact that the machinations of the political leadership illustrate the pervasive nature of politicking and of political tactics throughout the ABC. This lends credence to the description of the ABC as a Political Arena (Mintzberg, 1985).
2 These acronyms were noted in the fieldwork notes. It is not clear what they refer to, and they are included here as being indicative of the type of language used by both the assessors and the officers of the ABC.

7 The negotiation of leadership and the dynamic of resource acquisition

1 In order to maintain the confidentiality of the officers in this section, the comments will remain anonymous. The respondents were above Service Manager level.

9 The negotiation of leadership and the dynamic of politics

1 The ADS is situated in a separate building from the main civic hall. While from the exterior the building looks austere and foreboding (it is a Victorian school building),

the inside is very corporate. The reception lobby is quite different in presentation from other buildings within the authority. It represents contemporary design, with lots of chrome and aluminium on show. Present also are examples of successful projects and literature, including internal and external marketing materials. From this aspect, the ADS does not look like it is part of the ABC; it has established its own visual identity.

Inside, however, the presentation of the organization changes, as the workspace and desks are entirely representative of those seen in the rest of the authority: functional and depersonalized.

10 The agency of followers and the dynamic of game playing

1 This appears to be a reference to the negative perspective one adopts in Edward de Bono's *Six Thinking Hats* (2000).

Bibliography

ABC. 2007. Corporate Leadership Team Minutes. July.

ABC. 2008. Council Business Plan 2008 to 2011. March.

Ackroyd, S. 1996. Organization contra organisations: Professions and organizational change in the United Kingdom. *Organization Studies*, 17(4): 599–621.

Ackroyd, S., Kirkpatrick, I. and Walker, R. M. 2007. Public Management reform in the UK and its consequences: A comparative analysis. *Public Administration*, 85(1): 9–26.

Alimo-Metcalfe, B. and Alban-Metcalfe, J. 2001. The development of a new transformational leadership questionnaire. *The Journal Of Occupational and Organizational Psychology*, 71: 1–27.

Alimo-Metcalfe, B. and Alban-Metcalfe, J. 2004. Leadership in public sector organizations. In Storey, J. (ed.) *Leadership in Organizations: Current Issues and Key Trends*, London: Routledge, 173–202.

Alimo-Metcalfe, B. and Alban-Metcalfe, J. 2005. Leadership: Time for a new direction. *Leadership*, 1(1): 51–71.

Alvesson, M. 1993. *Cultural Perspectives on Organizations*. Cambridge: Cambridge University Press.

Alvesson, M. 1996. Leadership studies: From procedure and abstraction to reflexivity and situation. *The Leadership Quarterly*, 7(4): 455–485.

Alvesson, M. 2001. Knowledge work: Ambiguity, image and identity. *Human Relations*, 54(7): 863–886.

Alvesson, M. and Deetz, S. 2006a. *Doing Critical Management Research*. London: Sage.

Alvesson, M. and Deetz, S. A. 2006b. Critical Theory and postmodernism approaches to organizational studies. In Clegg, S. R., Hardy, C., Lawrence, T. B. and Nord, W. R. (eds) *The Sage Handbook of Organization Studies*, 2nd edn, London: Sage Publications, 255–283.

Alvesson, M. and Sköldberg, K. 2005. *Reflexive Methodology: New Vistas for Qualitative Research*. London: Sage.

Alvesson, M. and Spicer, A. 2011. *Metaphors We Lead By: Understanding Leadership in the Real World*. Oxford: Routledge.

Alvesson, M. and Sveningsson, S. 2003a. Good visions, bad micro-management and ugly ambition: Contradictions of (non-) leadership in a knowledge-intensive organization. *Organization Studies*, 24(6): 961–988.

Alvesson, M. and Sveningsson, S. 2003b. The great disappearing act: Difficulties in doing "leadership". *Leadership Quarterly*, 14(3): 359–381.

Alvesson, M. and Willmott, H. 2001. *Making Sense Of Management: A Critical Introduction*. London: Sage.

Alvesson, M. and Willmott, H. 2002. Identity regulation as organizational control: Producing the appropriate individual. *Journal of Management Studies*, 39(5): 619–644.

Ammeter, A. P., Douglas, C., Gardner, W. L., Hochwarter, W. A. and Ferris, G. R. 2002. Toward a political theory of leadership. *The Leadership Quarterly*, 13(6): 751–796.

Anderson, B. 1986. Thatcherites who would prefer to be without Thatcher, *The Spectator*.

Antonakis, J. and Atwater, L. 2002. Leader distance: A review and a proposed theory. *The Leadership Quarterly*, 13(6): 321–357.

Ashforth, B. A. and Lee, R. T. 1990. Defensive behavior in organizations: A preliminary model. *Human Relations*, 43: 621–649.

Ateş, H. 2004. Management as an agent of cultural change in the Turkish public sector. *Journal of Public Administration Research and Theory*, 14(1): 33–38.

Aucoin, P. 1990. Administrative reform in public management: Paradigms, principles, paradoxes and pendulums. *Governance*, 3(2): 115–137.

Aucoin, P. 1996. Designing agencies for good public management: The urgent need for reform. *Choices: Institute for Research on Public Policy*, 2(4): 5–19.

Avolio, B. 1991. *The Full Range of Leadership Development: Basic and Advanced Manuals*. Binghampton, NY: Bass, Avolio and Associates.

Avolio, B. J., Gardner, W. L., Walumbwa, F. O., Luthans, F. and May, D. R. 2004. Unlocking the mask: A look at the process by which authentic leaders impact follower attitudes and behaviors. *The Leadership Quarterly*, 15(6): 801–823.

Baimyrzaeva, M. 2011. Kyrgyzstan's public sector reforms: 1991–2010. *International Journal of Public Administration*, 434(9): 555–566.

Barzelay, M. 2001. *The New Public Management: Improving Research and Policy Dialogue*. Berkeley, CA: University of California Press.

Bass, B. M. 1960. *Leadership, Psychology and Organizational Behavior*. New York: Harper.

Bass, B. M. 1985. *Leadership and Performance Beyond Expectations*. New York: Free Press.

Bass, B. M. 1998. *Transformational Leadership: Industrial, Military, and Educational Impact*. Mahway, NJ: Lawrence Erlbaum.

Bass, B. M. 1999. Two decades of research and development in transformational leadership. *European Journal of Work and Organizational Psychology*, 8(1): 9–32.

Bass, B. M. 2000. The future of leadership in learning organizations. *Journal of Leadership and Organizational Studies*, 7(3): 18–40.

Bass, B. M. and Avolio, B. 1990. *Transformational Leadership Development: Manual for the Multifactor Leadership Questionnaire*. Palo Alto, Calif: Consulting Psychologists Press.

Bass, B. M. and Avolio, B. J. (eds) 1994a. *Improving Organizational Effectiveness through Transformational Leadership*. Thousand Oaks, CA: Sage.

Bass, B. M. and Avolio, B. J. 1994b. Shatter the glass ceiling: Women may make better managers. *Human Resource Management*, 33(4): 549–560.

Berg, E., Barry, J. and Chandler, J. 2004. New public management and higher education: A human cost? In Dent, M., Chandler, J. and Barry, J. (eds) *Questioning the New Public Management*. Aldershot, UK: Ashgate.

Beyer, J. 1999. Taming and promoting charisma to change organizations. *The Leadership Quarterly*, 10(2): 307–330.

Bin Sarat, M. 2009. Strategic planning directions of Malaysia's higher education: University autonomy in the midst of political uncertainties. *Higher Education*, 59(4): 461–473.

Blackler, F. 2006. Chief executives and the modernization of the English National Health Service. *Leadership*, 2(1): 5–30.

Bolman, L. G. and Deal, T. E. 1991. *Reframing Organizations: Artistry, Choice, and Leadership*. San Francisco: Jossey-Bass.

Boltansky, L. and Chiapello, E. 2005. *The New Spirit of Capitalism*. London: Verso.

Boyne, G. A. 1996. The intellectual crisis in British public administration: Is public management the problem or the solution? *Public Administration*, 74(4): 679–694.

Boyne, G. A. 1998. *Public Choice Theory and Local Government: A Comparative Analysis of the UK and the USA*. London: Macmillan.

Boyne, G. A. and Chen, A. A. 2007. Performance targets and public service improvement. *Journal of Public Administration Research and Theory*, 17(3): 455–477.

Bresnen, M. J. 1995. All things to all people? Perceptions, attributions and constructions of leadership. *The Leadership Quarterly*, 6(4): 495–513.

Brown, J. 1998. Public service ethics – A viewpoint from local government. *Public Money and Management*, 18(1): 7–8.

Bryman, A. 1992. *Charisma and Leadership in Organizations*. London: Sage.

Bryman, A. 1996. Leadership in organizations. In Clegg, S. R., Hardy, C. and Nord, W. R. (eds) *Handbook of Organization Studies*, London: Sage, 276–292.

Burns, J. M. 1978. *Leadership*. New York: Harper and Row.

Burrell, G. and Morgan, G. 1979. *Sociological Paradigms and Organizational Analysis*. London: Heinemann Press.

Cabinet Office. 1982. *Efficiency and Effectiveness in the Civil Service*. Whitehall: The Stationery Office.

Cabinet Office. 1999. *Modernising Government*. Whitehall: The Stationery Office.

Cabinet Office. 2000a. *Citizens First*. Whitehall: The Stationery Office.

Cabinet Office. 2000b. Freedom of Information Act. Whitehall: The Stationery Office.

Cabinet Office. 2001. Prime Minister calls for stronger public sector leadership. Available at: www.cabinetoffice.gov.uk/strategy/news/press_releases/2001/010327.aspx.

Calás, M. B. and Smircich, L. 1991. Voicing seduction to silence leadership. *Organization Studies*, 12(4): 567–602.

Campbell, C. and Wilson, G. 1995. *The End of Whitehall: Death of a Paradigm*. Oxford: Blackwell.

Chakraverti, S. 2004. Management mantras: Make way for new public administration. *Times of India*, July 14. Available at: http://timesofindia.indiatimes.com/articleshow/msid-776848,prtpage-1.cms (accessed 12 August 2010).

Chaleff, I. 2003. *The Courageous Follower: Standing Up to and For Our Leaders*. San Francisco: Berrett-Koehler.

Chemers, M. M. 2003. Leadership effectiveness: Functional, constructivist and empirical perspectives. In van Knippenberg, D. and Hogg, M. (eds) *Leadership and power: Identity processes in groups and organizations*: 5–17. London: Sage.

Christensen, T. and Lægreid, P. (eds) 2007. Transcending New Public Management: The Transformation of Public Sector Reforms. Aldershot, UK: Ashgate.

Clarke, J. and Newman, J. 1994. The Managerialisation of public services. in: Clarke, J. A., Cochrane, A. and McLaughlin, E. (eds) *Managing social policy*. London: Sage.

Clarke, J., Gewirtz, S. and McLaughlin, E. 2000. Reinventing the Welfare State. In McLaughlin E. Clarke J. Gewirtz S. (eds) 2000. *New managerialism, new welfare?* London: Sage.

Cole, M. 2001. Local Government Modernisation: The Executive and Scrutiny Model. *The Political Quarterly*, 72(2): 239–245.

Collingridge, D. 1992. The management of scale: Big organizations, big decisions, big mistakes. London: Routledge.

Collins, J. 2001. *Good to Great: Why Some Companies Make the Leap ... and Others Don't*. London: Random House.

Collinson, D. L. 1994. Strategies of resistance: power, knowledge and subjectivity in the workplace. In Jermier, J. M., Knights, D. and Nord, W. (eds) *Resistance and Power in Organizations*. London: Routledge.

Collinson, D. L. 1999. Surviving the rigs: Safety and surveillance on North Sea oil installations. *Organization Studies*, 20(4): 579–600.

Collinson, D. L. 2003. Identities and insecurities: Selves at work. *Organisation*, 10(3): 179–189.

Collinson, D. L. 2005. Dialectics of leadership. *Human Relations*, 58(11): 1419–1442.

Collinson, D. L. 2006. Rethinking followership: A post-structuralist analysis of follower identities. *The Leadership Quarterly*, 17(2): 179–189.

Common, R. K. 1998. Convergence and transfer: A review of the globalisation of New Public Management. *International Journal of Public Sector Management*, 11(6): 440–450.

Common, R. K. 2001. *Public Management and Policy Transfer in South East Asia*. Aldershot: Ashgate.

Conger, J. A. and Kanungo, R. A. 1987. Toward a behavioral theory of charismatic leadership in organizational settings. *Academy of Management Review*, 12: 637–647.

Conger, J. A. and Kanungo, R. A. (eds) 1998. *Charismatic Leadership in Organizations*. Thousand Oaks, CA: Sage.

Cooke, H. 2006. Seagull management and the control of nursing work. *Work, Employment and Society*, 20(2): 223–243.

Damiran, T. and Pratt, R. 2006. Institutional change in Mongolia: Balancing waves of reform. In Ahmad, R. (ed.) *The Role of Public Administration in Building a Harmonious Society*, selected proceedings from the Annual Conference of the Network of Asia-Pacific Schools and Institutes of Public Administration and Governance (NAPSI-PAG).

Dansereau, F. 1995. A dyadic approach to leadership: Creating and nurturing this approach under fire. *Leadership Quarterly*, 6(4): 479–490.

de Bono, E. 2000. *Six Thinking Hats*. London: Penguin.

Deem, R. and Brehony, K. J. 2007. Management as ideology: The case of "New Managerialism" in higher education. *Oxford Review of Education*, 31(2): 217–235.

Dent, M. 2005. Post-New Public Management in public sector hospitals? The UK, Germany and Italy. *Policy and Politics*, 33(4): 623–636.

Dent, M., Chandler, J. and Barry, J. (eds) 2004. *Questioning the New Public Management*. Aldershot, UK: Ashgate.

Denzin, N. and Lincoln, Y. (eds) 1994. *Handbook of Qualitative Research*, 2nd ed. Thousand Oaks, CA: Sage.

Digman, J. M. 1990. Personality structure: Emergence of the five factor model. *Annual Review of Psychology*, 4, Palo Alto, CA Annual Reviews: 417–440.

Dionne, S. D., Yammarino, F. J., Howell, J. P. and Villa, J. 2005. Substitutes for leadership, or not. *The Leadership Quarterly*, 16(1): 169–193.

du Gay, P. 2006. Machinery of government and standards in public service: Teaching new dogs old tricks. *Economy and Society*, 35(1): 148–167.

Dunleavy, P. and Hood, C. 1994. From old public administration to New Public Management. *Public Money and Management* 14(3): 9–16.

Dunleavy, P., Margetts, H., Bastow, S. and Tinkler, J. 2005. New public management is dead – long live digital-era governance. *Journal of Public Administration Research and Theory*, 16(3): 467–494.

Efficiency Unit. 1988. *Improving Management in Government: The Next Steps*. London: HMSO.

Eisenberg, E. M. 1984. Ambiguity as strategy in organizational communication. *Communication Monographs*, 51: 227–242.

Eisenberg, E. M. 2007. *Strategic Ambiguities: Essay on Communication, Organization and Identity*. Thousand Oaks, CA: Sage.

Elcock, H. 2005. Public administration: British art versus European technocracy. *Public Money and Management*, 25(2): 75–81.

Enteman, W. F. 1993. *Managerialism*. Madison, WI: University of Wisconsin Press.

Fairholm, G. W. 1993. *Organizational Power and Politics: Tactics in Organizational Leadership*. Westport, CT: Praeger.

Farrell, C. M. and Morris, J. 2003. The "neo-bureaucratic" state: Professionals, managers and professional managers in schools, general practices and social work. *Organization*, 10: 129–156.

Ferris, G. R. and Judge, T. A. 1991. Personnel/human resources management: A political influence perspective. *Journal of Management*, 17(2): 447–488.

Ferris, G. R., Treadway, D. C., Perrewé, P. L., Brouer, R. L., Douglas, C. and Lux, S. 2007. Political skill in organizations. *Journal of Management*, 33: 290–321.

Fiedler, F. E. 1967. *A Theory of Leadership Effectiveness*. New York: McGraw-Hill.

Flinders, M. 2005. The politics of public–private partnerships. *The British Journal of Politics and International Relations*, 7(2): 215–239.

Flynn, N. and Strehl, F. (Eds) 1996. *Public Sector Management in Europe*. London: Prentice Hall.

Fry, G. K. 1988. The Thatcher government: The financial management initiative and the "new civil service". *Public Administration* 66(2): 1–20.

Gabriel, Y. 1999. *Organizations in Depth*. London: Sage.

Gemmill, G. and Oakley, J. 1992. Leadership – An alienating social myth. *Human Relations*, 42(1): 13–29.

Giroux, H. 2006. "It was such a handy term": Management fashions and pragmatic ambiguity. *Journal of Management Studies*, 43(6): 1227–1260.

Glaser, B. G. and Strauss, A. L. 1967. *The Discovery of Grounded Theory: Strategies for Qualitative Research*. New York: Aldine.

Golden-Biddle, K. and Locke, K. 1993. Appealing work: An investigation of how ethnographic texts convince. *Organization Science*, 4(4): 595–616.

Goldfinch, S. and Wallis, J. 2010. Two myths of convergence in public reform. *Public Administration*, 88(4): 1099–1115.

Greenaway, J. 1995. Having the bun and the halfpenny: Can old public service ethos survive in the new Whitehall? *Public Administration*, 73(3): 357–374.

Greenleaf, R. K. and Spears, L. C. 2002. *Servant Leadership: A Journey into the Nature of Legitimate Power and Greatness* (25th anniversary edn). New York: Paulist Press.

Greenwood, R. and Hinings, B. 2006. Radical organizational change. In Clegg, S. R., Hardy, C., Lawrence, T. B. and Nord, W. R. (eds) *The Sage Handbook Of Organization Studies*, 2nd ed., London: Sage Publications, 814–842.

Grint, K. (ed.) 1997. *Leadership: Classical, Contemporary and Critical Approaches*. Oxford: Oxford University Press.

Grint, K. 2005a. Problems, problems, problems: The social construction of "leadership". *Human Relations*, 58(11): 1467–1494.

Grint, K. 2005b. *Leadership: Limits and Possibilities*. Basingstoke, UK: Palgrave Macmillan.

Hales, C. 2002. Bureaucracy-lite and continuities in managerial work. *British Journal of Management*, 13: 51–66.

Hardy, C. and Clegg, S. R. 2006. Some dare to call it power. In Clegg, S. R., Hardy, C., Lawrence, T. B. and Nord, W. R. (eds) *The Sage Handbook of Organization Studies*, 2nd ed., London: Sage Publications, 754–775.

Haslam, S. A. and Platow, M. J. 2001. The link between leadership and followership: How affirming social identity translates vision into action. *Personality and Social Psychology Bulletin*, 27(11): 1469–1479.

Hassard, J. McCann, L. and Morris, J. 2009. *Managing in the Modern Corporation: The Intensification of Managerial Work in the USA, UK and Japan*. Cambridge: Cambridge University Press.

Hencke, D. 1998. Jobcentres fiddled the figures. *Guardian*, 8 January, 2.

Hersey, P. and Blanchard, K. H. 1984. *Utilizing Human Resources: Management of Organizational Behavior* (3rd edn). Englewood Cliffs, NJ: Prentice-Hall.

Hesse, J. J. Hood, C. and Peters, B. G. (eds) 2003. *Paradoxes of Public Sector Reform: Soft Theory and Hard Cases*. Berlin: Duncker and Humblot.

HM Treasury Spending Review 2010. London: The Stationery Office.

Hodgson, D. 2005. "Putting on a professional performance": Performativity, subversion and project management. *Organization*, 12(1): 51–68.

Hogg, M. A. 2001. A social identity theory of leadership. *Personality and Social Psychology Review*, 5(3): 184–200.

Hoggett, P. 1996. New modes of control within the public sector. *Public Administration*, 74(1): 9–32.

Hood, C. 1995. The "New Public Management" in the 1980s: Variations on a theme. *Accounting Organizations and Society*, 20(2/3): 93–109.

Hood, C. 1996. Exploring variations in public management reform of the 1980s. In Bekke, H., Perry, J. and Toonen, T. (eds) *Civil Service Systems in Comparative Perspective*. Bloomington and Indianapolis, IN: Indiana University Press.

Hood, C. 1998. *The Art of the State*. Oxford: Clarendon.

Hood, C. and Peters, G. 2004. The middle aging of New Public Management: Into the Age of Paradox? *Journal of Public Administration Research and Theory*, 14(3): 267–282.

Hood, C., Scott, C., James, O., Jones, G. W. and Travers, A. 1999. *Regulation Inside Government*. Oxford: Oxford University Press.

Hough, L. M. 1992. The "big five" personality variables – construct confusion: Description versus prediction. *Human Performance*, 5: 139–155.

House, R. J. 1971. A path-goal theory of leader effectiveness. *Administrative Science Quarterly*, 16: 321–339.

House, R. J. 1977. A 1976 theory of charismatic leadership. In Hunt, J. G. and Larson, L. L. (eds) *Leadership: The Cutting Edge*, Carbondale, IL: Southern Illinois University Press, 189–207.

House, R. J. and Aditya, R. N. 1997. The social scientific study of leadership: Quo vadis? *Journal of Management*, 23(3): 409–473.

Hughes, O. E. 1998. *Public Management and Administration: An Introduction*. Basingstoke: Paulgrave Macmillan.

Hunter, D. J. 1996. The changing roles of health care personnel in health and health care management. *Social Science and Medicine*, 43(5): 799.

Iedema, R., Rhodes, C. and Scheeres, H. 2006. Surveillance, resistance, observance: Exploring the teleo-affective volatility of workplace interaction. *Organization Studies*, 27(8): 1111–1130.

Jackson, B. and Parry, K. 2008. *A Very Short, Fairly Interesting and Reasonably Cheap Book About Studying Leadership*. London: Sage.

James, W. 2004. The impact of corporatisation and national competition policy: An exploratory study of organisational change and leadership style. *Leadership and Organization Development Journal*, 26(4): 289–309.

Jermier, J. M. and Kerr, S. 1997. Substitutes for leadership: Their meaning and measurement: Contextual recollections and current observations. *The Leadership Quarterly*, 8(2): 95–101.

Johnson, G. and Scholes, K. 1999. *Exploring Corporate Strategy* (5th edn). Harlow: Prentice Hall.

Jones, C. (1993) The Pacific challenge: Confucian welfare states. In Jones, C. (ed.) *New Perspectives on the Welfare State in Europe*. London: Routledge.

Jones, L. R. and Thompson, F. (eds) 1999. *Public Management: Institutional Renewal for the Twenty-first Century*. Volume 10: *Research in Public Policy Analysis and Management*. Greenwich, CT: Jai Press.

Kan, M. M. and Parry, K. W. 2004. Identifying paradox: A grounded theory of leadership in overcoming resistance to change. *The Leadership Quarterly*. 15(4): 467–491.

Keen, S. 2011. *Debunking Economics: The Naked Emperor Dethroned*. London: Zed Books.

Kelemen, M. and Rumens, N. 2008. *An Introduction to Critical Management Research*. London: Sage.

Kellerman, B. 2004. *Bad Leadership: What is it, How it Happens, Why it Matters*. Boston, MA: Harvard Business School Publishing.

Kellerman, B. 2008. *Followership: How Followers are Creating Change and Changing Leaders*. Boston, MA: Harvard Business School Publishing.

Kelley, R. E. 1992. *The Power of Followership: How to Create Leaders People Want to Follow, and Followers Who Lead Themselves*. New York: Doubleday.

Kelley, R. E. 2004. Followership. In Burns, J. M., Goethals, G. R. and Sorenson, G. J. (eds) *Encyclopaedia of Leadership*, Oxford: Sage Reference, 504–513.

Kerr, S. and Jermier, J. 1978. Substitutes for leadership: Their meaning and measurement. *Organization Behaviour and Human Performance*, 22: 374–403.

Kettl, D. F. 2005. *The Global Public Management Revolution* (2nd edn). Washington: Brookings Institution Press.

Kets de Vries, M. 2003. *Leaders, Fools and Impostors* (2nd edn). New York: iUniverse, Inc.

Kirkpatrick, I. 1999. The worst of both worlds? Public services without markets or bureaucracy. *Public Money and Management*, 19(3): 7–14.

Kirkpatrick, I. and Ackroyd, S. 2003. Transforming the professional archytype? The New Managerialism in UK social services. *Public Management Review*, 5(4): 511–531.

Kirkpatrick, I., Ackroyd, S. and Walker, R. 2005. *The New Managerialism and Public Service Professions: Changes in Health, Social Services and Housing*. Basingstoke, UK: Palgrave Macmillan.

Knights, D. and Willmott, H. 1992. Conceptualizing leadership processes: A study of senior managers in a financial services company. *Journal of Management Studies*, 29(6): 761–782.

Kudo, H. 2003. Between the "governance" model and the policy evaluation act: New public management in Japan. *International Review of Administrative Sciences*, 69(4): 483–504.

Kuhn, T. S. 1990. *The Structure of Scientific Revolutions* (3rd ed.). Chicago: University of Chicago Press.

Labour Party. 1982. *Labour's Programme.*

Laughlin, R. C. 1991. Environmental disturbances and organizational transitions and transformations: Some alternative models. *Organizational Studies*, 12 (2): 209–232.

Layder, D. 1994. *Understanding Social Theory.* London: Sage.

Lee, J. W., Rainey, H. G. and Chun, Y. H. 2009. On politics and purpose: Political salience and goal ambiguity of US federal agencies. *Public Administration*, 87(3): 457–484.

Light, P. 1993. *Monitoring Government: Inspectors-general and the Search for Accountability.* Washington, DC: Brookings.

Local Government Act. 1988. c29, 1 June. London: The Stationery Office.

Local Government Changes for England Regulations 1994. 1994. 12 April.

Local Government, Planning and Land Act. 1980. c65, 13 November. London: The Stationery Office.

Locke, R. R. and Spender, J. C. 2011. *Confronting Managerialism: How the Business Elite Threw our Lives out of Balance.* London: Zed Books.

Lord, R. G. and Brown, D. J. 2001. Leadership, values and subordinate self-concepts. *The Leadership Quarterly*, 12(2): 133–152.

Lord, R. G., DeVader, C. and Alliger, G. M. 1986. A meta-analysis of the relation between personality traits and leadership perceptions: An application of validity generalization procedures. *Journal of Applied Psychology*, 3: 402–410.

Lundin, S. C. and Lancaster, L. C. 1990. Beyond leadership: The importance of followership. *Futurist*, 24: 18–22.

Manning, N. 2000. The legacy of the New Public Management in developing countries. *International Review of Administrative Sciences*, 67: 297–312.

Maor, M. 1999. The paradox of managerialism. *Public Administration Review*, 59(1): 5–18.

Margetts, H. 1999. *Information Technology in Government: Britain and America.* London: Routledge.

Meindl, J. R. and Ehrlich, S. B. 1987. The romance of leadership and the evaluation of organizational performance. *Academy of Management Journal*, 30: 91–109.

Meindl, J. R., Ehrlich, S. B. and Dukerich, J. M. 1985. The romance of leadership. *Administrative Science Quarterly*, 30: 78–102.

Mintzberg, H. 1982. If you're not serving Bill and Barbara, then you're not serving leadership. In Hunt, J. G., Sekaran, U. and Schriesheim, C. A. (eds) *Leadership: Beyond Establishment Views.* 239–259. Carbondale, IL: Southern Illinois University Press.

Mintzberg, H. 1985. The organization as a political arena. *Journal of Management Studies*, 22(2): 133–154.

Mintzberg, H. 2004. *Managers not MBAs.* Harlow: Pearson Education Ltd.

Morgan, G. 1997. *Images of Organisation* (2nd edn). Thousand Oaks, CA: Sage.

Morgan, G. and Smircich, L. 1980. The case for qualitative research. *Academy of Management Review*, 5(4): 491–500.

Moynihan, D. 2006. Managing for results in state government: Evaluating a decade of reform. *Public Administration Review*, 66(1): 77–89.

Mumby, D. K. 2005. Theorizing resistance in organization studies: A dialectical approach. *Management Communication Quarterly*, 19(1): 19–44.

Muramatsu, M. and Matsunami, J. 2003. The late and sudden emergence of New Public Management reforms in Japan. In Wollmann, H. (ed.) *Evaluation in Public Sector Reform: Concepts and Practice in International Perspective.* Cheltenham, UK: Edward Elgar.

Napier, B. J. and Ferris, G. R. 1993. Distance in organizations. *Human Resource Management Review*, 3(4): 321–357.

Naschold, F. 1995. *The Modernization of the Public Sector in Europe.* Helsinki: Ministry of Labour.

National Audit Act. 1983. c 44. 13 May. Whitehall: The Stationery Office.

Noordegraaf, M. and Abma, T. 2003. Management by measurement? Public management practices amidst ambiguity, *Public Administration*, 81(4): 852–871.

O'Reilly, D. and Reed, M. 2010. Leaderism: An evolution of managerialism in UK public sector reform. *Public Administration*, 88(4): 960–978.

Orr, K. and Vince, R. 2007. Traditions of local government. *Public Administration*, 87(3): 655–677.

Osborne, D. and Gaebler, T. 1992. *Reinventing Government*. Reading, MA: Addison-Wesley.

Pal, L. A. 2007. Inversions without end: The OECD and global public management reform. Paper presented at the OECD and Global Governance Workshop, Carleton University, Ottawa, January 19–20.

Pandey, S. K. and Wright, B. E. 2006. Connecting the dots in public management: Political environment, organizational goal ambiguity, and the manager's role ambiguity. *Journal of Public Administration Research and Theory*, 16(4): 511–532.

Parker, L. D. and Guthrie, J. 1993. The Australian public sector in the 1990s: New accountability regimes in motion. *Journal of International Accounting, Auditing and Taxation*, 2(1): 59–81.

Parry, K. and Bryman, A. 2006. Leadership in organizations. In Clegg, S. R., Hardy, C., Lawrence, T. B. and Nord, W. R. (eds) *The Sage Handbook of Organization Studies*, 2nd ed., London: Sage Publications, 447–468.

Parry, K. W. 1998. Grounded theory and social process: A new direction for leadership research. *The Leadership Quarterly*, 9(1): 85–105.

Performance and Innovation Unit. 2001. *Strengthening Leadership in the Public Sector*. March. Whitehall: The Stationery Office.

Peters, B. G. 2010. *The Politics of Bureaucracy: An Introduction to Comparative Public Administration* (6th edn). Abingdon, UK: Routledge.

Peters, T. and Waterman, R. 1982. *In Search of Excellence: Lessons from America's Best Run Companies.* New York: Harper Row.

Pfeffer, J. 1981. *Power in Organizations*. Boston: Pitman.

Pollitt, C. 1993. *Managerialism and the Public Services: The Anglo-American Experience.* London: Macmillan.

Pollitt, C. 2000. Is the Emperor in his underwear? An analysis of the impacts of public management reform. *Public Management*, 2(2): 181–199.

Pollitt, C. 2002. Clarifying convergence: Striking similarities and durable differences in public management reform. *Public Management Review*, 4(1): 471–492.

Pollitt, C., Girre, X., Lonsdale, J., Mul, R., Summa, H. and Waerness, M. 1999. *Performance or Compliance? Performance Audit and Public Management in Five Countries.* Oxford: Oxford University Press.

Porter, L., Allen, R. W. and Angle, H. L. 1981. The politics of upward influence in organization. In Staw, B. and Cummings, L. (eds) *Research in Organizational Behavior*, Vol. 3. Greenwich, CT: JAI Press.

Potter, E. H., Rosenbach, W. E. and Pittman, T. S. 2001. Followers for the times: Engaging employees in a winning partnership. In Rosenbach, W. E. and Taylor, R. L. (eds) *Contemporary Issues in Leadership* (5th ed.). Boulder, CO: Westview Press.

Power, M. 1999. *The Audit Society*. Oxford: Oxford University Press.

Pratchett, L. and Wingfield, M. 1996. Petty bureaucracy and woolyminded liberalism? The changing ethos of local government officers. *Public Administration*, 74(4): 639–656.

Raelin, J. 2003. *Creating Leaderful Organizations*. San Francisco: Berrett-Koehler.

Raelin, J. 2004. Don't bother putting leadership into people. *The Academy of Management Executive*, 18: 131–135.

Reeves, E. 1970. *The Dynamics of Group Behavior*. New York: American Management Association Inc.

Reichard, C. 2003. Local public management reforms in Germany. *Public Administration*, 81(2): 345–363.

Reicher, S., Haslam, S. A. and Hopkins, N. 2005. Social identity and the dynamics of leadership: Leaders and followers as collaborative agents in the transformation of social reality. *The Leadership Quarterly*, 16: 547–568.

Rhodes, R. A. W. 1991. The New Public Management. *Public Administration*, 69(1): Introduction.

Rickards, T. and Clark, M. 2006. *Dilemmas of Leadership*. Abingdon, UK: Routledge.

Rosenau, J. 2004. Followership and discretion. *Harvard International Review* (fall): 14–17.

Rost, J. 1993. *Leadership for the Twenty-First Century*. Westport, CT: Praeger.

Sahlin-Andersson, K. 2001. National, international and transnational constructions of New Public Management. In Christensen, T. and Laegreid, P. (eds) *New Public Management: The Transformation of Ideas and Practice*. Aldershot, UK: Ashgate.

Samaratunge, R., Alam, Q. and Teicher, J. 2008. The New Public Management reforms in Asia: A comparison of South and Southeast Asian countries. *International Review of Administrative Sciences*, 74(1): 25–46.

Savoie, D. 1995. What is wrong with the New Public Management? *Canadian Public Administration*, 38(1): 112–121.

Sayer, A. 2000. *Method in Social Science* (2nd edn) London: Routledge.

Seteroff, S. 2003. *Beyond Leadership to Followership*. Victoria, Canada: Trafford.

Shamir, B. 1995. Social distance and charisma: Theoretical notes and an exploratory study. *Leadership Quarterly*, 6(1): 19–47.

Smircich, L. and Morgan, G. 1982. Leadership: The management of meaning. *The Journal of Applied Behavioral Science*, 18(3): 257–273.

Social Services Inspectorate. 1998. *Someone Else's Children: Inspections of Planning and Decision Making for Children Looked After and the Safety of Children Looked After, Social Care Group*. London: Department of Health.

Stech, E. L. 2004. Psycho-dynamic approach. In Northouse, P. G. (ed.) *Leadership Theory and Practice*, London: Sage, 235–263.

Stodghill, R. M. 1948. Personal factors associated with leadership: A survey of literature. *Journal of Personality*, 25: 35–71.

Strang, S. E. and Kuhnert, K. W. 2009. Personality and leadership developmental levels as predictors of leader performance. *The Leadership Quarterly*, 20(June): 421–433.

Suleiman, E. 2003. *Dismantling Democratic States*. Princeton, NJ: Princeton University Press.

Talbot, C. 1996. Ministers and agencies: Responsibility and performance. In *Second Report – Ministerial Accountability and Responsibility*, HC313–ii. London: Public Service Select Committee/HMSO.

Talbot, C. 1997. UK Civil Service personnel reforms: Devolution, decentralization and delusion. *Public Policy and Administration*, 12(4): 14–34.

Ter Bogt, H. 1999. Financial and economic management in autonomized Dutch organizations. *Financial Accountability and Management*, 51(3/4): 329–351.

Thomas, J. 1993. *Doing Critical Ethnography*. Newbury Park, CA: Sage.

Thompson, F. and Miller, H. T. 2003. New public management and bureaucracy versus business values and bureaucracy. *Review of Public Personnel Administration*, 23: 328–343.

Tolstoy, L. 1869. *War and Peace*. Edited translation, 1991, Oxford: Oxford University Press.

Toynbee, P. 2009. These rottweilers do the work of the Tories for them. *Guardian*, 10 February. Available at: www.guardian.co.uk/commentisfree/2009/feb/10/taxpayers-alliance-public-sector.

van Kippenberg, D., van Kippenberg, B., Cremer, D. D. and Hogg, M. 2004. Leadership, self and identity: A review and research agenda. *The Leadership Quarterly*, 15: 825–856.

Van Wart, M. 2003. Public-sector leadership theory: An assessment. *Public Administration Review*, 63(2): 214–228.

Wallis, J. and McLoughlin L. 2009. Public value-seeking leadership: Its nature, rationale and development in the context of public management reform. In Goldfinch, S. and Wallis, J. (eds) *International Handbook of Public Management Reform*. London: Edward Elgar.

Watkins, P. 1989. Leadership, power and symbols in educational administration. In Smyth, J. (ed.) *Critical Perspectives on Educational Leadership*. Lewes, UK: Farmer Press.

Western, S. 2008. *Leadership: A Critical Text.* London: Sage.

Wildavsky, A. 1988. *Searching for Safety*. New Brunswick, NJ: Transaction.

Yadamsuren, B. 2006. Citizens' participation in local budgeting: The case of Mongolia. In Ahmad, R. (ed.) *The Role of Public Administration in Building a Harmonious Society*, selected proceedings from the Annual Conference of the Network of Asia-Pacific Schools and Institutes of Public Administration and Governance (NAPSIPAG).

Yamamoto, H. 2003. *New Public Management: Japan's Practice*, IIPS Policy Paper 293e. Tokyo: Institute for International Policy Studies.

Yukl, G. 1989. Managerial leadership: A review of theory and research. *Journal Of Management*, 15(2): 251–289.

Yukl, G. 1999. An evaluative essay on current conceptions of effective leadership. *European Journal of Work and Organizational Psychology*, 8: 33–48.

Yukl, G. 2002. *Leadership in Organizations* (5th edn). New Jersey: Prentice Hall.

Zanzi, A. and O'Neill, R. M. 2001. Sanctioned versus non-sanctioned political tactics. *Journal of Managerial Issues*, 13(2): 245–263.

Zoller, H. M. and Fairhurst, G. T. 2007. Resistance leadership: The overlooked potential in critical organization and leadership studies. *Human Relations*, 60(9): 1331–1361.

Index

Page numbers in **bold** denote figures.